An Atlas of EEC Affairs

Ray Hudson, David Rhind and Helen Mounsey

AN ATLAS OF EEC AFFAIRS

AN ATLAS OF EEC AFFAIRS

Ray Hudson, David Rhind and Helen Mounsey

METHUEN
LONDON AND NEW YORK

First published in 1984 by
Methuen & Co. Ltd
11 New Fetter Lane, London EC4P 4EE

Published in the USA by
Methuen & Co.
in association with Methuen, Inc.
733 Third Avenue, New York, NY 10017

© 1984 Ray Hudson, David Rhind and Helen Mounsey

Typeset by Scarborough Typesetting Services
Printed in Great Britain at the
University Press, Cambridge

British Library Cataloguing in Publication Data
Hudson, Ray
  An atlas of EEC affairs.
  1. European Economic Community
  I. Title   II. Rhind, David
  III. Mounsey, Helen
  341.24'22   HC241.2

  ISBN 0–416–30910–0
  ISBN 0–416–30920–8 Pbk

Library of Congress Cataloging in Publication Data
Hudson, Raymond.
  An atlas of EEC affairs.

  Bibliography: p.
  Includes index.
  1. European Economic Community.   2. European Economic
Community—Maps.   I. Rhind, David.   II. Mounsey, Helen.
III. Title.   IV. Title: Atlas of E.E.C. affairs.
HC241.2.H83 1984   341.24'22   84–501
ISBN 0–416–30910–0
ISBN 0–416–30920–8 (pbk.)

CONTENTS

LIST OF FIGURES

LIST OF TABLES

LIST OF PLATES

ACKNOWLEDGEMENTS

Those who know us will have little difficulty in recognizing the primary division of labour involved in the production of this Atlas: David Rhind and Helen Mounsey produced the maps, Ray Hudson the text (with the exception of the technical appendix). Nevertheless, its production depended upon assistance and help from many other people and organizations. We wish to acknowledge the invaluable assistance of the University of Durham which, through its Special Projects Research Fund, provided the resources for a research project to develop a computerized regional information and mapping system. Ray Hudson also acknowledges financial support from the European Cultural Foundation and the European Economic Community, the Nuffield Foundation and the University of Durham for various research projects on regional and national development in the Community, the results of which have been drawn upon in what follows. We also thank the technical and secretarial staff of the Department of Geography at Durham, without whom the manuscript would never have reached the publishers in a legible form, and for their assistance in producing many of the maps which could not be produced by computer mapping; likewise, we thank the staff of the Computer Unit of Durham University for their invaluable help with producing the maps that were produced by computer. Finally, our thanks to Mary Ann Kernan not only for originally putting the idea into our heads but also for her patience as we successively passed a series of deadlines.

RAY HUDSON
DAVID RHIND
HELEN MOUNSEY

PREFACE

The beginning of the 1980s may well mark a watershed in the history of the European Community. While the EEC developed relatively smoothly in the 1960s environment of rapid economic growth, this changed dramatically after 1973 so that the 1980s dawned in the midst of recession, slow or even nil economic growth and mounting problems such as those of energy, industrial decline and rising unemployment. Can the European Community respond effectively to the challenges which these pose?

Our aims in this Atlas are modest: to describe in maps and words recent trends, current problems, and to some extent future prospects, in important aspects of economic, social and political life in the Community. Wherever possible, we present information not only at the national level but also at the regional scale using the Community's own EUROSTAT data for the most part. While the nation state remains the principal focus of political authority in the Community and the only meaningful level for considering some issues, the degree of variability between regions within countries as well as between regions in different countries provides cogent reasons for this. To the extent that maps at the regional scale form a central element, however, our selection of issues has to a degree been constrained by the availability of comparable regional data. A related point is that data for Greenland are not available so that what was until recently the Community's largest single areal unit is absent from the maps presented here, a reflection of its marginal status in terms of population and levels of socio-economic development.

Furthermore, focusing on the regional scale raises two other sorts of problems. There is a great variation in size among regions (to be precise, among the level II regions of the European Community), which in itself creates difficulties in the interpretation of regional patterns, while there is also considerable intra-regional heterogeneity. In addition, at the time of writing the most up-to-date available regional data generally referred to the latter part of the 1970s. Nevertheless, despite the constraints imposed on choice of variables, and the problems posed by the dates for which data were available and by the varying sizes of the areal units themselves, the case for examining – even if only in a preliminary manner – the great variety between regions in the Community in terms of economic, political and social conditions was overwhelming. For this great spatial variability raises questions of considerable practical and theoretical importance: for example, in many of the member states of the Community a considerable de-centralization of power has recently occurred or is occurring to regions or other sub-national spatial units (Belgium, France, Greece and Italy are cases in point) while the role of space and spatial uneven development has recently come to be realized as centrally important in the overall process of social and economic development. We would stress, however, that our ambitions here are much more limited than attempting to answer such questions.

For our aims here – to repeat – are to describe rather than to explain, to raise issues and questions rather than resolve and answer them, and in this way provide an intro-duction to important issues in the life of the Community for students of geography, European studies and related social-science disciplines in sixth forms, polytechnics and universities, and for all those with an interest in the affairs of the European Community.

In part, our primary focus on describing spatial patterns, on relating who and what are where, rather than attempting to explain why they are there, is a reflection of the character of the variables for which data are available, the spatial units and time periods for which the variables are available. For example, the regional boundaries often reflect administrative convenience rather than any fundamental and meaningful partitioning of the European Community space in terms of social and economic processes. Similarly, the time periods for which data are available are often equally arbitrary. Thus the links between regional or national patterns and generative processes are not always easy to disentangle. Furthermore, and a more serious barrier militating against attempts at explanation, these relationships between pattern and process are complicated ones (for example, not only does spatial pattern reflect the effects of a variety of interacting processes but also the unevenness in spatial distribution itself may be a crucial element in shaping these processes) and it was simply infeasible to begin to tackle them seriously within the limits on the length of this text. For those interested in pursuing these issues of why the European Community displays the particular internal human geography that it does, extensive references are provided which do address themselves directly to the question of *why* particular spatial patterns have been developed (although these have been generally limited to publications available in English).

1

THE EUROPEAN COMMUNITY: HISTORY; ORGANIZATIONAL STRUCTURE; POWERS AND POLICIES

1.1 The historical background to the European Community

There are those (for example, Kerr, 1977: 1–5) who would trace the germ of the idea of a united Europe back to the final days of the Roman Empire; a unity based upon a common, shared civilization and culture. In succeeding centuries a measure of cultural and linguistic unity undoubtedly did reappear among at least some social strata in Europe: for example, until the sixteenth century, Latin remained the common language of European scholars and ideas of European unity sporadically recurred, primarily in response to the depredations of recurrent wars.

With the rise of industrial capitalism and its corollary, the nation state and the fostering of nationalist sentiment, in the nineteenth century, the threats posed by war were aggravated, not least because the technological capacity to wage war was tremendously increased as scientific knowledge advanced. The struggle for national power led to imperialist policies of expansion in what later was to be termed the 'Third World', and to wars aimed at territorial aggrandizement within Europe, culminating in the carnage of the First World War.

It is in the responses to this war that the modern origins of the movement towards European unity, one product of which was the European Community, lie. One reaction, by no means confined to Europe, was a concern for peace which resulted in the formation of the League of Nations and in fact the term 'Common Market', as the European Community is often if incorrectly referred to, was coined by Aristide Briand, a French diplomat, in a scheme for a European union which he proposed to the League in 1929. In 1930 he submitted it to all European governments. The scheme was not adopted and in retrospect it is easy to see why, for the reaction of national governments in western Europe to the depression of the inter-war years was manifested in policies of protectionism and the fostering of nationalism rather than internationalism, a reaction which attained its most extreme form in the Fascist or related regimes of Germany, Italy and Spain and culminated in the Second World War rather than European integration. After 1945, however, a series of moves towards economic and political integration, initially heavily influenced by a desire for lasting peace in Europe, was set in motion which culminated in the formation of the European Economic Community in 1957 (for a fuller discussion, see Blacksell, 1977).

1.1.1 Moves towards economic integration, 1945–57

The cessation of the Second World War was accompanied by the realization that the 'old' nations of western Europe had lost their global economic pre-eminence, eclipsed by the rise of the USA and USSR. There were several strands to this. First the ravages of war had resulted in the destruction of much of Europe's industrial capacity and a considerable indebtedness to the USA. Second, export markets for manufactured goods in the Third World had been lost to the USA during the war. Third, the break-up of the European colonial empires was imminent, although the continuing British orientation to its Commonwealth was to have a decisive effect on the subsequent path of European integration. Fourth, the domestic markets of the individual European nations were increasingly too small, given changes that were taking place in the scale of production, associated with the trend to bigger companies and production units.

In 1947 a serious crisis hit the European economy, which re-emphasized its dependence upon economic aid from the USA to enable a reconstruction programme to be implemented. This the USA was prepared to grant under the Marshall Plan, subject to the crucial condition that the receiving states establish a joint organization to manage it and develop a common economic policy. In the same year, the Benelux (Belgium, Netherlands, Luxembourg) Union, a mini-Common Market, and the more general Economic Commission for Europe (ECE) were set up, the latter based in Geneva (see Figure 1.1). The ECE was a regional organization of the United Nations, intended to foster European co-operation on a continental basis – an intention rapidly overtaken by events as the 'Cold War' descended upon Europe, dividing the continent into two ideologically opposed blocs. This led in 1948 to the formation of the Organization for European Economic Co-operation (OEEC) from the western remnants of ECE which later, in 1961, evolved into the Organization for Economic Co-operation and Development (OECD). In one respect, though, the formation of the OEEC was of great importance in furthering economic growth and integration within Europe. For it established the European Payments Union (EPU) to deal with the problem of currency convertibility, the European countries' lack of dollars, the hard currency of international trade, a solution to which was a vital pre-condition for guaranteeing free trade. A year later, in 1949, the Council of Europe was founded.

The establishment of these two institutions, OEEC and Council of Europe, was important in that it presaged the beginnings of a division between the two groups of countries that were later to form the EEC and the European Free Trade Area (EFTA). At this stage, the emphasis among the former group, particularly the French, was upon 'supranationalism' – the creation of institutions which transcended national boundaries and the authority of individual nation states. The latter group were opposed to this and the attitude of Britain was crucial here. With its colonial interests largely intact and its horizons still global, Britain vigorously opposed any idea of 'supranationalism' and a

Figure 1.1
Significant events
in the evolution of
the European
Community

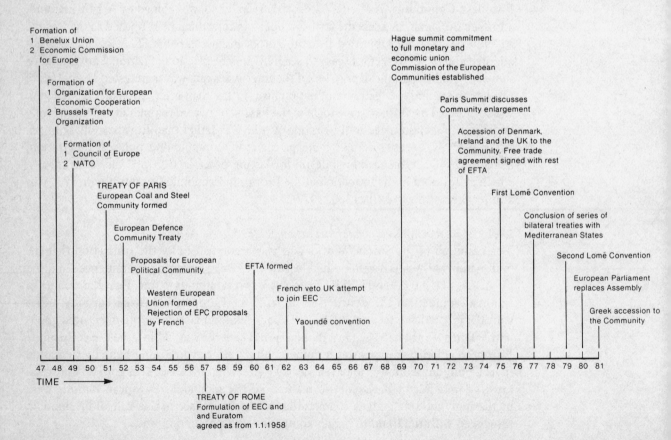

'European interest', emphasizing instead that the route to European unity lay in inter-governmental co-operation rather than the surrender of national sovereignty to European institutions.

This parting of ways went one step further in 1951. Following the Schuman proposals of 9 May 1951, the Treaty of Paris was signed, forming the European Coal and Steel Community (ECSC), without Britain and the Scandinavian countries. The proximate causes of the formation of the ECSC lay in the perceived threat to the security of western Europe following the Stalinist rise to ascendancy in Czechoslovakia and Hungary and the creation of Soviet satellite states in eastern Europe. An effective response to this required German re-armament but the French were implacably opposed to this unless it could be carried out in such a way as to rule out absolutely any possibility of a further Franco-German war. How could Germany's reviving economy be made into the basis for guaranteed peace within Europe and a stronger safeguard against external threats? The 'obvious' solution was to integrate inextricably the coal, iron and steel industries, the industries central to armaments production. There were also, as Swann (1975: 20 ff.) points out, other advantages in such a solution: it provided a way of tackling the 'Saar Question' between Germany and France; it gave Germany a passport to international respectability; and it was attractive to European federalists disillusioned with the OEEC and Council of Europe. In fact, the Treaty of Paris was to provide a model for many of the administrative and decision-making structures built into the Treaty of Rome in 1957 (see section 1.2 below) but gave the ECSC stronger powers than were later given to the EEC. Two reasons are important in accounting for this difference: first, the powers of the ECSC lay in a relatively narrow, specialized area so that there was less opposition from national governments; second, it was meant to ensure the impossibility of another war in Europe at a time when this was seen as a vital objective.

1.1.2 Moves towards political integration, 1945–57

Paralleling and interrelated to moves towards greater economic integration were attempts to bring about closer political integration. The starting point for these was the formation in 1948 of the Brussels Treaty Organization (whose members were Belgium, France, Luxembourg, the Netherlands and the UK), which agreed to a pact of mutual assistance in time of war in Europe. In 1949 this was considerably broadened into the North Atlantic Treaty Organization (NATO).

The outbreak of the Korean War in 1950 was of great significance for developments within Europe for it led to the USA suggesting German re-armament, a suggestion opposed by France. In response, though, Plevan, the French Prime Minister, suggested the creation of a European army, an idea that was subsequently taken up by the members of the ECSC who signed a European Defence Community (EDC) Treaty in May 1952. This in turn presupposed a common foreign policy which itself implied moving further towards full political integration. Two other forces were pushing in this direction at this time: the need for democratic control of such an army; and the desire, especially of the Netherlands, for greater economic as well as military integration.

Consequently, in 1953 a draft outlining a European Political Community (EPC) was produced by the ECSC Assembly, in collaboration with co-opted members from the Consultative Assembly of the Council of Europe. In essence, this proposed a European parliament and executive. However, these EPC proposals collapsed in 1954 when the French national assembly refused to consider them. There were several reasons for this: opposition to the supranational elements of the proposals, in sharp contrast to earlier French attitudes; opposition of the French left to German re-armament; opposition of the French right to foreign control of the French army; and British aloofness to the idea.

This French rejection effectively killed off any immediate hopes of a deeper political union within Europe. Those who wished to attain this goal had to alter their tactics;

rather than tackle political union head-on, a more effective approach seemed to be to proceed more cautiously and concentrate in the short term on consolidating and extending economic union, keeping political and military union in the background as long-term goals.

1.1.3   Compromises, 1954–7

In 1954 the Brussels Treaty Organization was broadened into the Western European Union by the addition of (FR) Germany and Italy and this was followed in 1955 by the circulation of a memorandum from the governments of the Benelux countries calling for a general common market and specific action in the spheres of energy and transport. It thus recognized that while the ultimate goal was political union, the short and medium-term objectives should be economic integration. This memorandum met with a favourable response at a meeting involving ministers of the Six, held at Messina in 1955. Subsequently the UK joined the discussions, only to withdraw in November 1955 because of opposition to the proposals for supranational institutions.

Thus on 25 March 1957 the Treaty of Rome was signed by the Benelux countries, France, Germany and Italy, and on 1 January 1958 the European Economic Community (EEC) and the European Atomic Energy Community (Euratom) came into being, continuing in parallel with the ECSC until their fusion in 1969. The immediate objectives of the EEC were to promote economic growth and the free movement of capital and labour within it. This implied (*inter alia*): no customs duties between members of the Community; 'equivalent taxes' or quota restrictions on goods moving between member countries; uniform customs duties for imports from outside the Community; the right of companies to operate in any country of the EEC; rules to prevent governments aiding 'unfair competition', although perhaps paradoxically regional policy measures were exempt from this; unrestricted inter-country movement of people, capital and money – although this latter presupposes a common currency which did not and does not exist so that controls have periodically emerged on such movements.

The Treaty of Rome made explicit provision for policies on agriculture, energy (which already in part existed through the ECSC), social affairs and transport, and such policies have subsequently emerged to varying degrees (see section 1.4 below). Other policies, notably industrial and regional, have also developed, though not specifically catered for in the Treaty.

1.1.4   The emergence of the European Free Trade Area

As much of the subsequent expansion of the original EEC from six to nine, ten and possibly twelve countries has involved the incorporation of EFTA members, it is worth briefly discussing EFTA's origins. During 1955–6 the UK government came to recognize that it had underestimated the determination of the Six, and in response initiated a policy shift. In July 1956, prompted by the UK, the OEEC began a study of a free trade area that would include the Six and which, unlike the customs union of the Six, would allow each nation to set its own tariffs on exports and imports. In January 1957 the results of the study were published in a report, which concluded that such a free trade area was feasible.

As a result, discussions began in March 1957 aimed at concluding a treaty for a European Industrial Free Trade Area (EIFTA). These dragged on until their demise at the end of 1958, the French being particularly hostile to the suggestion. There were several reasons for the failure of these talks: the Six were suspicious of the UK's motives (probably correctly), as they saw EIFTA as a means of wrecking the embryonic EEC; the UK's insistence on free trade for industrial goods within the area while retaining national autonomy – and in its own case Commonwealth preferences – in world trade; the omission of agriculture from the UK proposals, so as to allow continued imports of cheap food from the Commonwealth; and also the problems of harmonizing, for example, social security charges.

As a consequence of these developments, the signing of the Stockholm convention on 4 January 1960 by Austria, Denmark, Portugal, Norway, Sweden, Switzerland and the UK created EFTA, and the division of most of western Europe into two economic groupings.

1.1.5 The evolution of the European Community, 1957–80

The early years of the Community, until 1962–3, were relatively smooth. There were several reasons for this: memories of the destruction of the Second World War were still sharp; there were Christian Democratic governments in all of the Six, which shared a fear of the spectre of communism; and last but by no means least, the Six were experiencing rapid rates of economic growth in this period and average living standards were rising in real terms (see Chapters 3, 4 and 5). By 1962, the Common Agricultural Policy (CAP) had begun and steps had been taken to bring in anti-monopoly legislation and allow the free movement of capital and labour (see Chapter 2).

In the same year, however, the evolving Community met with its first serious difficulties following the application (in November 1961) for membership by Denmark, Ireland, Norway and the UK. Though supported by the other five, France (in the person of President de Gaulle) vetoed the UK's application. In the event, none of the applicants joined and the result was rancour and an end to further serious discussion of political union among the Six themselves.

Nevertheless in succeeding years the development of the Community progressed. In 1963 the Yaoundé Convention was signed, giving preferential trade arrangements with eighteen African states by which the EEC secured supplies of food and raw materials in return for aid and guaranteed markets; later in 1975 this was to evolve into the more general Lomé Convention (see section 1.4.6 below). In 1965 the fusion of the executives of the ECSC, EEC and Euratom began, their merger to form the Commission of the European Communities (CEC) being completed in 1969. Then in 1968 the formation of the customs union and the removal of internal tariffs was completed, ahead of schedule.

This was followed in 1969 by a further significant advance agreed at the Hague Summit, which went beyond the explicit provisions of the Treaty of Rome and embraced the idea of both economic and monetary union. In the following year, the Commission submitted a plan for full economic and monetary union by 1980 – a goal yet to be achieved, as the currently operating European Monetary System (EMS) falls far short of full monetary union.

In the same year, de Gaulle having departed, the UK renewed its application to join the Community, along with Denmark, Ireland and Norway. An important consequence of the subsequent discussions was the recognition by the Community, at the 1972 Paris Summit, of the need for an EEC regional development fund (see section 1.4.5 below). This commitment was ultimately insufficient to persuade the Norwegians to join the Community (entry being rejected in a referendum), but on 1 January 1973 Denmark, Ireland and the UK all joined. The Community was further enlarged with the entry of Greece on 1 January 1981, following the restoration of democracy there, and Portugal and Spain are likely to join by the mid-1980s (see Chapter 6). Thus despite the pressures generated by the impact of the 1970s recession (see Chapter 4) the Community has continued to develop and expand, although at the price of considerably increasing economic and social heterogeneity within it. Dealing successfully with this diversity presents a major challenge for the Community in the years to come – but this is to anticipate matters (see Chapter 6).

Figure 1.2
The organiza-
tional and
decision-
making
structure of
the European
Community

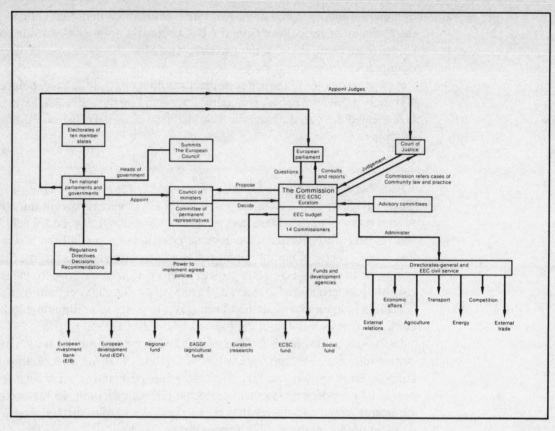

1.2 Organizational and decision-making structure

1.2.1 Administrative structures

Briefly, the most important elements of this may be summarized as follows (see Figure 1.2). The Community is a confederation of national states, which remain the chief locus of political authority and power. Its ultimate governing authority is the Council of Ministers, made up of representatives appointed by each national government. The Council effectively constitutes the link between national governments and the Commission. Unlike the Commission, the Council is not a fixed body of people, its composition varying with the topic under discussion. In principle, unanimous agreement is not generally required for Council decisions to become Community policy, a two-thirds majority being sufficient except on key issues such as admission of new membership where unanimity is a requirement. In practice, however, even in those areas where a majority agreement is, in principle, sufficient, unanimity is in practice necessary, the major exception (since 1966) being in the area of budgetary matters. The presidency of the Council rotates at six-monthly intervals and during this period the European Council, comprising the heads of national governments, holds a summit meeting in the capital of the country which holds the presidency; in addition, a third annual summit is held in Brussels.

Since May 1979, the European Parliament has consisted of members directly elected by national electorates, 61 per cent of whom took the trouble to vote in the first election. The election results and the resultant composition of the European Parliament are shown in Figures 1.3 and 1.4. Overall, the parliamentary balance is a fairly even one between left and right: the broad right (Conservatives and Christian Democrats) obtained 162 seats and the broad left (Communists and Socialists) 156 seats, with the broad centre (Liberals and Progressive Democrats) obtaining 68 seats and the remaining 24 seats being distributed among a very heterogeneous group composed of the extreme right or left, nationalists, independents, anti-EEC, etc. At national level there were considerable variations in the proportions of members of different parties, reflecting variations in political affiliations and party strengths within the various member states.

Figure 1.3
National voting
patterns in the first
election to the
European
Parliament, May
1979

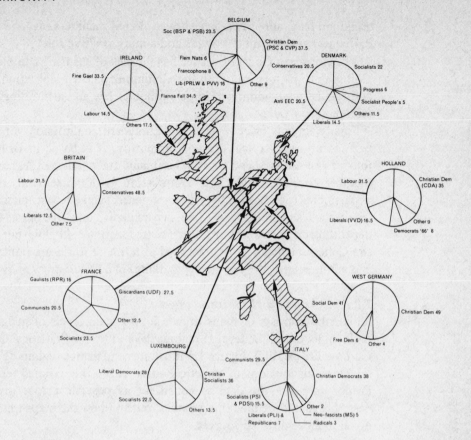

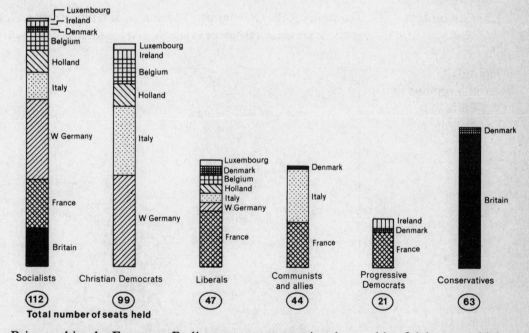

Figure 1.4
The
composition
of the first
elected
European
Parliament

Prior to this, the European Parliament was an appointed assembly of delegates which immediately before the switch to direct elections numbered 198. The Parliament's major sanction lies in its power to dismiss the Commission if two-thirds of European MPs agree to this line of action, but even in the improbable event of its being exercised, member states could then simply re-appoint the same commissioners. At present its functions are mainly consultative rather than legislative, its lack of legislative powers being one of its distinguishing characteristics. It tends instead to work through a dozen small, specialized committees, which review policy-making and the composition of the budget – indeed, control of the latter is the Parliament's main practical power. The transition from appointed delegates to elected members may, however, be leading to a Parliament seeking more powers and a more positive role.

The European Court of Justice has the task of ensuring compliance with the various Community treaties and with the Community's own legislation (decisions, directives and regulations), administering Community law and arbitrating in disputes involving Community treaties.

Finally, in this brief review, the European Commission is the executive arm, the permanent civil service, of the Community. It is based in Brussels and directed by fourteen commissioners: France, Germany, Italy and the UK have two, the remaining member countries one. The Commission is organized into twenty administrative departments each headed by a director-general and a few specialized services (statistics; legal; spokesman's group). The departments, or directorates-general, vary in size depending on the tasks they undertake (see section 1.4 below) but in general the work of the Commission can be summarized in terms of initiating policy, drafting legislation and administering the day-to-day workings of a Community of over 250 million people.

1.2.2 EC status and statistical areas
This Atlas consists of maps drawn at two main levels of geographical detail – the national level and the level II regions devised by the Statistical Office of the European Community (SOEC). Figure 1.5 illustrates and names regions. The level II regions are *ad hoc* amalgamations of statistical areas within the national territories, grouped in a fashion to make the data as consistent as possible across the EC. The appendix describes in outline how this is carried out and how the maps were made; references are given to more detailed sources.

1.3 The budget

The ability of the Community to formulate and implement policy is crucially dependent upon the financial resources available to it for these purposes. Until 1 January 1979 the

Figure 1.5
Level II regions in
the European
Community

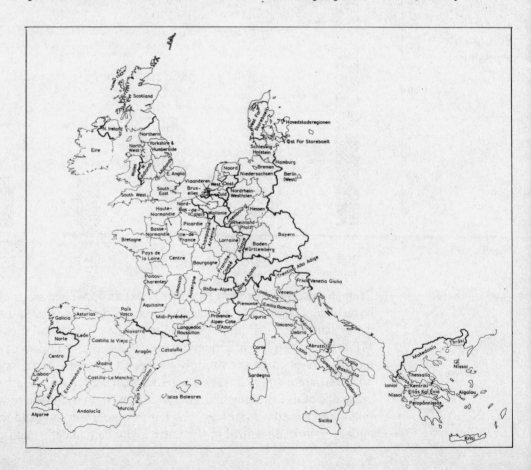

Community's budget was financed by member states via a sliding scale, based largely on size and wealth. Consequently FR Germany tended consistently to be the largest gross contributor to the budget in this period, Luxembourg the smallest (see Table 1.1). Of greater political significance, however, have been the net, rather than the gross, national contributions to the budget – that is, the difference between payments and receipts (see Table 1.2). The reasons for national variations in net contributions to the budget are closely related to the sectoral distribution of Community funds, which in turn reflect perceived policy priorities, an issue developed in the next section. While Germany maintains its position as the chief contributor in net as well as gross terms, the position

Table 1.1 Financing the general budget of the European Community Institutions, 1973–9

	Receipts			
	1973	*1979*	*1973*	*1979*
	(millions units of account)		*(% share)*	
Belgium	337.3	966.5	7.4	6.7
Denmark	51.3	337.4	1.1	2.4
France	1,135.5	2,886.5	24.8	20.1
FR Germany	1,331.5	4,407.2	29.0	30.7
Ireland	12.7	104.6	0.3	0.7
Italy	872.2	1,793.2	19.0	12.5
Luxembourg	8.2	19.4	0.2	0.1
Netherlands	432.8	1,344.1	9.4	9.3
UK	402.5	2,513.5	8.8	17.5
EEC Nine	4,584.0	14,372.4	100.0	100.0

Source: Eurostat, 1981: Table 1.1.7

Table 1.2 Total payments to member states, 1979 (millions units account)

	Payment (adjusted MCAs)[1]	*Differences between payment to and from the budget*	*% payment attributable to member states within the EEC*
Belgium	842.9	+123.6	6.6
Denmark	703.5	+366.1	5.5
France	2,648.5	−238.0	20.6
FR Germany	2,753.2	−1,654.0	21.4
Ireland	629.3	+524.7	4.9
Italy	2,166.1	+372.9	16.9
Luxembourg	15.2	−4.2	0.1
Netherlands	1,546.8	+202.7	12.0
UK	1,541.1	−972.4	12.6
EEC Nine	12,846.6		
Payments to non-members or not attributable to specific countries	1,520.5		
Total	14,367.1	−1,278.6[2]	100.6[3]

Source: Eurostat, 1981: Tables 1.1.7 and 1.1.9

Notes: 1 Monetary Compensatory Awards.
2 The total net contribution from member states in 1979 (−1,278.6) does not equal the difference between total and internal spending with the EEC due to differences in the timings of payments, etc.
3 Does not total to 100.0 because of rounding errors.

of the UK as the second largest net contributor at a time of economic decline and deflationary national policies, which cut average living standards for those in work and raised unemployment to over three million (see Chapter 3), became an issue of considerable importance. Neither the temporary solutions agreed partially to patch over this apparent anomaly nor the more general changes introduced since 1 January 1979 in the method of financing the Community budget have effectively countered the domestic opposition to the UK's continuing as a member of the Community. Nor have these more general changes, which involve financing the budget via a combination of agricultural levies, customs duties and 1 per cent of revenues raised by Value Added Tax, resolved the overriding problem of funding the budget (which in practice largely revolves around funding the price support provisions of the CAP, as we show in the next section). The danger of expenditure exceeding income is a more or less ever-present one which increases as the Community expands and ultimately can probably only be erased by fundamental reform of the CAP (see Chapter 6).

1.4 Community policies and funding

At one level, the Community has developed an impressive array of policies, ranging over agricultural, economic, energy, industrial, regional and social affairs (see Figure 1.2). In practice, however, many of these remain weakly developed and scarcely implemented. Among the more important reasons for this is the fact that the Community consists essentially of a confederation of ten countries which are in the process of cumulatively delegating broad areas of economic policy to a common machinery, with the result that decision-making is located between the Commission and national governments, with the latter retaining power in many areas, particularly where these are perceived to be vital to national interests. Related to this is the point that the Community's budget is of minor importance compared to those of national governments: in 1978, for example, it amounted to 0.8 per cent of Community gross domestic product and 2.5 per cent of the combined national budgets of the Nine (Brouwers, 1979: 33). Furthermore, until recently, in several key areas there was no apparent need for active Community policy involvement as the combination of general economic growth and the distributive mechanisms of the market, guided by national policies, seemed satisfactory: only with the impacts of the post-1973 recession, for example, has it seemed necessary for a positive Community policy initiative in the areas of energy and industry (although specific provisions for coal and iron and steel pre-date this by some two decades: see de Bauw, 1979: 80). Energy, industry and transport, to say nothing of agriculture, will continue to pose major policy challenges to the Community in the future, a theme we return to in Chapter 6.

In practice, despite the comparatively minor role that agriculture plays in the Community's economy (see Chapters 3 and 4), Community policy has largely been synonymous with the implementation of the CAP and, in particular, with the price support (guarantee) section of that policy (see Table 1.3). For even within the area of agricultural policy, national governments have been more important in financing policies designed to bring about structural reform in agriculture than has the Community: for example, in 1975 national government expenditures on structural reform exceeded those of the Community by a factor of ten (see Mackerron and Rush, 1976: 290). The Commission's proposals contained in the Mansholt Plan for radical structural change in agriculture were never implemented, not least because of their implication as to the addition of five million to the unemployment total at a time when it was already beginning to rise sharply (see Kerr, 1977: 62–9, and Chapter 3). Indeed, this rise in the 1970s provided cogent reasons for increasing the level of expenditure through the regional and social funds, particularly given the spatially uneven distribution of unemployment increases, at a time when there were already problems of balancing the Community's budget.

The sectoral imbalance in the allocation of the Community's budget largely accounts

Table 1.3 Expenditures of the general budget of the European Community Institutions, 1973–9

	1973	1979	1973	1979
	(millions units of account)		(% share)	
Administration	239.4	772.9	6.0	5.4
EAGGF				
Guarantee section	3,174.2	10,434.5	79.3	72.6
Guidance section	123.7	403.4	3.1	2.8
Social fund	49.9	595.7	1.2	4.1
Regional fund	—	513.1	—	3.6
Research and investment	72.3	225.1	1.8	1.6
Co-operation with developing countries	104.8	405.4	2.5	2.8
Other sectors	3.7	117.1	0.1	0.8
Reimbursement to member states (10% of own resources)	236.5	899.9	5.5	6.3
Total	4,004.5[1]	14,367.1[1]	99.5[2]	100.0

Source: Eurostat, 1981: Table 1.1.8

Notes: 1 Totals differ from those of receipts in these years as expenditures relate to payments against appropriations for the relevant year, plus those carried over from past years.
2 Does not total to 100.0 because of rounding errors.

for national differences in net contributions to it. For example, while in 1979 the UK took almost one-third of expenditures from the regional and social funds, less than 10 per cent of expenditure on agricultural price support was allocated to it (see Table 1.4). In general, countries which obtained a relatively large share of expenditure on price support obtained a net positive transfer of funds via the budget, although in the case of Italy, which did relatively badly from the CAP because its large agricultural sector did not specialize in the northern products most favourably treated by CAP regulations, the

Table 1.4 Payments by funds to member states, 1979

	EAGGF		Percentages of total sectoral payment			Percentage of total overall payment[1]
	Guarantee[2]	Guidance	Social fund	Regional fund	Reimbursement	
Belgium	7.2	4.2	1.3	0.6	8.1	6.6
Denmark	6.1	3.7	4.1	1.8	2.1	5.5
France	21.6	24.6	15.7	20.2	13.6	20.6
FR Germany	22.3	29.4	10.3	9.0	27.2	21.4
Ireland	4.4	7.0	6.5	6.4	0.9	4.9
Italy	15.7	8.7	26.2	28.0	13.2	16.9
Luxembourg	0.1	0.1	*	*	*	0.1
Netherlands	13.6	6.3	1.9	1.7	11.7	12.0
UK	8.9	15.9	33.9	32.3	23.2	12.6
EEC Nine	99.9	99.9	99.9	100.0	100.0	100.6[3]

Source: Calculated from Eurostat, 1981: Table 1.1.9

Notes: 1 This refers to the total, excluding administrative expenses, research and investment, co-operation with developing countries and other sectors – expenditure not attributable to specific member countries.
2 Adjusted MCAs.
3 Does not total to 100.0 because of rounding errors.

* Less than 0.1%

large share of both regional and social fund expenditures is important. In the case of Germany and, to a much lesser degree, France, the magnitude of its gross budget contribution more than offsets the funds received from the price support scheme.

1.4.1   The Common Agricultural Policy

The objectives of this are specified in articles 38–47 and 110 of the Treaty of Rome: to establish a common market and free movement of agricultural goods; to increase agricultural productivity; to provide a fair standard of living for those in agriculture; to provide stability in agricultural markets; to guarantee security of food supplies; to ensure reasonable food prices for consumers; to support the harmonious development of world trade. Two points are relevant here. First, many of these objectives are loosely specified: what, for example, are a fair standard of living or reasonable prices? Second, and more important, many of these objectives are mutually incompatible, particularly given the emphasis upon price support policies as the single instrument employed to achieve them. Of these goals, in fact, only security of supply has seemingly been achieved to date, with some degree of attainment of market stability – but only at the price of increased dependence on imports of farming inputs (fertilizers, animal feedstuffs), over-production and high consumer prices (see, for example, Commission of the European Communities, 1975 and 1980; Mackerron and Rush, 1976; Bergmann, 1977). While other changes have taken place in agriculture which coincide with objectives of the CAP, such as the increase in agricultural productivity, these have often taken place despite rather than because of the CAP due to the influence of market forces and national government policies (see Baker, 1961; Mayhew, 1970, 1971; Bergmann, 1977).

Furthermore, implementation of the CAP has had further unintended and undesirable consequences within the Community, widening spatial inequalities both at national and regional level in direct opposition to the aims of the Treaty of Rome, the preamble to which asserted that the contracting parties 'were anxious to strengthen the unity of their economies and to ensure their harmonious development by reducing the differences existing between the various regions and the backwardness of the less favoured regions'. At national level the CAP has tended to transfer resources from poor to rich countries not only because of differences in the size of the agricultural sector (see section 1.4 above) but also because high food prices mean a net transfer to food exporting from food importing countries, notably Italy and the UK, while at regional level the pattern of price support for northern rather than Mediterranean products has served to widen regional inequalities both within individual countries (France, Italy) as well as at Community level, so that on average farm incomes in the richest farming regions are six times those in the poorest (*Economist*, 1979: 6; see also Bowler, 1975). Moreover, this problem can only be exacerbated by the expansion of the Community into the Mediterranean area (see Chapters 3, 4 and 6).

1.4.2   Industrial policy and Community attitudes towards multinationals

In contrast to agriculture which is politically pre-eminent in the Community's concerns but of minor economic importance, manufacturing industry remains vital to the Community's economic well-being yet there is no explicit overall policy for it, over and above the general commitment to create a common market. One important reason for this absence of coherent Community-level policies is that national governments have developed industrial policies to protect what are regarded as key national interests in this area. Another is that prior to 1973 the manufacturing sector was growing strongly and there was no apparent need for a positive industrial policy. This is not to say that there are not specific policies or attempts to create policies for particular branches of manufacturing. Four examples will suffice to illustrate this point. Firstly, policies for iron and steel lay at the heart of the formation of the ECSC and remain of central importance to the Community, not least because of the regional implications of restructuring steel production (see Chapters 2 and 3). Secondly, the Euratom treaty contained elements of an industrial policy. Thirdly, there were Commission proposals in 1980, which eventually came to nothing, for a 'scrap and build' scheme to boost demand in Community shipyards. Finally, in the micro-electronics sector in July 1980 the Commission revealed a plan to help the Community catch up with the USA and Japan, which would involve the Community contributing half of £60 million in subsidies to the industry over the period 1980–4.

This last example in fact touches on two related, often contradictory, concerns of long standing: the relative technological backwardness of Community manufacturing industry, and the Community's attitude to and relations with multinationals (not only in manufacturing but also in energy). Somewhat paradoxically, given the Community's overall orientation, fears of a growing 'technology gap' between the USA and Europe in the early 1960s (see Mandel, 1975b: 151) led not only national governments but also the Commission to encourage mergers within Europe to counter the technological dominance of bigger US companies and prevent domination of the European market by US multinationals in key branches of manufacturing (on the penetration of European manufacturing by American companies, see Stubenitsky, 1973: Ch. 2). Such fears persist today, although increasingly the threat of technological domination is posed by Japan rather than the USA. From the point of view of both the Community and national governments, the greatly increased significance of multinational companies poses threats to political sovereignty and increasingly undermines conventional tools of economic management, but at the same time the fortunes of the Community and its constituent areas have become increasingly dependent upon the investment and disinvestment decisions of such companies (see also Chapter 4).

1.4.3 Energy policy

In many ways, there are striking parallels here with industrial policies. Despite the great dependence of the European economy upon energy, there is no real co-ordinated Community energy policy (Alting von Gesau, 1975; Lucas, 1977); indeed, the issue has only been seriously placed on the agenda since the oil price rises of November 1973. In essence, there was no policy at Community level prior to then because there was no perceived need for one: the price of energy had fallen in real terms and this was conducive to rapid rates of economic growth within the Community (see Chapter 4). This change was a result of a fundamental restructuring of the European energy market – the demise of domestically produced coal and the rise of imported oil which was cheaply available in large quantities on the world market from the late 1950s and, to a lesser degree, natural gas (see Chapter 4). This restructuring was more or less unrelated to any co-ordinated Community energy policy; rather it reflected a combination of the policies of (US) oil multinationals and national governments (see O'Dell, 1976).

The absence of a general energy policy did not mean that there were no Community policies for parts of the energy sector. Through the ECSC, the Community was involved in coal: in the 1950s via policies to maximize output as the Community's economy was heavily reliant on this source of energy, and in the 1960s in the rationalization of coal production, the reconversion of coalfield regions via attempts to introduce new industries and alternative sources of employment, and coping with the social costs of reducing coal output. Furthermore, through Euratom the Community was involved in encouraging the use of nuclear power as an energy source (see Chapter 4). Increasingly from 1973, however, pressures have grown for a more co-ordinated, comprehensive Community energy policy, and though this may be gradually emerging (Bailey, 1976; Hafele and Wolfgang, 1978), as yet the goal of attaining such a policy remains a rather distant one (see also Chapter 6).

1.4.4 Transport policy

In many ways transport is inextricably linked with the costs of energy, so it is not surprising that prior to 1973 progress towards a Community common transport policy had been slow and partial, and limited to railroad and inland waterways (Despicht, 1969; Thomson, 1976). However, there were other barriers to the emergence of such a policy. National governments, albeit to varying degrees, were very heavily involved in the transport sector via policies of infrastructure provision and fare and rate subsidization (directly contrary to the free market aims of the Treaty of Rome) and in many cases were running public transport services directly. Second, since 1953 the European Conference of Ministers of Transport, a permanent body made up of eighteen European countries, had met with a view to developing transport at a European – rather than just a European Community – level, while more specific measures aimed at European integration had been put forward in the areas of air, rail and road transport. A third reason was that increasingly in the period leading up to 1973 grave inconsistencies came to be perceived between the strictly commercial character of policies towards transport as specified in the Treaty of Rome and the reality of transport provision within the Community, together with growing concern as to the environmental, social and (after

Table 1.5 The European Community's financial instruments with regional objectives

Instruments	Legal basis	Which regions?	Which sectors?	Types of financial assistance	Amounts from the beginning until 1977 in million EUA
ECSC fund	ECSC Treaty article 54, first paragraph	Coal and steel areas	Coal and steel industries	Loans at low rate of interest	2500
ECSC fund	ECSC Treaty article 54, second paragraph	Coal and steel areas	Worker's housing	Loans at 1%	400
ECSC fund	ECSC Treaty article 56, first paragraph	Coal and steel areas	New industries allowing regional conversion	Loans at low rate of interest	500
ECSC fund	ECSC Treaty article 56, first paragraph	Coal and steel areas	Tideover and resettlement allowances and retraining costs for coal and steel workers	50% grants	250
EIB	EEC Treaty article 130	Less-developed regions, conversion, common interest	All sectors	Loans at financial market rate	7000
EAGGF – guidance section	Regulation no. 17/64/EEC	Agricultural regions	Agricultural production and marketing structures	25% to 45% subsidies	2000
EAGGF – guidance section	Directives 75/268/EEC to 75/276/EEC	Mountain and hill farming areas and less favoured farming areas	Agricultural joint investment	25% subsidies	40
Social fund	EEC Treaty articles 123–6, Decision 71/66/EEC	All regions	Vocational training	50% grants	1000
Regional fund	Regulation (EEC) no. 724/75	Regions covered by the regional policies of member states	Artisans, industry, services, infrastructures	10% to 30% grants 20% grants	1350

Source: Romus, 1979: 113

1973 especially) energy cost implications of these (for example, over the loss of land to transport routes, over the atmospheric pollution resulting from petrol combustion engines and over the immobility of the carless in an era when policy concerns were directed towards the needs of those with cars – see Burt, 1972; OECD, 1973; Hillman *et al.*, 1973; Watkins, 1972).

Increasingly after 1973, though, a rather different approach to Community transport policy emerged. This was a reflection of a combination of the perceived limits to previous policies, the energy crisis and the enlargement of the Community from six to nine members. While the focus of policy remains on the market as the route to efficient resource utilization, the emphasis has switched from private to social marginal costs so as to encompass the many environmental and social costs generated by transport activities. Moreover, the emphasis has switched increasingly to infrastructure provision as the perceived key to a successful common transport policy (Commission of the European Communities, 1979a).

1.4.5 Regional policy

As we noted above (section 1.4.1) the preamble to the Treaty of Rome explicitly advocated the reduction of regional inequality within the Community although it contained no proposals for a regional policy as such. In fact, national governments have long pursued regional policies within their own territories (see Yuill *et al.*, 1980, for a full review) while other Community policies have had marked regional impacts – in the case of the CAP, an unintended and undesirable one of widening regional inequalities. Other policies, however, have been implemented with a deliberate intention of narrowing regional inequalities (see Table 1.5): for example, the European Investment Bank (EIB) functions very largely as a regional development bank, channelling almost 30 per cent of its total loans to the Italian Mezzogiorno (see Figure 1.6); the European social fund increasingly since 1971 has been directed to regions with persistent and serious

Figure 1.6

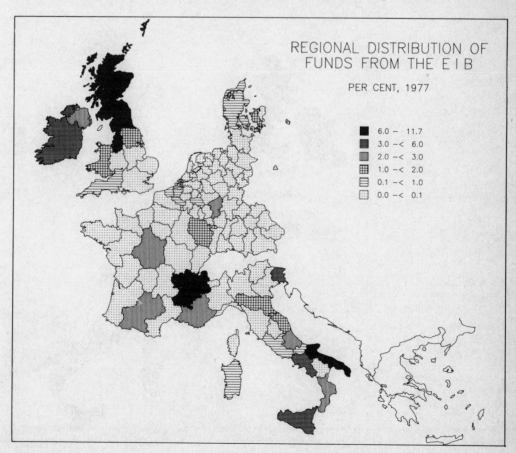

unemployment problems; and as a final example, the provisions of the ECSC allow for financial aid to be granted to help the reconversion of declining coal and steel regions.

It was not until 1969, however, that the Commission first proposed an explicit formal Community regional policy. In 1972, in the course of the discussions at the Paris Summit concerning Community enlargement from six to nine members, it was agreed to establish a specific instrument to implement such a policy, the European Regional Development Fund (ERDF), by the end of 1973 (see Carney and Hudson, 1979). In fact, because of disagreement as to the size of its budget, it was not set up until March 1975. Grants from the ERDF are limited to regions and areas benefiting from national systems of regional aid (see Figure 1.7) and, in principle, are meant to be additional to national aid rather than a means whereby national governments can cut their own levels of public expenditure. Given the mounting tide of unemployment and the Community's probable enlargement to twelve members (see Tsoukalis, 1981; also Chapter 3), the nature and scope of Community regional policy is likely to be a central issue in the 1980s (see Armstrong, 1978; also Chapter 6).

1.4.6 Policies towards areas outside the Community

A detailed examination of the Community's foreign policy is clearly beyond the scope of the present Atlas (for example, see Twitchett, 1975). Nevertheless within this broad area (see Figure 1.8) three areas of special interest in the realm of aid and trade policies can be identified in terms of their implications for past and future Community development − non-member countries within Europe (especially those of EFTA); the large and internally heterogeneous block of countries referred to as the Third World; and the emerging dialogue between the Community and the Arab League.

Figure 1.7

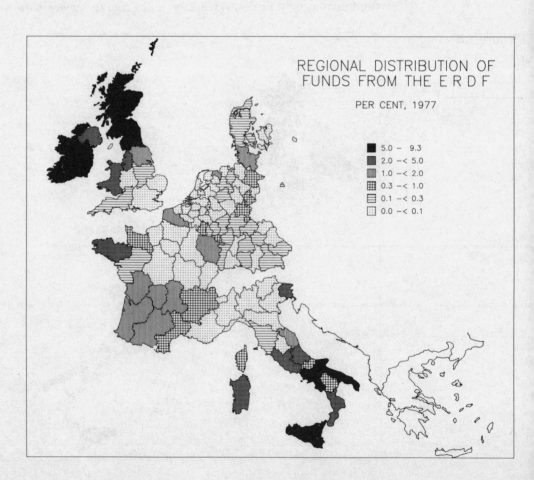

REGIONAL DISTRIBUTION OF
FUNDS FROM THE E R D F

PER CENT, 1977

5.0 − 9.3
2.0 −< 5.0
1.0 −< 2.0
0.3 −< 1.0
0.1 −< 0.3
0.0 −< 0.1

Figure 1.8
Links between the
European
Community and
non-Community
areas

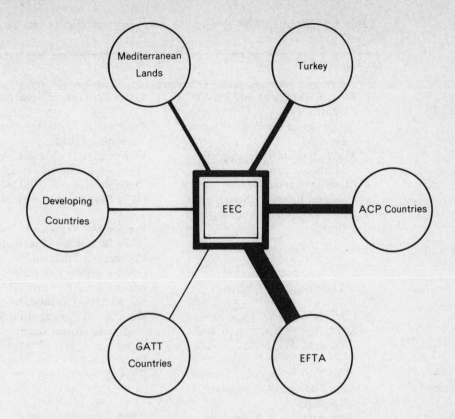

1.4.6.1 Relations with the remaining members of EFTA A series of trade arrangements
was concluded during 1972/3 (see Commission of European Communities Spokesman's
Group, 1980). These established a free trade area between the Community and the
remaining members of EFTA (Austria, Finland, Iceland, Norway, Portugal, Sweden
and Switzerland) for industrial as well as certain agricultural processed products.
Agriculture was not, as such, included although some concessions were made on both
sides to run parallel with the agreements concluded for industrial products.

1.4.6.2 Relations with the Third World Unlike the policies towards the countries of
EFTA, those relating the EEC to the Third World countries also involve aid as well as
trade agreements. Although the Treaty of Rome provided no explicit mandate for an
overall policy towards the Third World and it was not until the Paris Summit of 1972
that the Community began explicitly to develop such a policy, nevertheless since 1957
the Community has evolved a complex web of relationships between itself and the
diverse countries of the Third World. This has been evocatively summarized as a
'pyramid of privilege' (Mishalani *et al.*, 1981) and is set out in Table 1.6 (although, as
the inclusion of countries such as Israel, Portugal and Spain demonstrates, this pyramid
encompasses more than just Third World countries).

The main provisions of these various types of agreement may be summarized as
follows (see Warren, 1977; Lacroix and Perini, 1979: 176–8). The Lomé Convention
first signed in 1975 and renewed in 1980 until 1985 provides for co-operation between
the Community and African, Caribbean and Pacific (ACP) members in several areas,
most notably: freedom of access to the Community for nearly all products originating in
the ACP states; stabilization of the ACP countries' export earnings via the 'Stabex'
system; sales of cane sugar at annually negotiated guaranteed prices from the ACP states
to the Community; measures designed to promote ACP industrialization, especially via
the transfer and adaptation of technology; financial and technical aid to the ACP
countries. The fifty-six (as of March 1979) ACP countries receive about 75 per cent of
all Community aid.

Table 1.6 Relationships between the European Community and the countries of the Third World

Countries	Agreements
1 African, Caribbean and Pacific countries	Lomé Convention (1980 for 5 years)
2 Applicants to the EEC – Spain Portugal	Preferential Trade Agreement (1970), Free Trade Agreement (1972)
3 Maghreb countries – Algeria, Morocco, Tunisia	Preferential Trade and Co-operation Agreements (1976 for unlimited period)
4 Mashreq countries – Egypt, Jordan, Lebanon, Syria	Preferential Trade and Co-operation Agreements (1977 for unlimited period)
5 Other Mediterranean countries –	
Israel	Preferential Trade and Co-operation Agreement (1975 for unlimited period)
Yugoslavia	Preferential Trade and Co-operation Agreement (1980 for unlimited period)
Turkey, Malta, Cyprus	Association Agreements (1980, 1971 and 1973 respectively, for unlimited periods)
6 Other ldcs (except Taiwan)	Generalized System of Preferences
7 South Asia – Bangladesh, India, Pakistan, Sri Lanka	Non-preferential Commercial Co-operation Agreements (1976, 1974, 1976, 1975 respectively, for 5 years)
8 ASEAN – Indonesia, Malaysia, the Philippines, Singapore, Thailand	(One agreement, 1979 for 5 years)
9 Latin America – Argentina, Brazil, Mexico, Uruguay	(1972, 1974, 1976, 1975 respectively, for 3 to 5 years)
10 China, Romania	Non-preferential Trade Agreements (1979 for 5 years, and 1980 for 5 years, respectively)

Source: Adapted from Mishalani *et al.*, 1981: 61

Second, in 1976 and 1977, the Community concluded a revision of a series of bilateral agreements with countries in the southern Mediterranean – Algeria, Egypt, Israel, Jordan, Lebanon, Morocco, Syria and Tunisia – based on their eliminating customs duties on imports from the Community in return for grants and loans to finance agricultural modernization, industrial development and economic diversification, and provisions covering industrial co-operation, patents and private investment (Taylor, 1980). In addition, in the case of Algeria, Morocco and Tunisia, provisions were included relating to the 800,000 migrant workers from those countries in the Community (see Chapter 2). Third, the Community has a variety of commercial co-operation and trade agreements with countries in Asia and Latin America, as well as preferential trading links with over 110 Third World countries via the Generalized System of Preferences (GSP). The GSP involves imports to the Community of manufactured goods or processed agricultural products from the Third World entering duty-free or at reduced rates of duty.

Thus, despite the fact that aid forms a small part of the Community budget, a seemingly impressive web of various types of aid relationships has been established between the Community and semi-peripheral and Third World countries (trade patterns are examined more fully in Chapter 4). Moreover, by 1972 the Community had overtaken the USA as the main source of Third World aid, providing 40 per cent as compared to the USA's 39 per cent. Nevertheless, questions can be raised concerning the aid policies pursued by the Community and its member states. For example, of the total 'aid' granted in 1972, 44 per cent was in the form of direct private investment, often directed at securing access to cheap labour for manufacturing industry (see Frobel *et al.*, 1980; Balassa, 1981) or securing supplies of food or key raw materials for industry: for example, in 1977 over 80 per cent of oil imports to the Community and 32 per cent of those of raw materials for industry originated from the Third World (Lacroix and Perini, 1979: 171), and while 99.5 per cent of the exports from signatories of the Lomé Convention enter the Community duty-free, this is because most of them are agricultural or industrial raw materials (Hewitt and Stevens, 1981: 35). Where manufactured products that would threaten 'sensitive' industries within the Community are concerned, protectionist policies tend to prevail; for example, the second Multi-Fibre Agreement (MFA), signed in 1977, which was coupled with bilateral agreements with some thirty non-member low-cost textile and clothing producing nations (Tsoukalis, 1981: 174). Put another way, Community trade concessions are only granted in those areas where they do not conflict with the interests of Community members but, rather, are necessary to guarantee these.

1.4.6.3 Relations with the Arab world The rise in oil prices in 1973 was a sharp reminder to the Community of its dependence upon the oil-exporting countries of the Arab world; indeed, this trade involvement subsequently evolved to the point where the countries of the Arab League became the most important trading partners of the European Community (Commission of the European Communities Spokesman's Group, 1978). This closer economic tie served as a trigger in the launching of the Euro-Arab dialogue in 1974, encompassing not just economic relations but also social and cultural linkages. So far some progress has been made in relation to international migration and investment flows, as well as on matters relating to energy. While the progress of the dialogue has been rather halting and uneven, less rapid than originally intended, it does mark an important development in so far as it represents a further step in the Community's attempt to evolve a policy towards and linkages with a significant bloc of countries outside of its boundaries. To a degree, there is both overlap and conflict with the Community's emerging policies towards both the Mediterranean and Third World. For example, several countries in North Africa fall both within the Arab world and the Mediterranean world, a point taken up in Chapter 6.

1.5 Concluding comments

From this brief review of its origins and subsequent development, it is clear that while progress has been made towards greater unity within the Community, the road has not always been a smooth one; progress has neither been equal in all directions nor as great as those committed to the ideal of a united Europe would have wished. In the one area where Community policy has developed most fully, agriculture, its effects are not necessarily only those designed and intended. Community policies generally remain, however, poorly developed and ineffective, the sources of real political power within the Community remaining with national governments rather than having been transferred to Community level. Even so, the powers of national governments to influence events for the better are themselves limited, as the 1970s vividly demonstrated and the 1980s continue to demonstrate.

It is against the background of these remarks, then, that we proceed to review recent trends, current issues and to some extent future prospects in the economic, political and social life of the Community, beginning with a consideration of population structures, trends and forecasts. Following from this, recent trends and problems of the labour market and the economy are discussed, leading to a review of lifestyles and living conditions in the Community. Finally, some important issues and problems for the future are identified, problems which of necessity may have to be solved at Community level if the Community itself is to develop further or perhaps even survive in its present form.

THE CHANGING POPULATION OF THE EUROPEAN COMMUNITY

2.1 Introduction

The size and spatial distribution of the population are issues of central importance, both in terms of their implications for living conditions and the quality of individuals' lives, and for employment and the economy. These issues are considered in succeeding chapters but we begin here by outlining some of the basic demographic and locational characteristics of the Community's population. The chapter begins by examining the changing population numbers and densities within the Community. Next the components of change, birth and death rates and net migration, are examined, leading into some discussion of changing population structures. Finally, some of the public expenditure implications of these changing structures are examined.

2.2 Population numbers and densities

2.2.1   Community and national trends

By 1978 the population of the Community stood at almost 260 million, the bulk of which was concentrated in four of the then nine member countries (see Figure 2.1). Together, France, Germany, Italy and the UK accounted for 87 per cent of this total (see Figure 2.2; see also Kosinski, 1970), although the highest densities occurred in the smaller states of Belgium and the Netherlands: in 1978 densities (persons/sq. km.) were as follows: Netherlands, 339; Belgium, 332; Germany, 247; UK, 229; Luxembourg, 138; Denmark, 118; France, 98; Ireland, 47; giving an EEC average of 170 (Commission of the European Communities, 1981a: Annex Table 2.6). Overall, however, viewed in an international comparative context, the Community had assumed a position of considerable importance in terms of the size of its population relative to those of the USA and USSR, easily exceeding the 222 million of the former and being only marginally less than the 261 million of the latter (World Bank, 1980). Indeed, if one were to include the tenth member of the Community, Greece, which in 1978 had a population of some 9.4 million, then the Community population would exceed that of the USSR. The probable future expansion of the Community southwards into the Mediterranean to incorporate Portugal and Spain, which in 1978 had populations of 9.8 million and 37.1 million, would further reinforce the Community's superiority relative to the USA and USSR in terms of population numbers.

Irrespective of expansion due to the addition of new members, there has been a considerable growth in the Community's population in the post-war period in any case; one of the more striking features of the demographic situation has been the great increase in the numbers of people within the Community. This can be considered in two complementary ways. First, in terms of absolute numbers, the total population of the Community rose from almost 216 million in 1950 to over 259 million in 1978, this increase of almost 43 million representing about 20 per cent of the 1950 total. This growth was concentrated in the pre-1970 period, rather more so in the 1960s than 1950s. Second, these increases can be considered in relative terms and in terms of rates of change. For the Community as a whole, the annual average rate of growth over the period 1950–75 was 0.6 per cent per annum, although by the late 1970s this was slowing down markedly. Indeed, in demographic as well as economic terms (see Chapters 3 and 4), 1974 marked a watershed, with a very sharp fall in population growth rates occurring after that date.

THE CHANGING POPULATION OF THE EUROPEAN COMMUNITY

Figure 2.1

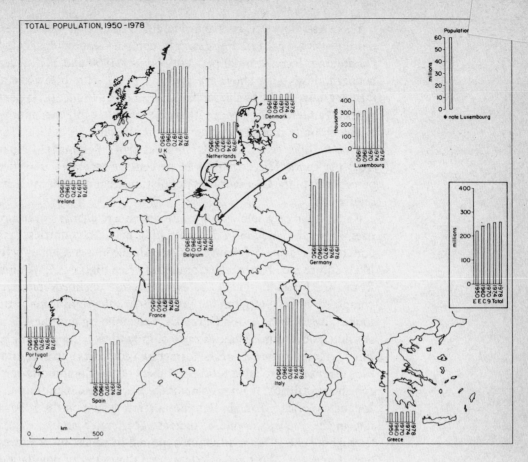

TOTAL POPULATION, 1950-1978

Figure 2.2

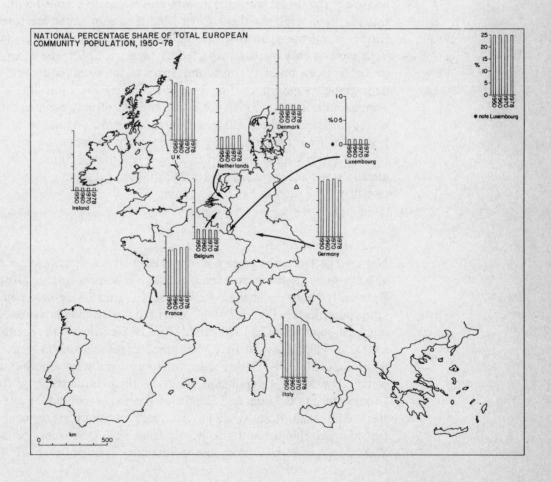

NATIONAL PERCENTAGE SHARE OF TOTAL EUROPEAN
COMMUNITY POPULATION, 1950-78

There has, however, been considerable variation at national level around this Community average pattern. For example, comparing individual countries with the overall Community increase of 20 per cent between 1950 and 1978 reveals a clear dichotomy between those with above-average and those with below-average increases. In the former group are the Netherlands (32.4 per cent), France (27.4 per cent), Germany (22.6 per cent) and Italy (20.9 per cent), with these latter three accounting for over 80 per cent of the absolute increase in numbers, in all some 36 million. In the latter group are Ireland (9.0 per cent), the UK (10.4 per cent), Belgium (14.3 per cent) and Denmark (16.3 per cent). These changes in percentage increases are reflected in the changing percentages of the Community's population accounted for by each member country (see Figure 2.2).

Rather than rely solely on overall percentage changes over a relatively long period, useful though these are in differentiating between countries, it is possible to consider annual average rates of change for individual countries, not only for the present but also likely future members of the Community (see Figure 2.3). A number of points emerge from this. First, in general, rates of increase declined considerably in the 1970s as compared to the 1960s, but within the 1970s, the significant turning point is 1974 and, indeed, by the later 1970s Germany, Luxembourg and the UK were all experiencing absolute population decline as rates of growth were replaced by gentle rates of decline. Furthermore, in the case of the former two countries and in contrast to the remainder of the current and probable future members of the Community this decline is forecast to continue until 1995 (Commission of the European Communities, 1978). Second, while Ireland experienced an absolute population decline in the 1950s and a modest growth rate in the 1960s, the rate of increase accelerated and was sustained at a high level throughout the 1970s, a situation expected to persist for the foreseeable future. Moreover, Greece and Portugal also increased their rates of population growth in the 1970s relative to the 1960s, while the growth rate for Spain declined only marginally from an initially high level. As these three Mediterranean states are forecast to experience further population growth of nine million by the end of the century (World Bank, 1980), with most of this increase expected to occur in Spain, the accession of Greece and probable accession of Portugal and Spain to the Community will be of considerable demographic significance. For it will increase upwards forecasts of the Community's population in the late 1970s for a Community of nine members (Commission of the European Communities, 1978), which anticipated a population growth of 0.2 per cent per annum from 1975 until 1985, to give a total population then of 261 million, followed by zero growth until 2015. In fact, by 1980 the Community of Nine's population already stood at marginally under 260 million, suggesting that these forecasts in any case may have been rather conservative.

2.2.2 Regional trends

Not unexpectedly, the pattern of population structure and change is much more variable at regional than national level, although in some ways there are marked similarities between the patterns at these two scales. In terms of regional populations and population densities (see Figure 2.4) the pattern in the later 1970s was one of great variability. Regional populations in 1978 varied from 16.8 million in the South East of the UK to 14,000 in Val d'Aosta in Italy. The three largest regions in terms of population (the South East of the UK, Ile de France and Lombardia in Italy) accounted for 13.8 per cent of the Community's population while the three smallest (Val d'Aosta, the region of Luxembourg in Belgium and Corsica in France) accounted for just 0.2 per cent of the total. More significantly, given the great variation in regional areas, population densities also fluctuated tremendously from 3396 inhabitants per square kilometre in West Berlin to 26 in Corsica (the Community average being 170: Commission of the

Figure 2.3

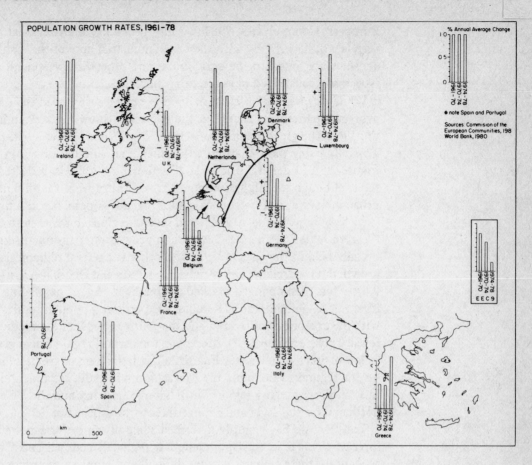

Figure 2.4

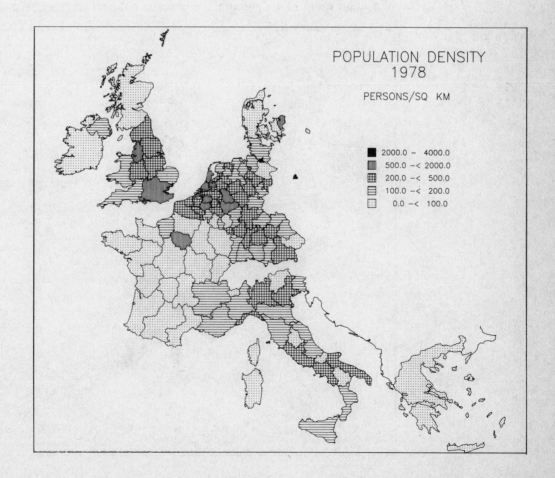

European Communities, 1981a). More generally, high regional population densities correlate quite strongly with the urban-industrial core of the Community while lower densities are found in the agricultural and otherwise peripheral areas – these other aspects are considered in succeeding chapters.

While this regional pattern in 1978 is much more varied than the national one, the aggregate patterns of change at the two scales show marked similarities. Thus during the 1960s the great majority of regions experienced growth, the differentiating factor generally being the rate of growth rather than whether or not growth took place (see Figure 2.5). In general, the pace of national growth was reflected in regional growth rates, although the highest regional growth rates were found outside the 'traditional' urban-industrial core: Corsica and Provence-Alpes-Côte d'Azur in France; Lazio (which contains Rome) in Italy; and several regions in the eastern Netherlands, outside the core region of the west. Although growth rates declined somewhat, this pattern broadly held in the early 1970s, with other peripheral regions also experiencing high growth rates – Ireland, East Anglia, Luneburg and Oberbayern in Germany (see Figure 2.6) – but then changed markedly after 1974. Again paralleling changes at national level, most German and UK regions experienced population decline, and elsewhere, with the exceptions of Ireland and the south and east of the Netherlands, growth rates fell sharply (see Figure 2.7). Moreover, forecasts of regional changes up to 1985 likewise follow national patterns (see Figure 2.8) with the areas of greatest forecast increase being several regions in Belgium, the Mezzogiorno in Italy, Ireland, and Nord-Pas-de-Calais in France, with many regions in Belgium, Germany and the UK as well as several in north and central Italy and France forecast to experience decline.

Thus far, we have simply described some of the major aspects of past changes and forecast changes in total population at regional, national and Community level. To account for these changes is more difficult and requires analysing the combined effects of a whole range of demographic, economic, political and social factors, some of which

Figure 2.5

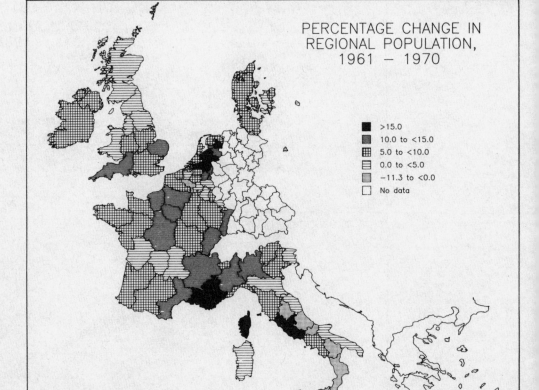

PERCENTAGE CHANGE IN
REGIONAL POPULATION,
1961 – 1970

■ >15.0
▨ 10.0 to <15.0
▦ 5.0 to <10.0
▤ 0.0 to <5.0
▨ −11.3 to <0.0
☐ No data

Figure 2.6

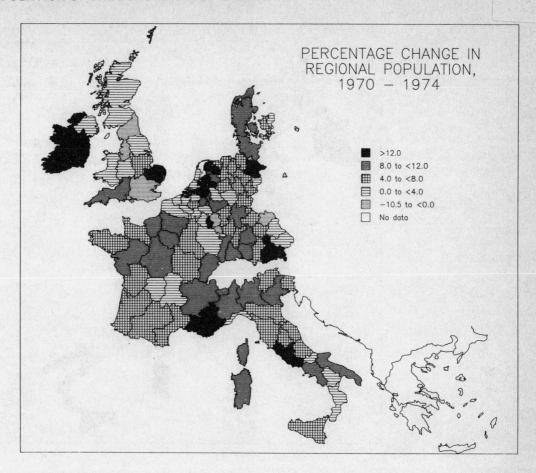

PERCENTAGE CHANGE IN
REGIONAL POPULATION,
1970 – 1974

>12.0
8.0 to <12.0
4.0 to <8.0
0.0 to <4.0
−10.5 to <0.0
No data

Figure 2.7

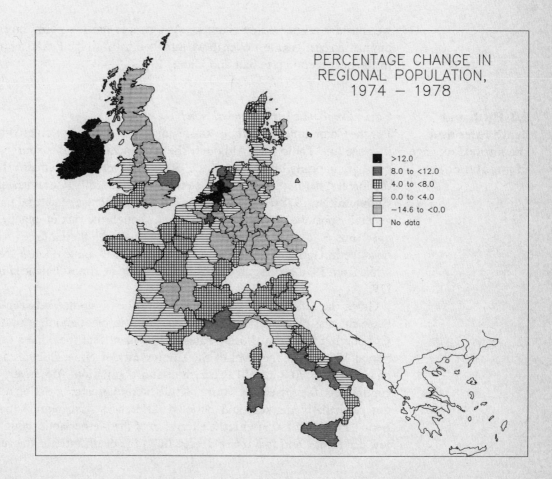

PERCENTAGE CHANGE IN
REGIONAL POPULATION,
1974 – 1978

>12.0
8.0 to <12.0
4.0 to <8.0
0.0 to <4.0
−14.6 to <0.0
No data

Figure 2.8

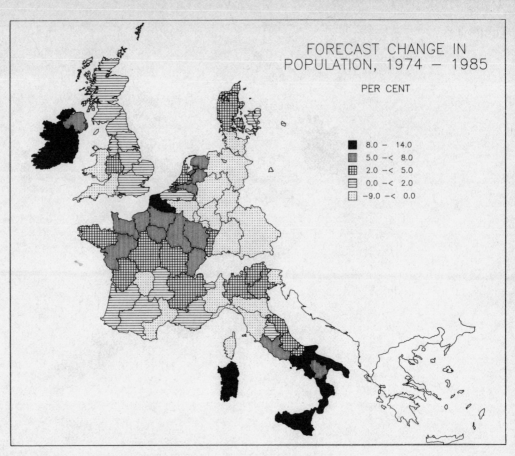

FORECAST CHANGE IN
POPULATION, 1974 − 1985

PER CENT

■ 8.0 − 14.0
▥ 5.0 −< 8.0
▦ 2.0 −< 5.0
▤ 0.0 −< 2.0
▨ −9.0 −< 0.0

we consider in succeeding chapters. As a simple starting point, however, these overall population changes are broken down into their natural change and migration components in the next section (see Salt and Clout, 1976).

2.3 Birth and death rates and the natural change of population

2.3.1 Community and national trends

For the Community as a whole, the major source of population growth has been natural increase (see Table 2.1). Although the increment from this source had slowed down quite dramatically by the end of the 1970s, it nevertheless remains the main element in the forecast net population increase for the Community (Commission of the European Communities, 1978). While at national level the balance of natural population change is generally positive throughout the period, though the rate of change has tended to fall over time − a good example of this being the Netherlands − natural change was negative in Germany throughout the 1970s and in Luxembourg from 1976 onwards, while from 1976 births and deaths were actually or almost balanced in Belgium and the UK.

Given the definition of natural change as the difference between births and deaths, these changes raise questions about variations in birth and death rates (see Table 2.2). Considering first annual death rates, it is evident that these have varied little over the period 1950−78 at the level of the Community of Nine, fluctuating within a narrow band between 10.7 and 11.0 per thousand population. Moreover, this is forecast to continue for the forseeable future. While there is greater variation at national level it is not particularly marked, and national differences have tended to decrease over the period so that by 1975 (with the exception of the Netherlands, which has an extremely low death rate, and to a lesser degree Italy) the death rates of the remaining countries

Table 2.1 Components of population change, 1950–78

	Changes per 100 inhabitants												
	1950–4		1955–9		1960–4		1965–9		1970–5		1976		1978	
	A	B	A	B	A	B	A	B	A	B	A	B	A	B
Belgium	0.5	0.0	0.5	0.2	0.5	0.2	0.3	0.1	0.1	0.2	0.0	0.1	0.1	
Denmark	0.9	−0.1	0.8	−0.1	0.8	0.0	0.7	0.0	0.5	0.1	0.2	0.1	0.2	
France	0.7	0.1	0.7	0.4	0.7	0.7	0.6	0.2	0.5	0.2	0.3	0.0	0.4	
FR Germany	0.5	0.5	0.5	0.7	0.7	0.4	0.5	0.2	−0.1	0.4	−0.2	−0.1	−0.2	
Ireland	0.9	−1.2	0.9	−1.5	1.0	−0.8	1.0	−0.6	1.1	0.0	1.1	−0.1	1.1	
Italy	0.9	−0.2	0.9	−0.2	1.0	−0.2	0.9	−0.2	0.6	0.1	0.4	0.1	0.3	
Luxembourg	0.3	0.3	0.4	0.2	0.4	0.7	0.3	0.3	0.0	1.0	−0.2	−0.4	−0.1	
Netherlands	1.5	−0.2	1.4	0.0	1.3	0.1	1.1	0.1	0.7	0.3	0.5	0.1	0.4	
UK	0.4	−0.2	0.5	0.0	0.7	0.0	0.6	−0.1	0.3	−0.1	0.0	0.0	0.0	
EEC Nine	0.7	0.0	0.7	0.1	0.8	0.1	0.7	0.0	0.4	0.2	n.a.	n.a.	0.1	

Not available (1978 B column)

Sources: Eurostat, 1976 and 1978; Commission of the European Communities, 1981a

Notes: A – natural change is calculated as the differences between births and deaths
B – migratory balance is calculated as the total change minus A

Table 2.2 Birth and death rates (annual per 1000 population), 1950–78

	1950		1960		1965		1970		1975		1977		1978	
	BR	DR	BR	DR	BR	DR	BR	DR	BR	DR	BR	DR	BR	DR
Belgium	16.8	12.5	16.9	12.4	16.5	12.2	14.8	12.3	12.2	12.2	12.4	11.4	12.4	11.7
Denmark	18.6	9.2	16.6	9.5	18.0	10.1	14.4	9.8	14.2	10.1	12.2	10.0	12.2	10.4
France	20.5	12.7	17.9	11.4	17.7	11.1	16.7	10.6	14.1	10.6	14.1	10.1	13.8	10.2
FR Germany	16.3	10.6	17.5	11.6	17.8	11.6	13.4	12.1	9.7	12.1	9.5	11.5	9.4	11.8
Greece	–	–	19.0	8.0	–	–	–	–	–	–	15.0	11.0	–	–
Ireland	21.4	12.7	21.4	11.5	22.1	11.5	21.9	11.4	21.5	10.6	21.3	10.3	21.1	10.0
Italy	19.3*	10.2*	18.1	9.6	19.1	10.0	16.8	9.7	15.1	10.0	n.a.	n.a.	12.6	9.5
Luxembourg	13.9	11.5	15.9	11.8	16.0	12.4	13.0	12.4	11.1	12.3	11.1	11.1	11.4	11.7
Netherlands	22.7	7.5	20.8	7.6	20.0	8.0	18.3	8.4	13.0	8.3	12.5	7.9	12.6	8.2
Portugal	–	–	24.0	11.0	–	–	–	–	–	–	19.0	11.0	–	–
Spain	–	–	21.0	9.0	–	–	–	–	–	–	18.0	9.0	–	–
UK	16.2	11.7	17.5	11.5	18.3	11.5	16.3	11.8	12.4	11.8	11.7	11.7	12.3	11.9
EEC Nine	18.2	11.0	17.9	10.9	18.3	10.9	15.9	11.0	12.9	11.0	n.a.	n.a.	12.1	10.7

Sources: Eurostat, 1976 and 1978; World Bank, 1979; Commission of the European Communities, 1981a

Notes: BR – birth rate
DR – death rate
* 1951 data

were clustered around the Community average; moreover Greece, Portugal and Spain also had death rates that were similar to those of the Nine in 1977.

In contrast, variations in birth rates (fertility) have been, currently are, and will continue to be the main determinant of the natural movement of the population.* From

---

* The most accurate method of assessing fertility changes is to consider the number of children born to women of particular generations. But while appropriate for considering historical movements over a long period, for the relatively short-term variations of the post-war period, the easier (from the point of view of data availability) although potentially more hazardous method (since it combines women from differing generations) of examining birth rates per annum of necessity must be adopted.

Figure 2.9

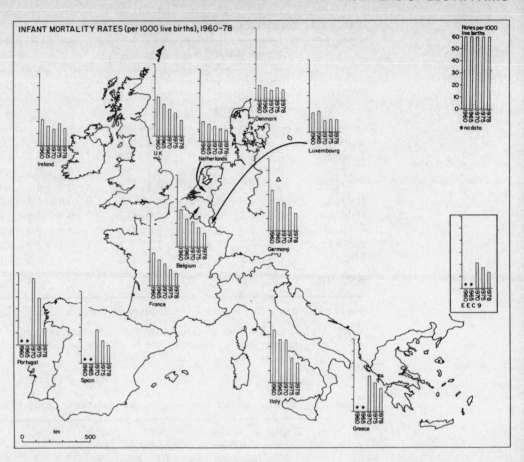

1950 to 1965, annual birth rates remained quite stable in the Community at about 17 to 18 per thousand population – but then fell sharply. With the major exception of Ireland, and to a lesser degree France, birth rates in the remaining member countries had converged at levels of around 11 to 12 per thousand by 1978, although the rate in Germany was well below average. At least in part, however, falling birth rates were offset by falling infant mortality rates (see Figure 2.9). In contrast to their similar death rates, there is a major difference between Greece, Portugal and Spain and the majority of the Community as regards birth rates, with the rates in these three countries being between those for France and Ireland in 1977, following a decline from initially much higher rates.

2.3.2 Regional trends

While the natural increase of the population has tended to fall at national level through-out the Community since 1961, there has been considerable variation between regions throughout the period (see Figures 2.10 to 2.13). For example, while in 1961 all regions except West Berlin experienced natural population increase, the rate of increase varied between 1.6 per thousand in Liège in Belgium and 17.7 per thousand in North Brabant in the Netherlands. Generally, regional variation at Community level broadly reflected national differences, although this is not to say that there were not considerable inter-regional variations within countries, especially between the Italian north and south. In contrast to 1961, by 1978 many regions were experiencing natural population decline – especially in Germany and the UK – but of the remaining member countries, only Ireland (itself a single region) and the Netherlands lacked regions of natural decrease. Of the remainder, with the exception of Ireland, the highest rate of increase had fallen to 9.7 per thousand in Campania in Italy.

Figure 2.10

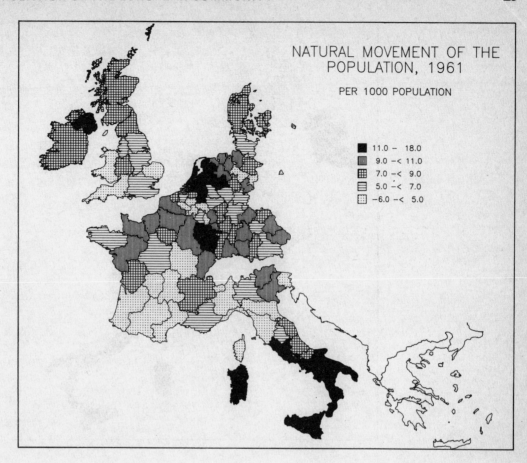

NATURAL MOVEMENT OF THE
POPULATION, 1961

PER 1000 POPULATION

■	11.0 – 18.0
	9.0 –< 11.0
	7.0 –< 9.0
	5.0 –< 7.0
	–6.0 –< 5.0

Figure 2.11

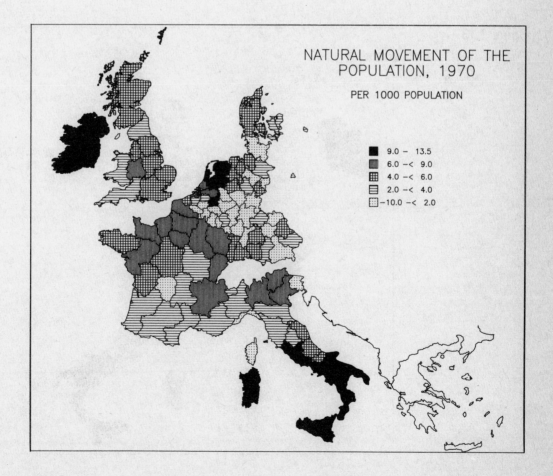

NATURAL MOVEMENT OF THE
POPULATION, 1970

PER 1000 POPULATION

■	9.0 – 13.5
	6.0 –< 9.0
	4.0 –< 6.0
	2.0 –< 4.0
	–10.0 –< 2.0

Figure 2.12

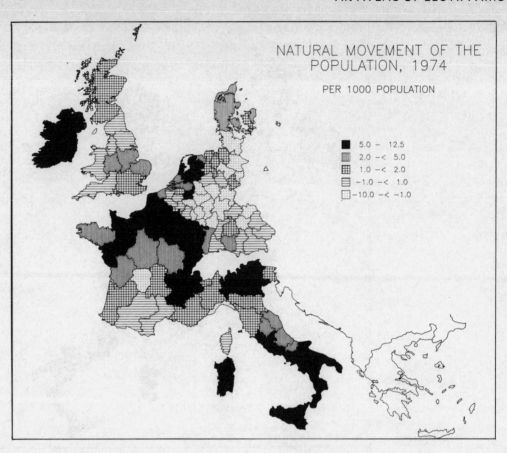

NATURAL MOVEMENT OF THE
POPULATION, 1974

PER 1000 POPULATION

5.0 – 12.5
2.0 –< 5.0
1.0 –< 2.0
–1.0 –< 1.0
–10.0 –< –1.0

Figure 2.13

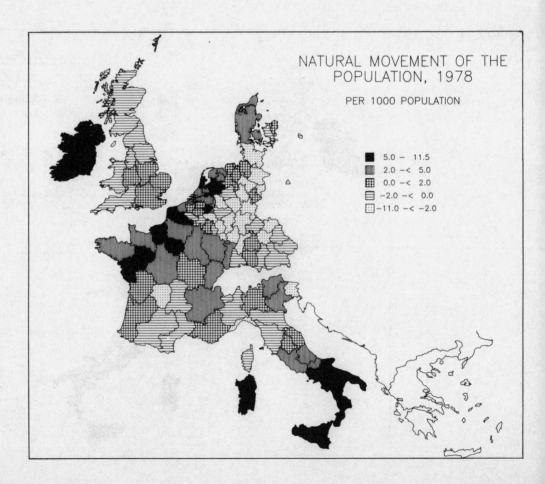

NATURAL MOVEMENT OF THE
POPULATION, 1978

PER 1000 POPULATION

5.0 – 11.5
2.0 –< 5.0
0.0 –< 2.0
–2.0 –< 0.0
–11.0 –< –2.0

Consideration of regional variations in birth and death rates (see Figures 2.14 to 2.17) reveals a similar pattern to that at national level with comparatively little temporal variation in death rates but marked declines in birth rates, with these falling below death rates in many regions by 1978, particularly in Germany but more generally across the Community. Nevertheless, although less markedly than in 1960, both death rates and more especially birth rates still exhibited considerable inter-regional variation in 1978, remaining highest in Ireland, parts of southern Italy and in Nord-Pas-de-Calais in France, as they had done in 1961.

2.3.3   Reasons for variation in natural changes of population

Thus far we have briefly described the pattern of population change resulting from the evolution of birth and death rates. Why should such changes have taken place? This is not an easy question to answer but we can briefly point to four sorts of influential factors (see also Ilberry, 1981: 14–16).

The first and most obvious factor is simply that different areas have varying population age structures and, indeed, for any particular area, be it the Community, a country or, especially, a region, the age distribution will vary over time. This issue is one we consider in the following section but, even if one standardizes population to consider age and sex-specific rates, considerable differences remain.

A second reason that one can suggest to help account for these variations is that of cultural and religious differences, particularly as these affect attitudes towards birth control. Those countries – Ireland and France, together with the prospective Mediterranean members – and parts of countries (such as southern Italy) where the Catholic church remains most influential tend to experience higher birth rates. This is not, of course, to claim that only they experience them.

A third relevant factor relates to the degree of incorporation of women into the wage-labour force (which is discussed more fully in the next chapter) although the links between this and birth rates depend upon broader social attitudes towards the role of women in society and on societal provision of child-care facilities.

A fourth factor is the difference in living conditions and standards – a theme we take up at greater length in Chapter 5. For the present, it is sufficient to note two points. In general, increased incomes are associated with smaller family sizes. In terms of its relationship to mortality patterns, rising affluence in general tends to be associated with lower death rates and with a different pattern of causes of death (so that, for example, deaths from certain specific causes, such as particular forms of cancer or heart disease, rise while deaths from infectious diseases, and diseases related to deprivation, fall). However, this is by no means a perfect correlation as those regions with the lowest death rates in the Community – the Netherlands and the Italian Mezzogiorno – are at opposite ends of the spectrum in terms of affluence (see Figure 2.17). As is shown below (Chapter 5), health care improved in the period after 1960 on several quantitative indicators, although unevenly between areas; so while there is some relationship between spatial variations in death rates and medical provision, it is by no means a perfect one.

2.4 Migration and population change

2.4.1   Community and national trends

At the level of the Community, net migration is comparatively unimportant as a source of population change (see Table 2.3). Seemingly paradoxically, at national level migration has been of the utmost importance in relation to such change; it has been argued that variations in national growth patterns have been determined above all by large-scale migrations (Commission of the European Communities, 1978). In fact

Figure 2.14

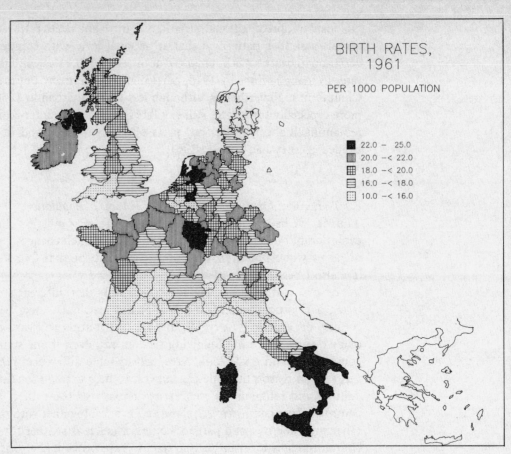

Figure 2.15

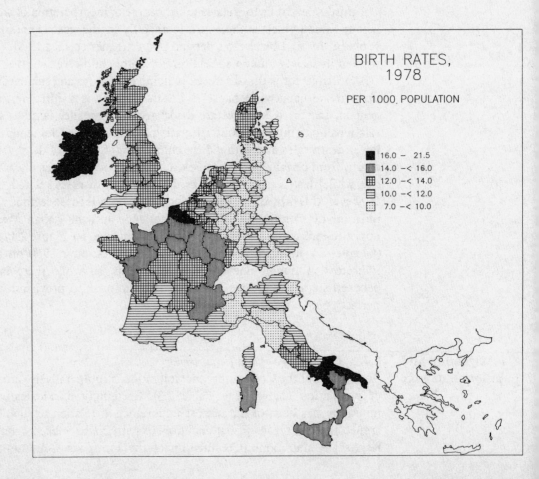

Figure 2.16

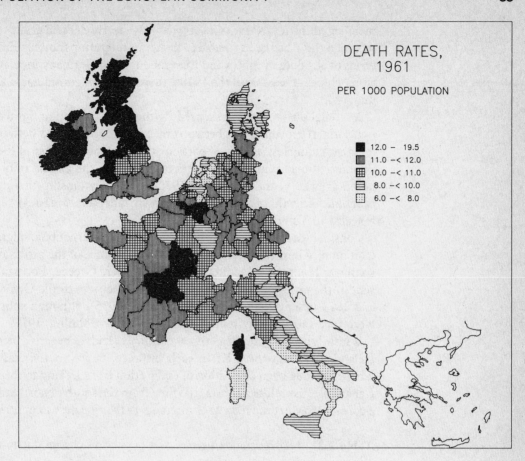

Figure 2.17

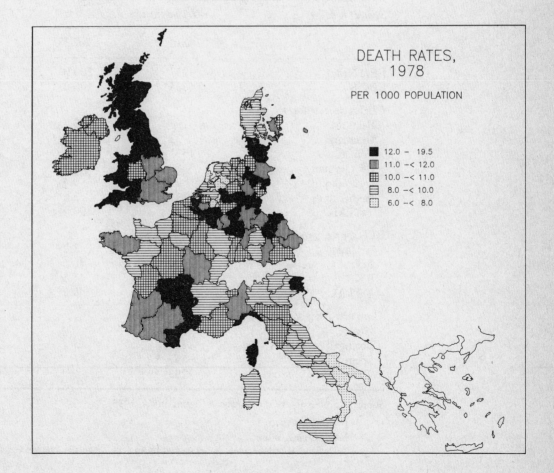

member countries fall into one of two fairly clearly defined groups (see Table 2.3): those
to which there has been considerable net in-migration (notably France and Germany in
terms of absolute numbers and Luxembourg and Germany in relative terms), and those
from which, at least until the 1970s, there has been considerable and sustained net out-
migration.

A crucial distinction is obscured by these net migration figures for they encompass
two sorts of movement – between member countries and between member and non-
member countries. This is of particular importance because of the decisive role played
by international migrant labourers from outside the Community as a source of population growth in the 1960s and 1970s (their relationship to and significance for the
economic growth process is taken up in Chapters 3 and 4). These differences are
revealed in Table 2.3.

Consideration of the main origin countries of international migrants from outside the
Community immediately points to the significance of the extension of the Community
southwards into the Mediterranean. Together, Greece, Portugal, Spain and Turkey
sent in the order of three million migrant labourers to the Community between 1963
and 1973 (see also Fielding, 1975; Mayer, 1975), although subsequently these flows
were very substantially reduced (Kayser, 1977; Böhning, 1979).

Within the Community, three countries had a negative net migration balance:
Ireland, Italy and the UK. In each instance, however, the reasons for this differed.
There has long been a tradition of emigration from Ireland to the UK and USA. In the
Italian case, as well as a substantial flow from the south to northern Italy, there has been
a considerable net movement of migrants to the remaining countries of the Community

Table 2.3 Total migration balance and population change due to migration in the EEC,
1963–73

Spatial unit	Net migration		Annual average population change due to migration[3]
	1000s	% EEC	
EEC Nine	3937	100.0	0.16
EEC Six	4635	100.0	0.25
EEC recipient states			
Belgium	197	3.7	0.17
Denmark	33	0.6	0.06
France	1531	28.2	0.28
FR Germany	3386	63.8	0.52
Luxembourg	23	0.4	0.63
Netherlands	137	2.6	0.12
TOTAL	5307	100.0	0.35
EEC source states			
Ireland	−111	8.1	−0.33
Italy	−638	46.6	−0.11
UK	−621	45.3	−0.10
TOTAL	−1370	100.0	−0.12
Main non-EEC source states			
Greece	−336		−0.35
Portugal[1]	−1122		−1.30
Spain	−657		−0.18
Turkey[2]	−793		−0.21

Source: Commission of the European Communities, 1978

Notes: 1 Excludes 1970
2 Gross emigration
3 Defined as annual average net migration in relation to the average resident population

(Werner, 1974; King, 1976 − although again after 1973 this flow became positive as return migrants outnumbered new emigrants from the Mezzogiorno, on which point see King *et al.*, 1984; King, 1984). Finally, considerable inflows of Commonwealth citizens to the UK were more than offset by out-migration of UK nationals.

The remaining countries of the Community (of Nine) were net recipients of international migrants − particularly France and Germany, which absorbed 93 per cent of net foreign migration between 1963 and 1973. In both cases, however, but again especially for Germany, these net movements conceal a large annual turnover − two-way flows in and out but with a positive net balance. There are, however, rather different patterns between these two countries in the origins of their international migrants (Commission of the European Communities, 1978). Over the period 1965−73, 71 per cent of those to Germany came from four countries: Turkey (27 per cent), Yugoslavia (20 per cent), Italy (14 per cent), Greece (10 per cent). Over the same period, 74 per cent of those to France also originated in four countries, although rather different ones: Portugal (25 per cent), Algeria (23 per cent), Spain (14 per cent), Italy (12 per cent). After 1973 these inflows fell sharply and in the case of Germany net migration was negative in 1975−6, as the impact of restrictions imposed in response to rising domestic unemployment triggered by the recession became apparent. When international migration flows into the Community recovered a little towards the end of the 1970s, this involved not so much a revival of out-migration to the Community from southern Europe but rather the increased incorporation of North African countries as sources of migrant workers (for example, see SOPEMI, 1980: 45) − an indication both of the structural necessity for international migrant workers in the Community's labour market and the wish to avoid the problems of temporary workers increasingly satisfying criteria for permanent residence.

2.4.2 Regional patterns and trends

It is virtually impossible to isolate consideration of inter-regional migration movements from those between rural and urban areas. Until quite recently, the long-established characteristic pattern of inter-regional migration within the countries of the Community has been from predominantly agricultural, rural regions to predominantly urban industrial ones. Superimposed upon this has been a net movement from declining to growing industrial areas. Such a pattern was broadly observable as recently as the 1960s and early 1970s for example (see Figures 2.18 and 2.19; see also Salt and Clout, 1976). These migration flows were associated with structural changes in regional economies (see Chapters 3 and 4) and characteristically were age- and sex-specific, with considerable ramifications for the development of both origin and destination areas: a reflection of this is the fact that net migration balance is often used as one indicator of regional well-being.

Indeed, more generally by the 1970s, quite closely associated with these changes in the pattern of urbanization (although these often occurred within, rather than between regions − themes that we return to in Chapter 5), there was evidence of a new, rather different pattern of inter-regional migration, with more complicated movement patterns than those commonly observed in the past. Especially after 1974, many major, predominantly urban, regions, especially in Germany, began to experience net migration loss (see Figures 2.19 and 2.20) and some even net population loss as a result (see Figure 2.7), although others continued to gain from net in-migration throughout: for example, Provence-Alpes-Côte d'Azur continued to experience both considerable net in-migration and growth in the urban population. At the same time, some mainly rural areas began to gain population through net in-migration (for example, Brittany and Pays de la Loire, most of the regions of central and north-east Italy and a few in the Mezzogiorno), with others continuing to experience net out-migration and in some cases overall population loss.

Figure 2.18

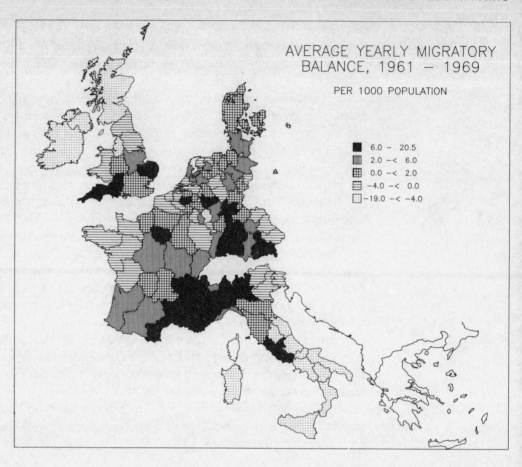

Figure 2.19

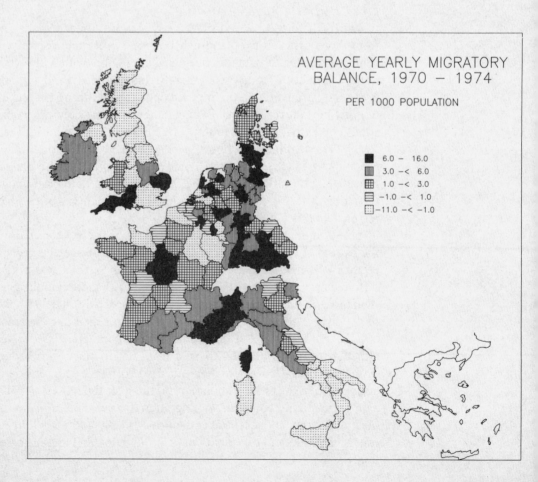

Figure 2.20

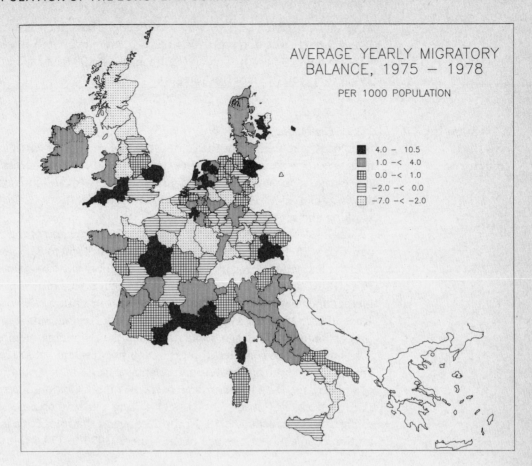

AVERAGE YEARLY MIGRATORY
BALANCE, 1975 – 1978

PER 1000 POPULATION

■	4.0 – 10.5
▦	1.0 –< 4.0
▦	0.0 –< 1.0
▤	–2.0 –< 0.0
▦	–7.0 –< –2.0

How can these migration trends be explained? Several, often interrelated factors need to be considered in accounting for them. First, there are the conditions of life in major urban areas which tend to push some people out of metropolitan areas. Basically these are factors associated with the cost of living, style and pace of life and so on – in a phrase the 'quality of life' in urban areas (see also Chapter 5). Such a decentralization into smaller towns and surrounding regions tends to be a selective out-migration, constrained by employment and income. Secondly, there is a set of factors related to changes in the spatial division of labour within both manufacturing and services (see Chapter 3). These are expressed in a variety of ways. In some 'old' industrial areas, continuing employment loss in old industries such as coal mining, iron and steel, textiles and clothing, had reduced job opportunities, compelling people to move in search of work. This, for example, explains accelerated migration losses from regions such as Lorraine and Nord-Pas-de-Calais in France and continuing losses from regions such as northern England and Scotland, with, as a corollary, regions such as the Italian Mezzogiorno gaining through return migration. A particular expression of this has been the sharp drop in demand for international migrant labour and the repatriation of such labourers, which was of decisive importance in twenty out of thirty German regions experiencing net migration loss between 1975 and 1978 and in regions in the Mezzogiorno gaining population via net migration over the same period. In contrast, the decentralization of parts of manufacturing and service industries into peripheral rural regions has been one reason for the positive migration balances in regions such as East Anglia and South West England, in parts of western France, north-east Italy and western Denmark (a topic developed in the next chapter). Such regions have also experienced net in-migration due to the growth of tourism and retirement there (Law and Warnes, 1976). Finally, one can mention the culturally based regionalist and nationalist revival in several peripheral regions which has led to areas which historically have lost population through net out-migration recently gaining through net in-migration: Brittany (Ardagh, 1982: 131–43), Corsica (Kofman, 1981; 1984) and Wales (Clavel, 1982; Nairn, 1977) would all fall into this category.

2.5 Changing population structures

2.5.1 Community and national trends

The focus here will be on the implications of changes in birth and death rates on age structures – male to female ratios are relatively constant across the Community, the percentage of males varying from 48.6 in the UK to 50.0 in Ireland in 1975 (Eurostat 1976: Tables 8 and 9) – in particular, on the proportions of the population of school, working and retirement ages.

Despite a considerable absolute increase, the proportion of the population of working age (that is 15–64 years) fell from 66.2 per cent in 1950 to 63.3 per cent in 1975 (Figure 2.21). This pattern broadly held at national level but two points are worthy of note. First, in some countries the percentage rose for a part of this period, especially in the Netherlands between 1960 and 1975 but also in France over the same period and in Luxembourg between 1970 and 1975. Second, Ireland consistently has a much lower proportion of working-age population than the remaining member countries.

If, however, one considers forecasts of future developments, a rather different picture emerges, with both an absolute and relative increase in the proportion of the population of working age. This (Commission of the European Communities, 1978) was forecast to rise to a peak of 66.9 per cent in 1985, falling a little to 65.8 per cent in 1995 and then rising to 66.1 per cent in 2015. In absolute terms, this implies an increase from the 163.4 million people of working age in the Nine in 1975 to 175.7 million in 1985 and 176.3

Figure 2.21

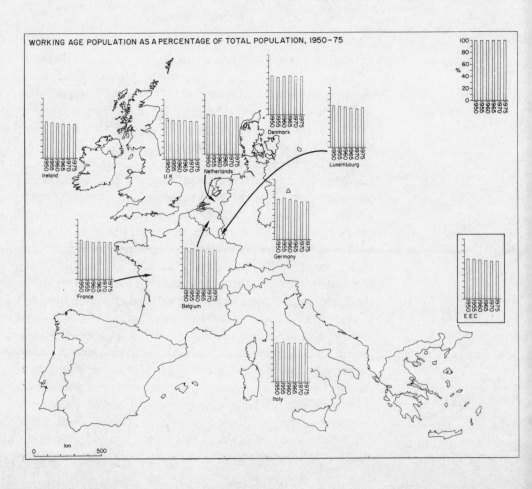

WORKING AGE POPULATION AS A PERCENTAGE OF TOTAL POPULATION, 1950–75

million in 1995, figures which make no allowance for the accession of Greece or possible accession of Portugal and Spain – the possible unemployment implications of these forecast increases are discussed in Chapter 3.

The percentage of the population of school age (0–14 years) rose quite sharply over the period 1950–75, increasing at an annual rate of 0.8 per cent and absolutely from 52.7 million in 1950 to a peak of 61.3 million in 1972 before beginning to decline by 1975. This decline is expected to continue to about 52.5 million by 1990, before increasing to 54 million by 1995. Thus as a percentage of the total population, this age group will fall from 23.4 per cent in 1975 to 19.7 per cent in 1990, then rise slightly to 20.2 per cent in 1995, with national variations around this ranging from some 15 per cent in the case of Germany to 30 per cent in that of Ireland.

Finally, if one considers the proportion of the population of retirement age (65 or more years), this expanded considerably between 1950 and 1975, growing at an average annual rate of 1.9 per cent; in absolute terms, this amounted to an increase of over 11 million people in this age group. Clearly, a marked 'ageing' of the Community's population was taking place over this period, reflecting increasing average life-spans. Furthermore, this process will continue, the number of people in this age group being forecast to rise from 34.3 million in 1975 to 37.6 million in 1995 and to continue to increase into the twenty-first century. This tendency towards an ageing population is especially marked in Germany but also in Denmark and the UK, which exceed the Community average in this respect.

2.5.2 Regional trends

The regional pattern of age-structures reveals quite considerable variations (see Figures 2.22 to 2.24). For example, the effects of past age-selective out-migration from agri-

Figure 2.22

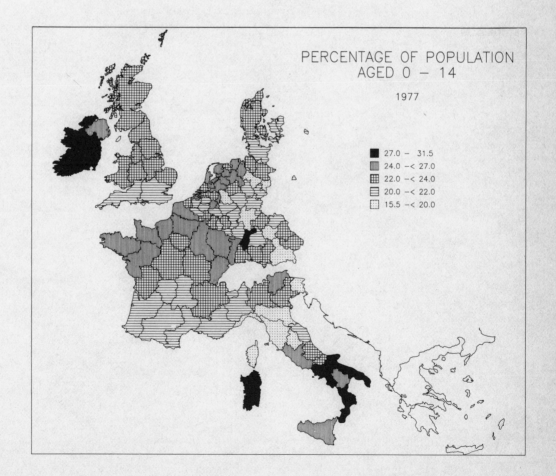

PERCENTAGE OF POPULATION
AGED 0 – 14

1977

27.0 – 31.5
24.0 –< 27.0
22.0 –< 24.0
20.0 –< 22.0
15.5 –< 20.0

Figure 2.23

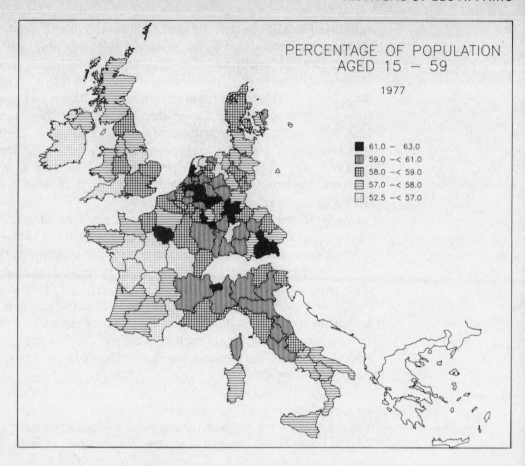

PERCENTAGE OF POPULATION
AGED 15 – 59

1977

■	61.0 – 63.0
	59.0 –< 61.0
	58.0 –< 59.0
	57.0 –< 58.0
	52.5 –< 57.0

Figure 2.24

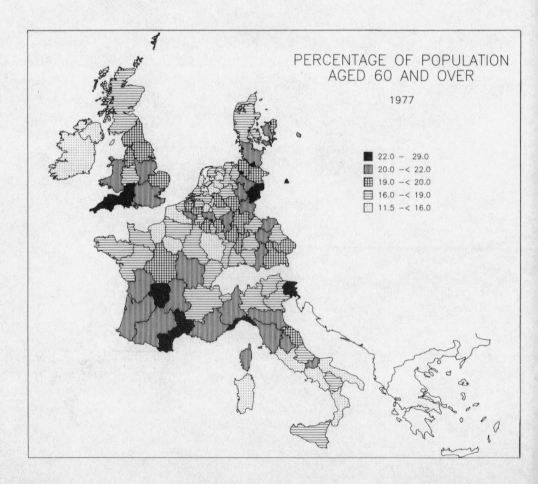

PERCENTAGE OF POPULATION
AGED 60 AND OVER

1977

■	22.0 – 29.0
	20.0 –< 22.0
	19.0 –< 20.0
	16.0 –< 19.0
	11.5 –< 16.0

cultural rural areas is shown in the high proportions of people of retirement age in regions such as Auvergne, Limousin, Midi-Pyrénées and Poitou-Charentes; others have such high proportions as a consequence of retirement to them, such as South West England. Paralleling the former set of rural regions, several old industrial ones have high percentages of people of retirement age because of industrial decline leading to selective out-migration: for example, Liguria. At the other end of the age spectrum there is, not surprisingly, a reasonable correlation between regions with a high percentage of children and those with high birth rates.

2.6 The public expenditure implications of demographic change

The increasing dependent percentage of the population between 1950 and 1975 was one reason for the considerable increase in public expenditure, both capital and revenue (see Chapter 4). A number of specific areas of demographic change can be identified as having implications for the level and pattern of public expenditure in the period to 1975; furthermore, future changes offer opportunities either to improve standards of provision of many basic public services or to trim the level of public expenditure. We briefly consider these here at Community and national levels.

The first of these is the considerable growth of expenditure on pensions, a result not only of the considerable (11 million) increase in numbers but also of the real level of benefits. Such increases were made possible by the generally rapid national economic growth experienced in this period (Chapter 4). Compared to this, the forecast increase of 3.5 million in the number of pensioners between 1975 and 1995 would seem not to pose any insurmountable problems in an even modestly expanding economy; however, in the present and foreseeable economic circumstances of the Community (see Chapter 4), it may pose quite acute problems for national governments of member countries.

Second, the rising number of children in the 1950s and 1960s led to increasing expenditure on family allowances. Conversely, the forecast fall in numbers to 1995 offers the possibility either to increase real per capita allowances or to cut aggregate expenditures – at the moment, the latter appears the more probable course of action.

Third, related to this, changing numbers of children have implications for the level and distribution of educational expenditure (see also Chapter 5). Within education, it is necessary to distinguish between nursery, primary and secondary, and tertiary. With respect to the first of these, the number of 0–4 year-olds peaked in the 1960s and while overall supply expanded, it lagged behind demand. Consequently, future reductions in this age group could allow a higher percentage of children to have access to such facilities without leading to (overall) surplus capacity, or alternatively expenditure could be cut back to maintain, or even decrease, participation levels. The next age group, primary and secondary, is forecast to fall considerably (from 42 million in 1975 to 34 million in 1995) with the primary minimum level being reached in the early 1980s, the secondary in the late 1980s and early 1990s. Again, this broadly presents two options: increase teacher to pupil ratios or cut back on the numbers of both teachers and schools, with the available evidence suggesting that currently it is the latter option that is generally being pursued.

The tertiary sector provides greater problems of forecasting likely demand for facilities since unlike school attendance – which by and large is compulsory – the participation ratio, which is the crucial variable here, is much more difficult to forecast. What can be forecast with some certainty is that the 15–24 age group will rise to a peak, then fall quickly, so that within the Community there will be 17 per cent fewer people in this age group in 1995 than in 1985. Even at the moment, however, despite rising numbers in this age group, there is evidence of reductions in public expenditure at this level of education in several member countries (for example Denmark and the UK).

A fourth area in which demographic change has public expenditure implications is that of health provision. Broadly speaking, health costs per capita are high for the very young, then fall sharply to a plateau before rising again with the onset of old age. In contrast to education, it seems likely that the recent increase of public expenditure on health provision within the Community will continue, reinforced by the changing population age structure. It has been calculated that 'ageing' will increase the average real health costs in the Community of Nine by 9 per cent between 1975 and 1995 (which implies that a rising share of gross domestic product be devoted to this; see Chapter 4). There would, however, be considerable national variations around this average, ranging from increases of 23 per cent in Ireland and 21 per cent in the Netherlands to 3.5 per cent in Germany and 2.5 per cent in Belgium.

What these figures fail to take account of − inevitably, as it is unprecedented − is the impact of the relatively large expected increase in numbers of very old people (aged 85 or more years), from 2 million in 1975 to 3.5 million in 1995. The significance of this is that it implies a considerably increased demand for residential care, which is expensive in per capita terms. Furthermore, within the Community this effect would especially be felt in Belgium, Germany, Luxembourg and the UK, narrowing the differentials between countries in increases on health expenditure as well as increasing aggregate spending within the Community. Indeed, residential care of the elderly may provide one of the few growth sectors in terms of employment in this period (see Chapters 3 and 4).

There is a fifth area in which demographic change is increasingly having implications for public expenditure − rising unemployment. The reasons for this are considered more fully in the following chapter but for the moment it is sufficient to note that to a considerable extent it can be related to demographic as well as economic change and that rising unemployment has considerable and potentially explosive implications for public expenditure.

A final comment: we have in this section broadly described the implications of population change at Community (of Nine) level, noting some national variations. However, given the present distribution of power between the Community and national governments, responses to demographic change in terms of public expenditure decisions will not only reflect the demographic peculiarities of each country but also political priorities within them. The forecasting of demographic change is a rather more straightforward matter than that of political evolution.

2.7 Concluding comments

While it is a fairly straightforward matter to describe selected aspects of population change at various spatial scales, it is considerably more difficult to explain them. Population changes are inextricably bound up with evolving cultural, economic, political and social processes and we have touched upon these at various points in this chapter and the preceding one. In succeeding chapters we discuss at greater length many of these interrelated questions.

THE LABOUR MARKET: PATTERNS AND TRENDS OF EMPLOYMENT AND UNEMPLOYMENT

3.1 Introduction

The operation of the labour market can be reduced to the interaction of the forces of supply and demand. While this is not necessarily the most revealing level of analysis, it is appropriate for an introductory Atlas such as this for it allows us to decompose aggregate changes in terms of supply and demand on the market. Labour supply is clearly related to population size, age and sex structure (issues investigated in the previous chapter). There is, however, no simple relationship between population size and the magnitude of the labour force in an area; the outcome of the mediating processes can be summarized in terms of activity rates and this chapter begins with an examination of these. Then, in somewhat greater depth, the demand side of the market is analysed, examining trends in effective demand for labour in aggregate, by sector and by sex. Particularly at regional level, the processes generating these changing patterns of demand are examined, for at this spatial scale data on variables such as fixed capital investment or labour productivity are rarely available in a consistent form for the whole Community over the post-war period (see Chapter 4). Thus such employment series are of necessity central to any examination of economic change at regional level. Finally, the crucial issue of unemployment is considered, this being a partial indicator of the mismatch of labour supply and demand.

3.2 Activity rates

3.2.1 Community and national trends

In Chapter 2 the growth of the population of working age was outlined. The extent to which this became translated into growth in the labour force depended upon the movement of activity rates – a measure of the degree of participation in the labour market of people of working age. Over the post-war period in the Community, there has been a tendency for male activity rates to fall and female rates, especially those for married women, to rise. For a variety of cultural, economic and social reasons, the degree of incorporation of women into the wage-labour force varied quite markedly at national level, so that by 1973 female activity rates ranged from over 50 per cent in Denmark to less than 25 per cent in the Netherlands (see Figure 3.1). In contrast, despite the growth of female rates, male rates were both at a higher level and much less variable between countries.

One response to the 1970s recession in several countries (Germany, Italy, Netherlands and the UK) has been for male activity rates to decline at an accelerating rate; in contrast, however, in Denmark the male rate rose. Similarly (except in Ireland) female activity rates continued to rise, further narrowing the gap between male and female rates within countries but not between female rates in different countries. This continuing increase in female activity rates was reflected in the changing balance of employment between men and women (see section 3.7 below) and had considerable implications for the trend of unemployment. It is also indicative of changing social attitudes towards the role of women in society and the division of wage and non-wage labour between the sexes.

Figure 3.1

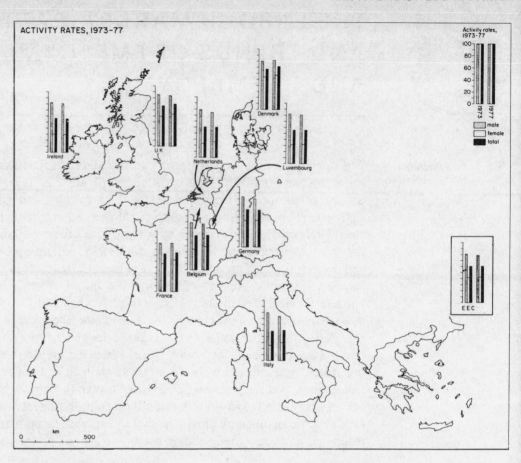

Figure 3.2

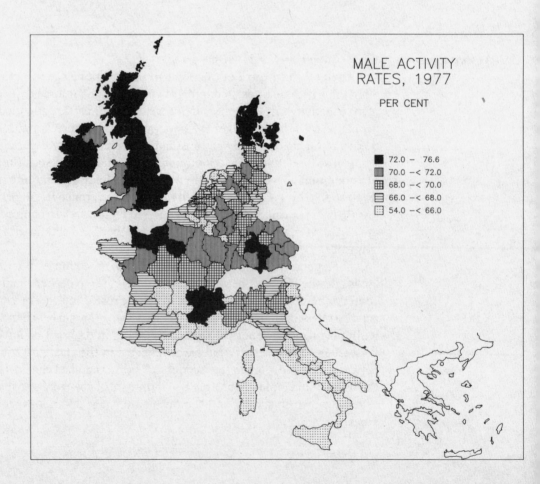

Figure 3.3

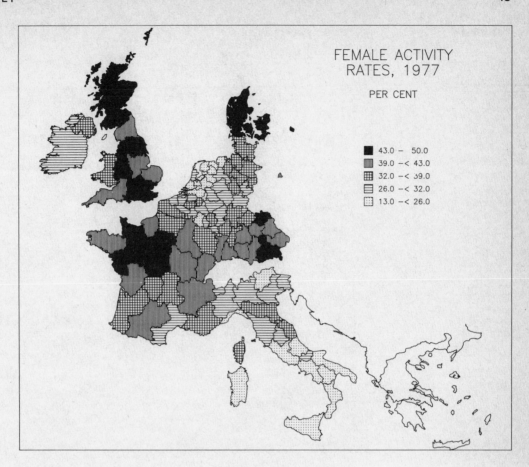

FEMALE ACTIVITY
RATES, 1977

PER CENT

■	43.0 – 50.0
▨	39.0 –< 43.0
▦	32.0 –< 39.0
▤	26.0 –< 32.0
▦	13.0 –< 26.0

3.2.2 Regional patterns

Male and female activity rates for 1977 are shown in Figures 3.2 and 3.3 and these reveal that as at national level the variation in total rates can largely be accounted for in terms of the latter. The regions with the lowest rates, both male and female, are concentrated in the Mezzogiorno and the north of the Netherlands. Conversely, those areas with the highest male and female rates are found in Denmark, much of France, south-east Germany and the UK. In other cases, however, regions with low male rates have high female ones and this reflects the combination of agricultural decline and new forms of industrial development there – for example, in parts of France (see sections 3.4 and 3.5).

3.3 Aggregate employment

3.3.1 Community and national trends

Reflecting the rising effective demand for labour associated with the growth of the European, indeed, the world economy in the post-war period, total employment in the Community grew strongly from 88 million in 1950 to 103 million in 1979 (see Figure 3.4). This growth was particularly concentrated in the 1950s, over half of the total increase (eight million) being recorded then as employment growth rates proceeded to fall with the passage of the 1960s and 1970s. Despite considerable natural increase of the population and of the resident labour force within the Community (see Chapter 2), much of this growth in labour demand was satisfied by international migration. In the 1950s movement from East to West Germany was particularly important in the aftermath of partition while in the 1960s and early 1970s flows of international migrant labourers from the Community's southern Mediterranean fringe played a decisive role in meeting labour demand (Drewer, 1974) and maintaining a degree of labour market

Figure 3.4

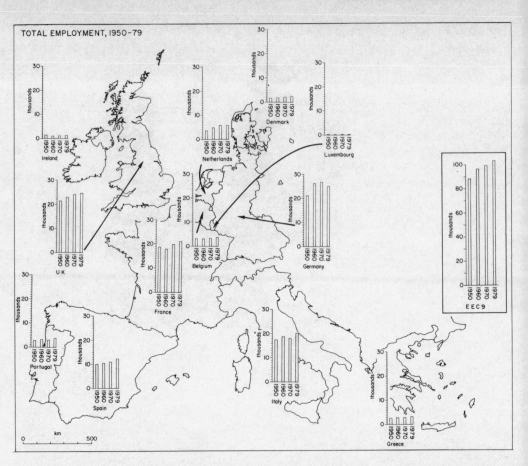

flexibility during a period of full employment (Schmid, 1971; Paine, 1977). Between 1965 and 1973, within the EEC of Six, immigrant workers from other member countries increased by 23 per cent but those from non-member states by 135 per cent (see also Castles and Kosack, 1973; Hume, 1973; Kane, 1978; Power, 1978). In aggregate, these migrant labour flows moved in rhythm with the economic cycle (see Figure 3.5 and also Chapter 2).

After 1974, however, as the oil price rises of November 1973 triggered a major global recession, employment fell sharply, recovering only weakly after 1975. In 1978 it still stood below the peak 1974 level. Among the consequences of this fall in labour demand were rising unemployment within the Community and the virtual cessation of net inflows of international in-migration to it.

At national level, patterns of change were similar to those experienced at Community level. Employment growth was particularly marked in Germany in the 1950s. In the remaining countries employment either grew more modestly or (in the case of Ireland) fell. In contrast, the 1960s and early 1970s witnessed a rather different pattern, employment levels stabilizing in Germany but rising in the remaining countries. International migrant labour flows into France and Germany were particularly important in this period (see Chapter 2). After 1974 employment declined in most countries and thereafter effective demand for labour recovered not only weakly but also unevenly; the major exceptions to this trend were Denmark, Italy and the Netherlands, where growth continued, albeit at a more subdued rate than in preceding years. The expansion in Italy − from many other points of view one of the Community's weakest economies (see Chapter 4) − was apparently striking but much of it reflected an increase in short-time work, rather than in full-time jobs, as a response to the recession and also, to some extent (as in Denmark and the Netherlands), central government public expenditure policies.

Figure 3.5
Inter-
national
migrant
labour
flows in
the
European
Com-
munity,
1958–76

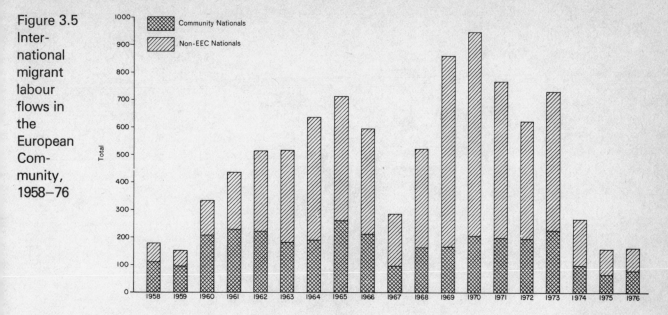

3.3.2 Regional trends

In the 1950s, a distinct polarization was visible between those regions experiencing aggregate employment growth and those experiencing decline (see Figure 3.6). Employment grew most quickly in German regions with regions of decline being mainly located in the Community's geographical periphery: the Mezzogiorno, Ireland, much of southern and western France, and also northern and central Belgium.

Figure 3.6

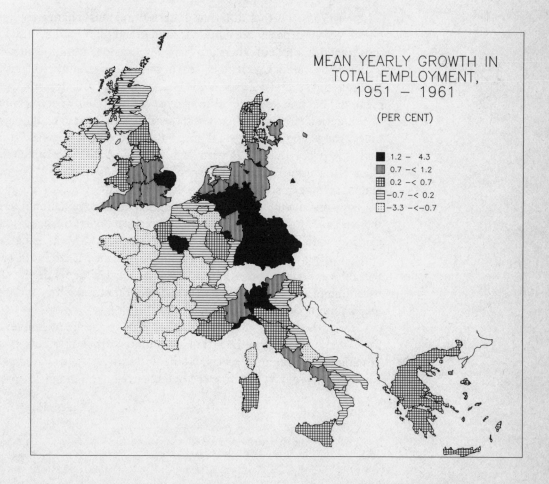

Figure 3.7

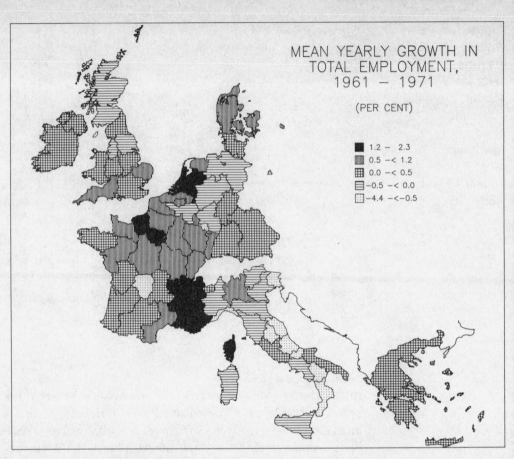

In the 1960s, a rather different pattern of regional change emerged (see Figure 3.7). Fewer regions experienced employment loss and there were several in Germany amongst those that did, while in others growth rates remained positive but were much lower than in the 1950s. Some UK regions also began to lose employment, having gained it in the 1950s, as did several regions in north-east and central Italy, with the result that employment loss became generalized over most of the Italian space economy.

The period 1970–7 again saw a rather different pattern of aggregate regional employment change established (see Figure 3.8). All German regions experienced net job loss, with the exceptions of Bayern and Schleswig-Holstein which had small gains. In France, in contrast, all regions except Auvergne, Brittany and Poitou-Charentes had net employment gains. In Italy and the UK a rather more varied pattern of regional employment change took place within their respective national territories. In the UK, the North, North West and South East regions registered net losses, the remainder net gains – with those in East Anglia and the South West being relatively large. The pattern within Italy was still more complicated: the Mezzogiorno (with the exception of Sardinia) experienced continuing employment decline while the rest of Italy (with the exception of Emilia-Romagna, Liguria and Trentino) either saw employment stabilize or, to varying degrees, increase.

Clearly, then, there have been marked changes in the overall level of employment in the Community, and in the intra-Community spatial distribution of employment, both at national and regional scales. To begin to understand why these aggregate changes came about, we next examine sectoral changes in employment patterns.

Figure 3.8

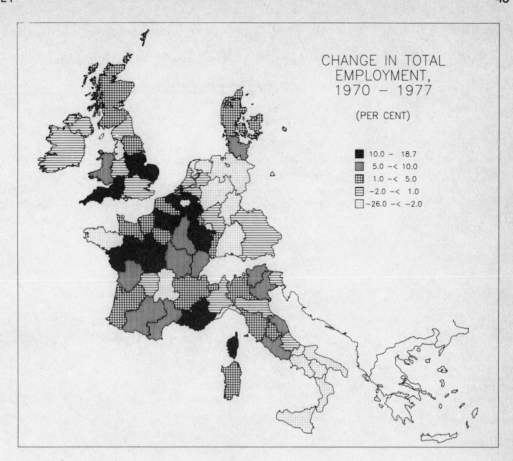

CHANGE IN TOTAL
EMPLOYMENT,
1970 – 1977

(PER CENT)

■ 10.0 – 18.7
▥ 5.0 –< 10.0
▦ 1.0 –< 5.0
▤ –2.0 –< 1.0
▨ –26.0 –< –2.0

3.4 Sectoral changes in employment: agriculture

3.4.1 Community and national trends

There has been a considerable and sustained decline, both in absolute and relative terms, in agricultural employment in the Community of Nine over the post-war period, especially since 1950 (see Figures 3.9 to 3.11). The concentration of decline prior to 1970 reflected the combined effects of a variety of forces: the penetration of capital and new farming techniques into agriculture, often for the first time, though this was an uneven process (see below); the effects of various government land-reform programmes (for example, see King, 1973); and the sustained demand for labour from other sectors of the economy (see below). In relative terms, agricultural employment fell from 25 per cent of total employment in 1950 to 6.7 per cent in 1979, although by the 1970s the rate of decline had fallen sharply. In absolute terms, it fell from 22 million in 1950 to 7.8 million in 1979, falling by slightly over 6 million in each of the decades of the 1950s and 1960s but only by 1.8 million between 1970 and 1979. The significance of the addition of Greece, Portugal and Spain to agriculture in the Community and to the CAP (Chapters 1 and 6) can be gauged from the fact that 4.5 million were employed in agriculture in these three countries in 1979.

The decline of agricultural employment within the Community reflects changes within agriculture itself, such as increasing mechanization and the consolidation of land holdings to give larger farms, as well as rising effective demand for labour in the industrial and service sectors. The sectoral reallocation of labour found expression in distinctive patterns of inter-regional and international migration (see Chapter 2). Despite the considerable structural changes that have taken place within agriculture, and the reduction of the total number of farms in the Community (for example, from over 5.75 million farms of one or more hectares in 1970 to 5.17 million in 1975: Eurostat, 1981: Table 5.5.6), there remain two distinct types of production within the Community. One is based on small, frequently subsistence-orientated and under-capitalized farms, based

Figure 3.9

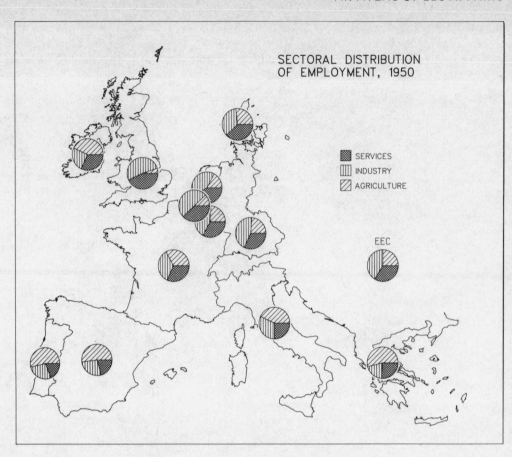

SECTORAL DISTRIBUTION
OF EMPLOYMENT, 1950

SERVICES
INDUSTRY
AGRICULTURE

EEC

Figure 3.10

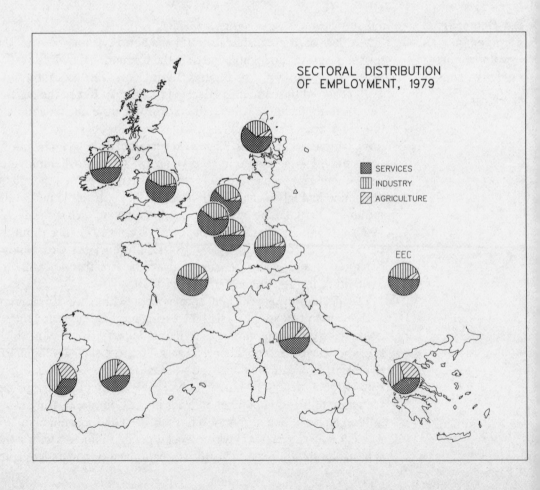

SECTORAL DISTRIBUTION
OF EMPLOYMENT, 1979

SERVICES
INDUSTRY
AGRICULTURE

EEC

Figure 3.11

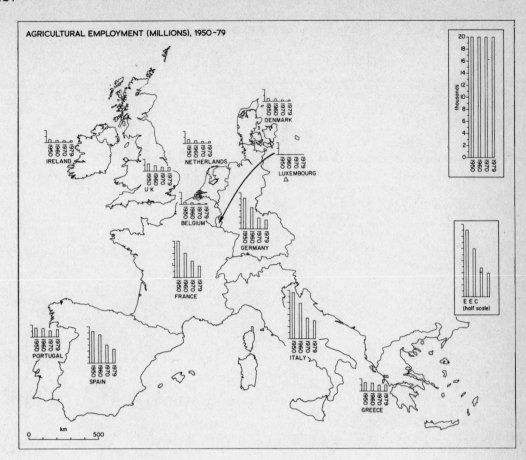

Figure 3.12

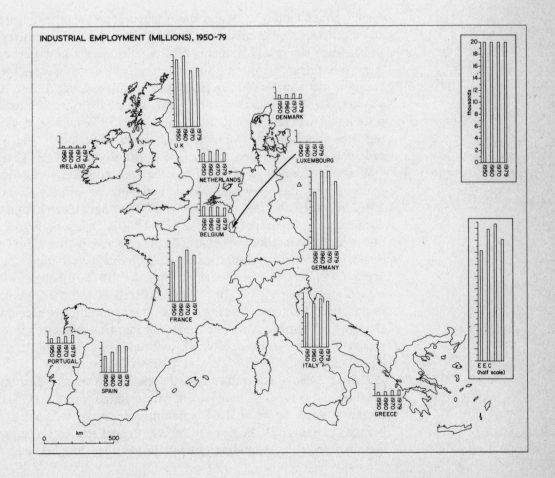

Figure 3.13

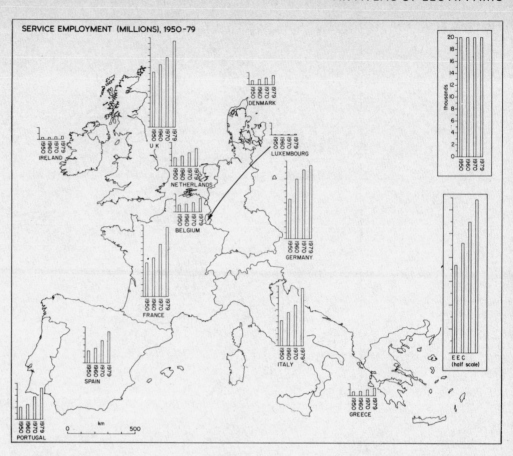

SERVICE EMPLOYMENT (MILLIONS), 1950-79

heavily on self-employment and family labour, and the other on large, capital-intensive and mechanized units producing primarily for the market based on self-employment and/or wage labour. This dual system is reflected not only in the size-distribution of farms (see Figure 3.14) but also in the much higher proportion of self-employed and family workers in agriculture (see Figure 3.15), as compared to that in industry and services. This is a pattern that the CAP has tended to reproduce by virtue of setting price levels with reference to the incomes of small farmers (and, as a by-product, creating large windfall profits for the much fewer larger ones), and which the Mansholt proposals, if implemented, would have drastically altered (see Chapter 1).

While the broad trend of a decline in the proportion employed in agriculture recurs at national level, there are considerable variations around the Community average. By 1950, in some countries – notably the UK – agricultural employment had already declined to a small proportion of the total while in Denmark, France, Ireland and Italy it exceeded the Community average of 25 per cent and, in the case of Greece, Portugal and Spain, was more than double this figure. This relative variation around the Community average was more or less maintained through to 1977, although by this date France had moved much nearer to it. In contrast, in Ireland and the Community's current and prospective Mediterranean fringe, agriculture continued to account for a much higher share of total employment – up to three or four times the average for the Nine. For this reason, if no other, the accession of Greece and possibly of Portugal and Spain will have a profound impact on the CAP (see Chapter 1).

There are also considerable national variations in the size distribution of agricultural holdings and in types of employment within agriculture. By 1975, the greatest concentration of small farms in the Community was in Italy – almost 70 per cent being between one and five hectares – but the modal size category in both Belgium and Germany (perhaps surprisingly) was also less than five hectares. Greek entry to the

Figure 3.14

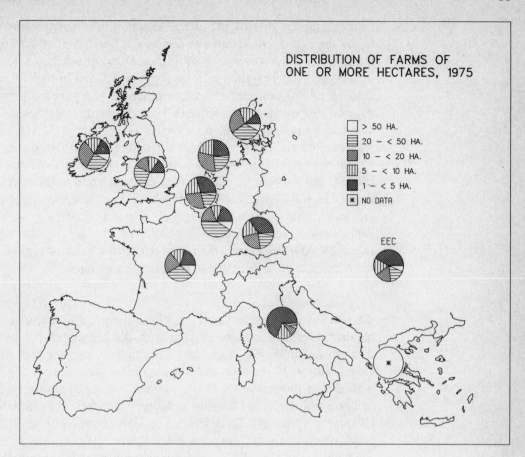

DISTRIBUTION OF FARMS OF
ONE OR MORE HECTARES, 1975

> 50 HA.
20 – < 50 HA.
10 – < 20 HA.
5 – < 10 HA.
1 – < 5 HA.
✳ NO DATA

EEC

Figure 3.15

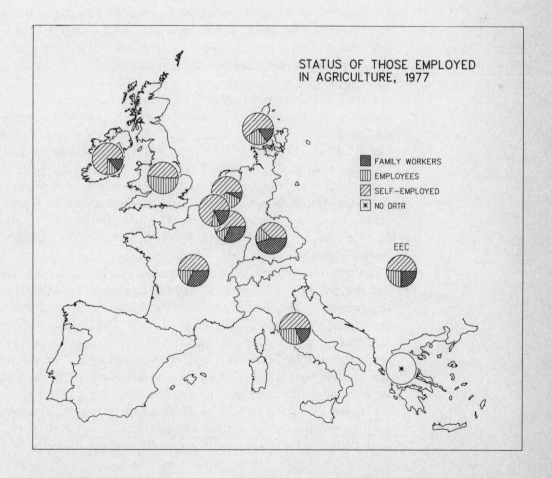

STATUS OF THOSE EMPLOYED
IN AGRICULTURE, 1977

FAMILY WORKERS
EMPLOYEES
SELF–EMPLOYED
✳ NO DATA

EEC

Community has sharply increased the numbers of small farms for 71 per cent of all Greek farms are five hectares or less in size (see Jones, 1984); in addition, such small farms suffer serious problems of fragmentation of holdings (see also Mouzelis, 1978). The biggest concentration of large farms was found in the UK with over 30 per cent comprising fifty or more hectares, compared to 11.6 per cent in France, the next highest national percentage (a difference that is of particular significance in terms of the UK's Community budget deficit: see Chapter 1). As well as the UK and France, Denmark, Luxembourg and the Netherlands also had relatively high percentages of larger farms. At national level, self-employment in agriculture is most marked in Belgium and Ireland, and exceeds the Community average share in the remaining countries other than Germany and the UK. Family labour, in contrast, is most heavily concentrated in Germany, with France and Luxembourg also exceeding the Community average. Employees in agriculture are concentrated in the UK, the Netherlands, Italy and Denmark. At national level then, the relationship between types of agricultural employ-ment and size of farm holdings is a complicated one.

3.4.2   Regional trends

To some extent, regional concentrations of agricultural employment in 1950 echoed national ones in that those regions with the highest shares (over 50 per cent) were concentrated in the Mezzogiorno (with Puglia having the highest concentration in the Community − 79 per cent) and western France (see Figure 3.16). Furthermore, regions with a high proportion of employment in agriculture were typically those in which labour supply exceeded demand and were characterized by high net out-migration (see Chapter 2). Other than Ile de France, the only regions with less than 10 per cent of their employment in agriculture were in the UK.

Between 1950 and 1960 agricultural employment fell absolutely in all regions of the Community. The greatest absolute losses (over 200,000 each) were recorded in four German regions (Baden-Wurtemburg, Bayern, Niedersachen and Nordrhein-Westfalen) and two Italian ones (Emilia-Romagna and Veneto, these related to land-reform pro-grammes: see Bethemont and Pelletier, 1983: 68–71) but the spatial pattern of annual rates of decline, a more sensitive indicator of change, shows a rather different configur-ation (see Figure 3.17). Annual average rates of decline of over 5 per cent were recorded in three French regions (Alsace, Corsica and Lorraine) and two German ones (Saarland and West Berlin, the latter a rather exceptional case) while in many others, rates of decline of between 4 per cent and 5 per cent were experienced: Niedersachen, Rhein-land–Pfalz and Schleswig-Holstein; Val d'Aosta and Veneto; much of western and southern France; the south and east of the Netherlands; Brabant in Belgium; and Luxembourg. Thus to some extent those French regions which in 1950 formed one of the major concentrations of agricultural employment in the Community experienced above-average rates of decline, while in contrast, in the other major concentration, the Mezzogiorno, rates of decline tended to be around or below the Community, or even the Italian, average.

Nevertheless, by 1960 the spatial pattern of concentration of agricultural employment had changed little, although in all regions the share of agricultural employment fell (so that only four regions now had more than 50 per cent employed in agriculture) and inter-regional differences had tended to narrow. The highest concentrations were still to be found in the Mezzogiorno (where the four regions exceeding 50 per cent were located, headed by Molise − 71 per cent) and western France. On the other hand, in several more regions (in Belgium, Germany, the Netherlands and the UK) the share of agricultural employment had fallen to less than 10 per cent.

Between 1960 and 1970 all regions again experienced absolute decline in agricultural employment. In addition to those that had also done so in the previous decade, Rhein-land–Pfalz and Piemonte now experienced an absolute decline in excess of 200,000.

Figure 3.16

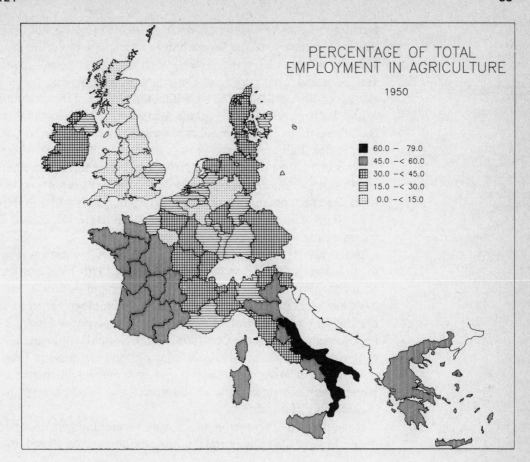

PERCENTAGE OF TOTAL
EMPLOYMENT IN AGRICULTURE

1950

60.0 – 79.0
45.0 –< 60.0
30.0 –< 45.0
15.0 –< 30.0
0.0 –< 15.0

Figure 3.17

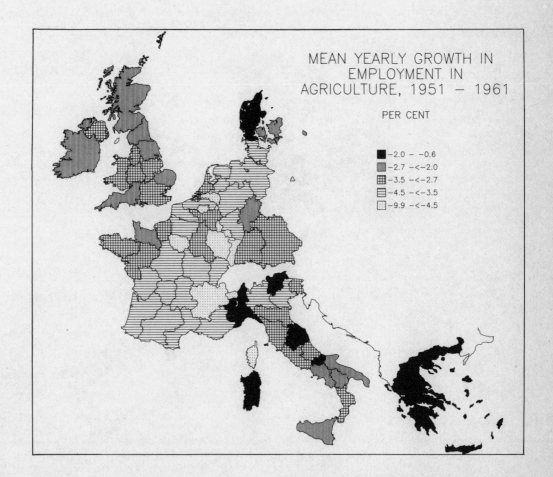

MEAN YEARLY GROWTH IN
EMPLOYMENT IN
AGRICULTURE, 1951 – 1961

PER CENT

-2.0 – -0.6
-2.7 –<-2.0
-3.5 –<-2.7
-4.5 –<-3.5
-9.9 –<-4.5

Furthermore, many regions experienced high annual rates of decline (see Figure 3.18), reflected in the rise of the Community average rate of decline from 3.2 per cent in the 1950s to 4.9 per cent in the 1960s. With the exception of the urban regions Bremen, Hamburg and West Berlin, all German regions experienced annual rates of decline in excess of 5 per cent, Saarland recording the highest in the Community − 15.1 per cent. Many Italian and Danish regions also exceeded the Community's average rate of decline. As in the 1960s, the effect of these changes has been to narrow the magnitude of inter-regional differences rather than fundamentally to alter their pattern.

Thus in 1970 western France, Ireland and the Mezzogiorno (headed by Molise with 46 per cent) remained the regions with the highest proportions of agricultural employment. Several more regions in Denmark, France, Italy and the Netherlands now had less than 10 per cent employed in agriculture, while the UK joined Belgium as a country where all regions fell into this category.

In contrast to − and indeed as a consequence of − the great magnitude of the preceding fall in agricultural employment, the period 1970–7 was characterized more by stasis than change as the forces that had produced rapid decline in earlier decades began to have a less potent effect. While the share of employment in agriculture continued to decline, in most regions it did so at a gentler pace (see Figure 3.19). In several more regions scattered over the Community, agricultural employment fell to less than 10 per cent of the total while in 1977 the Mezzogiorno and western France continued to have the greatest relative concentrations of employment in this sector (see Figure 3.20), which essentially reflects the spatial structure of 1950 but with the shares of all regions considerably reduced.

In addition to the overall percentage of employment in agriculture in 1977, the proportions of the agricultural workforce who were employed, self-employed or family

Figure 3.18

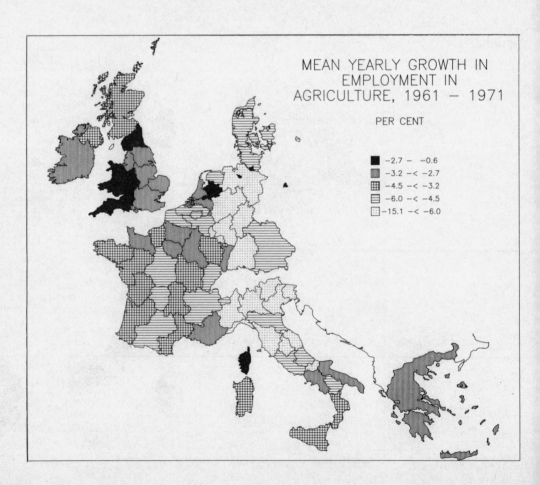

MEAN YEARLY GROWTH IN EMPLOYMENT IN AGRICULTURE, 1961 − 1971

PER CENT

- −2.7 − −0.6
- −3.2 −< −2.7
- −4.5 −< −3.2
- −6.0 −< −4.5
- −15.1 −< −6.0

Figure 3.19

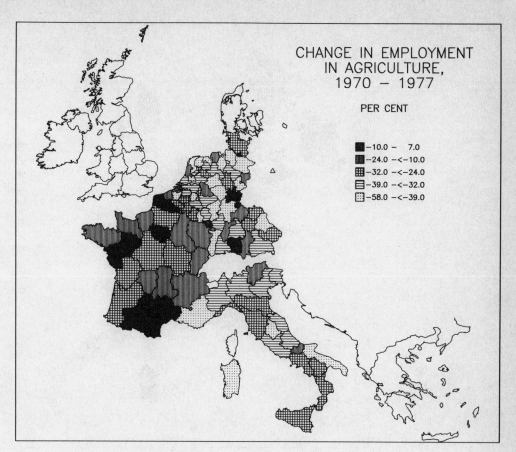

CHANGE IN EMPLOYMENT
IN AGRICULTURE,
1970 – 1977

PER CENT

–10.0 – 7.0
–24.0 –<–10.0
–32.0 –<–24.0
–39.0 –<–32.0
–58.0 –<–39.0

Figure 3.20

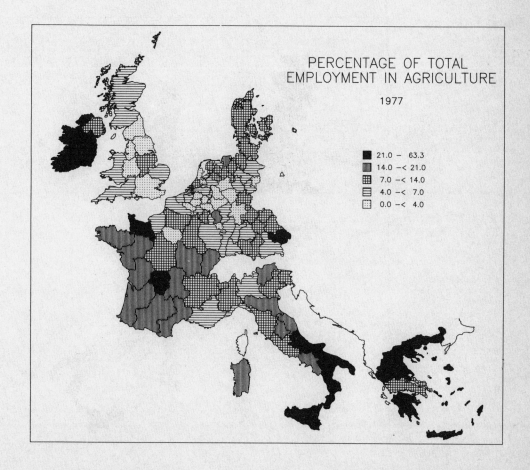

PERCENTAGE OF TOTAL
EMPLOYMENT IN AGRICULTURE

1977

21.0 – 63.3
14.0 –< 21.0
7.0 –< 14.0
4.0 –< 7.0
0.0 –< 4.0

Figure 3.21

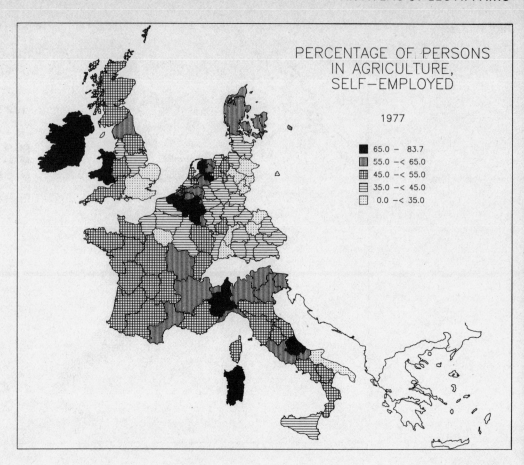

Figure 3.22

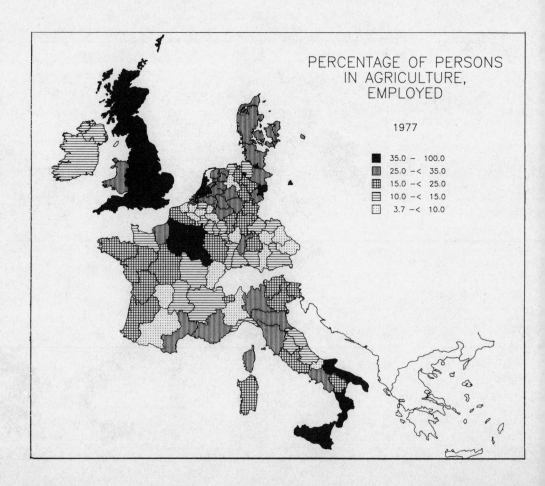

Figure 3.23

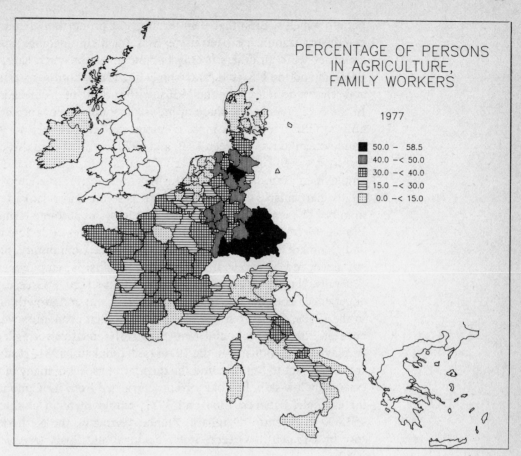

PERCENTAGE OF PERSONS
IN AGRICULTURE,
FAMILY WORKERS

1977

■ 50.0 – 58.5
▤ 40.0 –< 50.0
▦ 30.0 –< 40.0
▤ 15.0 –< 30.0
▫ 0.0 –< 15.0

workers can also be examined (see Figures 3.21–3.23). The greatest concentrations of employees are found in England and Scotland, northern France and the western Netherlands – essentially areas of large, efficient farms, producing primarily for the market – and parts of the Mezzogiorno (a legacy of the creation there in the Fascist era of large estates to grow grain: see Pugliese, 1984). Such workers are relatively uncommon in south-east Germany, southern Belgium and much of France and Italy, where there are higher proportions of self-employed and/or family labourers. Family labour is especially concentrated in south-east Germany.

3.5 Sectoral changes in employment: the onset of deindustrialization?

3.5.1 Community and national trends

In the Community of Nine, industrial employment stood at 36.6 million in 1950. It then rose by almost 7.1 million by 1960 and by a further 1.8 million by 1970 before falling by 5.2 million between 1970 and 1979 (see Figure 3.12). In the 1950s employment was growing both in coal mining and manufacturing in response to the demands of post-war reconstruction. With the switch to a multi-fuel from a single-fuel economy from the late 1950s, manufacturing gains in the 1960s were offset by coal-mining losses. In relative terms, industrial employment rose from 41 per cent of total employment in 1950 to 45 per cent in 1960 and 1970, before falling back to 41 per cent in 1977 (see Figures 3.9, 3.10 and 3.12). This was one symptom of the deindustrialization of the Community, reflecting the impacts of the 1970s recession, the increasing mechanization and automation in response to this, and changes in the international division of labour as certain types of production were relocated outside the Community, in the Mediterranean and in some Third World countries (see Chapter 1; also Frank, 1980; Frobel et al., 1980; Paine, 1980; Balassa, 1981).

At national level, however, there are considerable variations around this general pattern which suggest that – in terms of the proportion of employment in industry – deindustrialization has been under way for a considerable number of years in some countries while in others it only became apparent much later. In the first group are Belgium and the UK (see Anderson *et al.*, 1983), both registering continuing absolute and relative declines from the 1950s, with the rate of decline accelerating in the 1970s. In the Netherlands, the share of industrial employment rose between 1950 and 1960, only to fall thereafter. A more common pattern has been for the share of industrial employment to rise between 1950 and 1970, then fall – in this case, the distinguishing feature between countries has been the rates of expansion and decline. Thus industrial employment, especially manufacturing employment, has tended to fall generally in the 1970s, particularly after 1973, in both absolute and relative terms, within the Community. The majority of manufacturing losses in absolute terms were concentrated in France, Germany and the UK, but the highest rates of decline were found in Belgium and Denmark after 1973. In contrast within the Community, only in Italy was there a sustained, indeed accelerated, increase in industrial employment in the 1970s. More generally, the countries of the Mediterranean fringe – Greece, Portugal and Spain – experienced considerable industrial development and growth of industrial workforces in the 1960s, albeit from low base levels, as their economies were opened to the influence of external forces and tended to suffer relatively smaller falls in the share of employment in industry in the 1970s (see Tsoukalis, 1981; Hudson and Lewis, 1984a). It is important to bear in mind the qualitative aspect of many of these jobs, which were essentially low-skill, low-pay jobs decentralized from the Community's industrial core: for example, between 1965 and 1977, employment in clothing and textiles fell by 954,000 in Belgium, Denmark, France, Germany, the Netherlands and the UK, but rose by 285,000 in Greece, Italy, Portugal and Spain (*Financial Times*, 10 January 1980).

The net loss of industrial employment in the Community in the 1970s was then heavily concentrated in the manufacturing sector, especially after 1973 (see Table 3.1). In the period 1970–3 there was a net loss of 500,000 manufacturing jobs, over 80 per cent of them in textiles, clothing and leather. Almost two million manufacturing jobs were lost between 1973 and 1977 (and more subsequently) and while losses in textiles, etc., rose absolutely, the share of these declined to about 30 per cent of total losses and the recession became generalized over many more branches of manufacturing in the Community. Over 55 per cent of losses occurred in consumer-goods industries while another 20 per cent were in metal products and industrial machinery. Losses in metals production were relatively small (2.5 per cent) as the major restructuring of iron and steel production, which led to substantial, regionally concentrated job losses, came in the years following 1977.

Table 3.1 Changes in industrial employment, 1970–7

	Belgium		Denmark		France		FR Germany		Italy		Netherlands		UK		EEC Seven	
	70/73	73/77	70/73	73/77	70/73	73/77	70/73	73/77	70/73	73/77	70/73	73/77	70/73	73/77	70/73	73/77
(a) Absolute change (thousands)																
Fuel, power	−6	−8	0	1	−21	−9	−35	−19	−3	18	−6	−6	−101	−4	−172	−27
Manufacturing	−4	−137	−1	−59	183	−227	−155	−1060	26	138	−75	−113	−494	−487	−520	−1946
(b) Annual rates of change																
Fuel, power	−2.8	−2.9	−0.2	2.5	−2.3	−0.8	−2.2	−0.9	−0.6	2.5	−2.9	−2.4	−4.7	−0.2	−3.0	−0.3
Manufacturing	−0.1	−3.2	−0.0	−3.7	1.1	−1.0	−0.5	−2.8	0.2	0.6	−2.1	−2.6	−2.1	−1.6	−0.5	−1.5

Source: Commission of the European Communities, 1979b

3.5.2 Regional trends

The regional distribution of industrial employment in 1950 (see Figure 3.24) picks out the 'traditional' industrial belt of north-west Europe, based on the nineteenth-century development of coalfields and associated industries such as iron, steel, heavy engineering and shipbuilding. Thus those regions with particular concentrations (40 per cent or more) of total employment in industry were to be found in the UK, northern and eastern France, and in the regions around the Ruhr in Germany, with the remaining major concentration being in north-west Italy.

Between 1950 and 1960 industrial employment rose absolutely in all regions except Ireland and Wallonia (see Davin, 1969). The greatest absolute increases were recorded in German regions: Nordrhein-Westfalen (over one million); Baden-Wurtemburg (almost 750,000); Bayern (over 500,000); Niedersachen and Hessen (over 300,000 each). Elsewhere major increases occurred in south-east England (over 350,000), Lombardy (almost 390,000) and the Paris region (320,000). Thus these eight regions that were among the major concentrations of industrial employment in 1950 accounted for almost 70 per cent of the overall growth in the 1950s. In terms of growth rates, though, a rather different pattern emerges for while many of these eight recorded above-average rates (though not all, for example, South East England), so too did many regions that were less industrialized in 1950, notably the majority of Italian regions outside the north-west (see Figure 3.25). As a result of these various changes, the regional pattern of industrial employment in 1960 (see Figure 3.26) bore a marked resemblance to that of 1950.

In contrast to the preceding decade, industrial employment fell absolutely in several regions in the 1960s, including some of those that had earlier experienced the largest absolute gains, notably Nordrhein-Westfalen and South East England. More generally, regions experiencing absolute losses were confined to Belgium, Germany and the UK. These were often old industrial regions, the net loss in employment conflating two

Figure 3.24

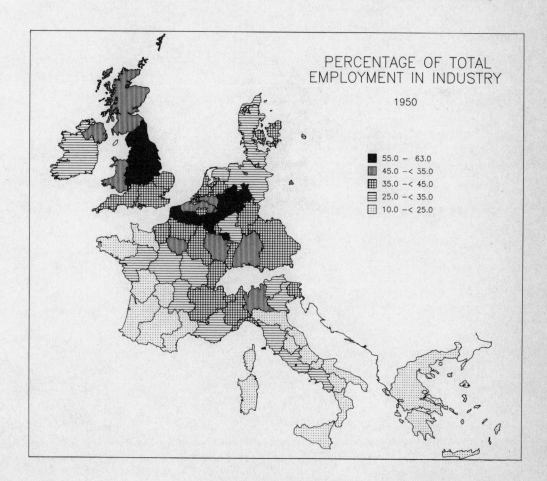

PERCENTAGE OF TOTAL
EMPLOYMENT IN INDUSTRY

1950

■ 55.0 – 63.0
▦ 45.0 –< 55.0
▦ 35.0 –< 45.0
▤ 25.0 –< 35.0
▨ 10.0 –< 25.0

Figure 3.25

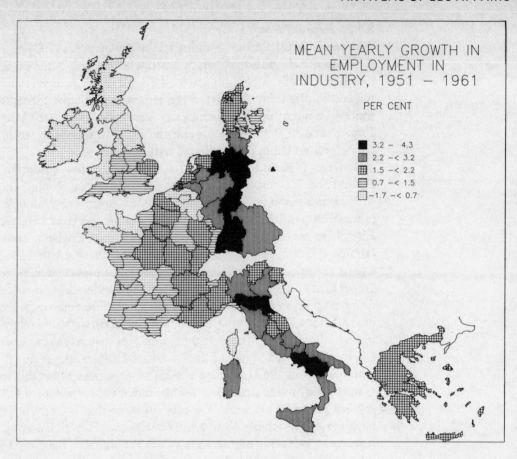

MEAN YEARLY GROWTH IN
EMPLOYMENT IN
INDUSTRY, 1951 – 1961

PER CENT

- 3.2 – 4.3
- 2.2 – < 3.2
- 1.5 – < 2.2
- 0.7 – < 1.5
- –1.7 – < 0.7

Figure 3.26

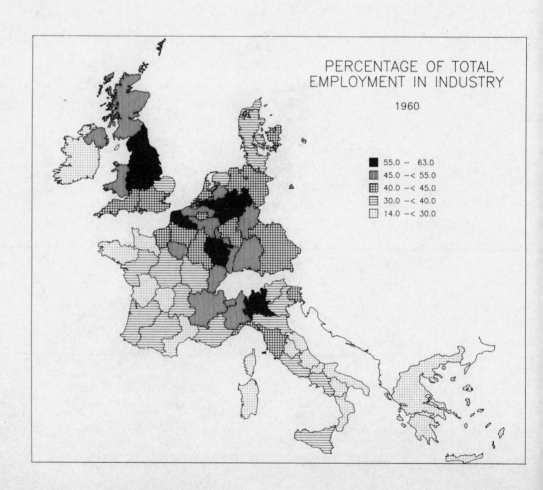

PERCENTAGE OF TOTAL
EMPLOYMENT IN INDUSTRY

1960

- 55.0 – 63.0
- 45.0 – < 55.0
- 40.0 – < 45.0
- 30.0 – < 40.0
- 14.0 – < 30.0

distinct tendencies: a loss of (largely male) jobs from coal mining (see Chapter 4) and traditional manufacturing industries and an expansion of new (often female) jobs in 'new' branches of manufacturing. Characteristically these new industries were in branch plants enticed to these regions by the combination of labour availability and regional policies (for example, see Morgan, 1979; Schröter and Zierold, 1980; Hudson, 1982a). In those regions where net employment continued to grow, it generally did so at a more muted pace than in the 1960s (see Figure 3.27). Indeed, the spatial pattern of growth rates also altered, the highest rates now being found in the more peripheral, agricultural regions, both within individual countries and at Community level, a pattern especially discernible in western France and the regions to the south and west of Paris (for example, see Lipietz, 1980), western Denmark (see Friis, 1980), north-east and central Italy (see Bagnasco, 1977; Borzaga and Goglio, 1981) and Ireland (see Perrons, 1980). This change in the relative distribution of industrial employment – the industrialization of the countryside and the absolute or relative deindustrialization of old, established 'industrial' regions – reflected changes in the spatial division of labour in industry within the Community. Increasingly, high-level administrative decisions and research and development were concentrated in a limited set of regions, usually those containing national capitals, while those parts of the production process needing skilled manual labour were, of necessity, retained in established industrial regions. At the same time, though, as pressures built up on wages in the tight, full-employment labour markets of these latter regions, companies sought to locate routine, labour-intensive operations in peripheral, agricultural regions which offered the possibility of cheaper labour, often with no tradition of factory work, trade union organization or militancy. This industrialization of the countryside characteristically took one of two forms (see Hudson, 1983a): branch plants of major national or multinational companies, in part attracted by the incentives of regional policies (for example, as in western France);

Figure 3.27

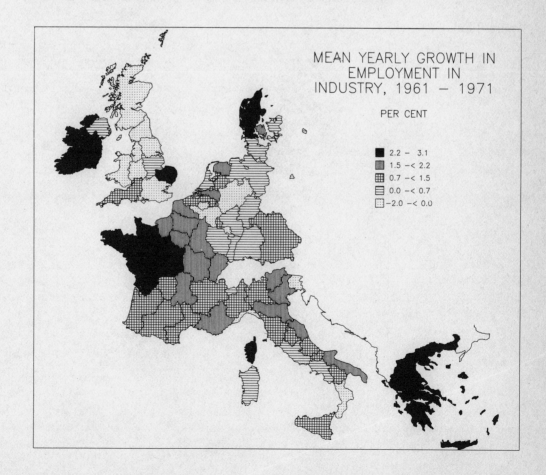

MEAN YEARLY GROWTH IN
EMPLOYMENT IN
INDUSTRY, 1961 – 1971

PER CENT

- 2.2 – 3.1
- 1.5 –< 2.2
- 0.7 –< 1.5
- 0.0 –< 0.7
- -2.0 –< 0.0

'diffuse industrialization', based on small firms or production units, often spontaneously relocating without reference to regional policies (for example, as in north-east Italy).

Thus by 1970 a considerable quantitative – if not qualitative – inter-regional equalization had taken place in terms of their shares of employment in industry (see Figure 3.28). By 1970 no region had less than 25 per cent or more than 60 per cent of its employment in industry (as compared to ranges of 10 per cent to 63 per cent in 1950 and 14 per cent to 63 per cent in 1960).

In the 1970s, a rather more varied pattern of regional changes emerged (see Figure 3.29 – though note that changes between 1970 and 1977 often conflate two opposing trends, before and after 1974). In general, industrial employment declined both absolutely and relatively. Only in a few peripheral regions that were relatively unindustrialized in 1970 (Haute Normandie, Limousin and Poitou-Charentes in France, Marche in Italy) did the proportion of industrial employment rise. Thus to some limited extent the trend of industrializing the countryside continued, though at the same time many peripheral rural regions that had above average growth rates in the 1960s experienced decline in the 1970s. Nevertheless, the most substantial losses were recorded not in these but in the Community's traditional industrial regions in Belgium, Germany, the Netherlands and the UK. Essentially, these regional changes reflected overall employment decline in these countries, brought about by structural changes in their national economies, accelerated or set in motion by the recession, and forming part of a more generalized changing international division of labour in industry. In terms of its spatial distribution within the Community, the net result of these changes was a further reduction in the differences between regions in terms of their shares of employment in industry (see Figure 3.30) – by 1977 the range was from 21 per cent to 55 per cent (both of these regions, Molise and Lombardia, being in Italy).

What was becoming of central importance by the end of the 1970s, given the changes taking place in the international division of labour, was the *type* of industries within

Figure 3.28

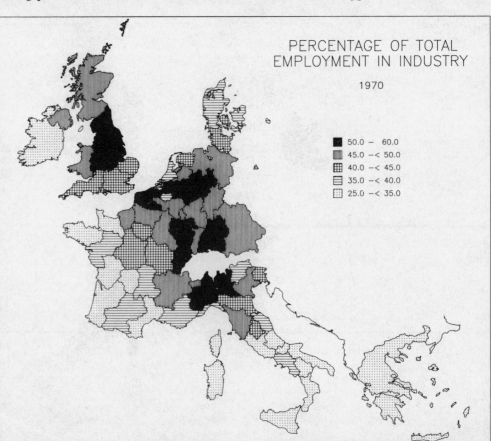

Figure 3.29

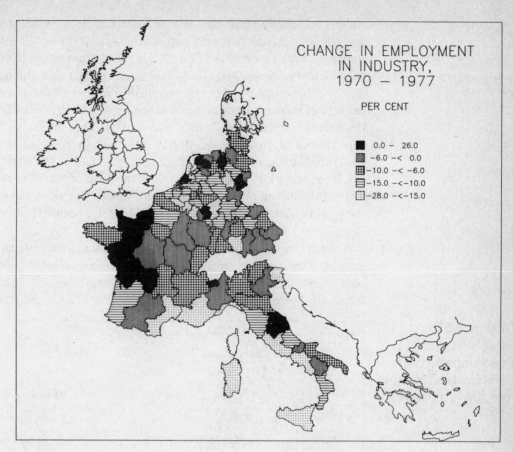

Figure 3.30

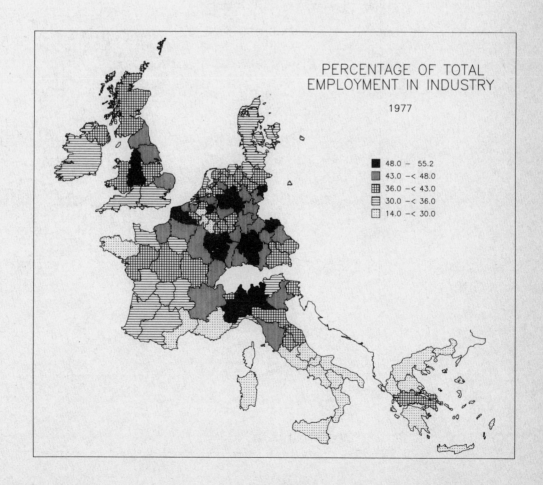

regions, especially so in the case of those regions dependent for employment upon branches of industry that were particularly susceptible to the joint pressures of foreign competition and recession: shipbuilding, steel and textiles (Commission of the European Communities, 1981a: 78–84). Despite the fact that shipbuilding employment is usually concentrated within regions, in 1977 it nevertheless accounted for more than 5 per cent of industrial employment in the regions of Bremen, Hamburg and Schleswig-Holstein in Germany and Zeeland and South Holland in the Netherlands, in the French departments of Bouches du Rhône and Var (in Provence-Alpes-Côte d'Azur) and Charente Maritime (in Poitou-Charentes), the counties of Belfast, Strathclyde and Tyne and Wear in the UK and in Denmark, of the Amts of Storestroms (in Ost for Storebaelt) and North Jutland (Vest for Storebaelt). Since 1977 there have been considerable job losses in Belfast, Hamburg, Schleswig-Holstein, South Holland and Tyne and Wear (see Figure 3.31).

While not as spatially concentrated within the Community as shipbuilding, employment in iron and steel production is nevertheless unevenly distributed, with twenty-nine regions in 1977 exceeding the Community average of 1.8 per cent employed in this sector. (If, however, one excludes those regions with insignificant steel employment, a

Figure 3.31
Regional
concentrations of
employment in
declining industries,
1977

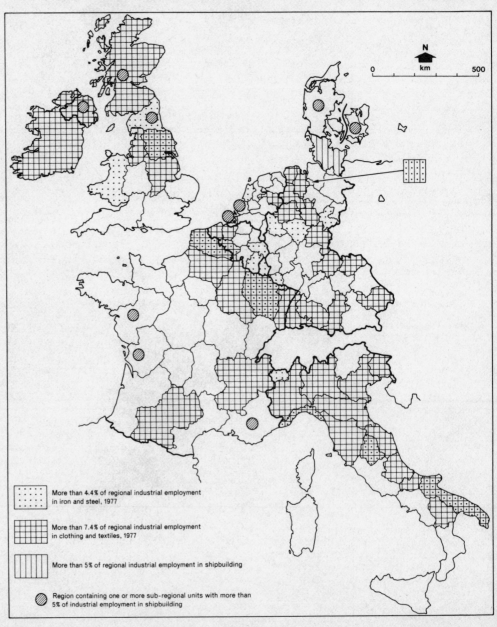

Plate 1   A sign of the times: protesting against Hoesch's plans to end steel making in Dortmund in the Ruhr

more realistic average for the remainder is 4.4 per cent.) Employment in iron and steel exceeded 4.4 per cent of total industrial employment in eighteen regions: in Luxembourg; in Arnsberg, Braunschweig, Bremen, Dusseldorf and Saarland in Germany; Lorraine and Nord-Pas-de-Calais in France; Liguria, Val d'Aosta, Puglia and Umbria in Italy; North Holland in the Netherlands; Hainault, Liège and Luxembourg in Belgium; and the Northern Region and Wales in the UK. In all of these regions employment in iron and steel has declined considerably in recent years and while in some cases this has been more or less passively accepted (see Hudson, 1982a; Hudson and Sadler, 1983a) in others it has sparked off violent protests, most notably to date in Lorraine and the Nord-Pas-de-Calais regions in France (see Chapter 6 and Carney et al., 1980; Hudson and Sadler, 1983b).

Regions with a high concentration of employment in clothing and textiles were still more widely distributed within the Community, with thirty-nine regions exceeding the Community average of 7.4 per cent: twelve in Italy, ten in Germany, seven in France, five in the UK, three in Belgium, together with one each in the Netherlands and Ireland. Of particular significance are the cases of those regions with above average shares of employment in two or all three of the clothing and textiles, shipbuilding and steel sectors: for example, both textiles and steel concentrations were found in Yorkshire and Humberside in the UK, Lorraine and Nord-Pas-de-Calais in France, Hainault in Belgium and Umbria and Puglia in Italy (see Figure 3.31).

Furthermore, as the recession has deepened and become more generalized, affecting an increasing range of industries (see Mandel, 1978), not least the 1960s' growth industries such as cars and chemicals, more and more regions, themselves often former growth regions, have been affected by industrial decline – the West Midlands in the UK perhaps being the most striking example.

3.6 Sectoral changes in employment: the tertiarization of society

3.6.1 Community and national trends
While many service occupations are found in the industrial sector and the service sector itself encompasses a wide range of diverse activities, so that generalizations can be dangerous, there is no denying the great and sustained absolute and relative increases in the tertiary sector's share of total employment in the Community: from 33 per cent in 1950 to 52 per cent in 1977 (see Figure 3.9, 3.10 and 3.13). In contrast to industrial employment, that in services continued to grow throughout the 1970s – in absolute terms, by over 5 million between 1970 and 1977 (see Figure 3.13). Slightly more of these were in market rather than non-market services (these being roughly synonymous with the private and public sectors) but the latter grew at an appreciably faster rate, though both rates fell after 1973 (see Table 3.2).

Table 3.2   Changes in service sector employment, 1970–7

	Belgium		Denmark		France		FR Germany		Italy		Netherlands		UK		EEC Seven	
	70/73	73/77	70/73	73/77	70/73	73/77	70/73	73/77	70/73	73/77	70/73	73/77	70/73	73/77	70/73	73/77
(a) Absolute change (thousands)																
Market services	102	96	11	18	557	467	218	−190	261	582	87	81	308	246	1544	1300
Non-market services	36	29	90	78	199	132	365	286	239	218	36	57	38	358	1345	1138
(b) Annual rates of change																
Market services	2.4	1.6	0.4	0.7	2.6	1.5	0.9	−0.6	1.5	2.3	1.5	1.0	1.1.	0.7	1.5	0.9
Non-market services	1.9	1.1	7.2	5.1	2.1	1.0	3.3	1.7	3.0	1.9	1.8	2.0	2.7	1.8	2.8	1.6

Source: As Table 3.1

Broadly similar patterns of change were experienced in the individual countries of the Community so that by 1977 the share of the tertiary sector in total employment varied from 46 per cent in Ireland to 59 per cent in Denmark. While tertiary employment also expanded in Greece, Portugal and Spain – some of this growth being associated with tourist developments (see Boissevain, 1980) – it remained smaller than average among the Nine in 1977.

While there was a degree of similarity in the magnitude of the service sector in different national economies in 1977, there were nevertheless considerable differences in its composition and in patterns of change in the preceding years of the decade. Perhaps the most striking feature is the growth rate of non-market services in Denmark, an indication of the scale of development of the Danish public sector (see Friis, 1980; also Chapter 4). Elsewhere, these growth rates were lower, though in some cases (Germany, Italy) still quite marked. The reduction in the rates of growth of non-market services after 1973 in all countries except the Netherlands reflected public expenditure cuts on the part of national governments as part of counter-inflation, deflationary policy packages. In most countries, growth in employment in market services was of greater importance, though growth rates tended to be lower – indeed, in Germany employment in this sector fell absolutely between 1973 and 1977.

3.6.2   Regional trends
In 1950 regional differences in the distribution of service sector employment were rather less pronounced than those in agriculture and industry. Even though the range was considerable – 55 per cent in Hamburg to 9 per cent in Molise – the generally more even distribution reflects the need to provide certain basic services in all areas. In general, regions with the highest proportions were those containing national or regional

Figure 3.32

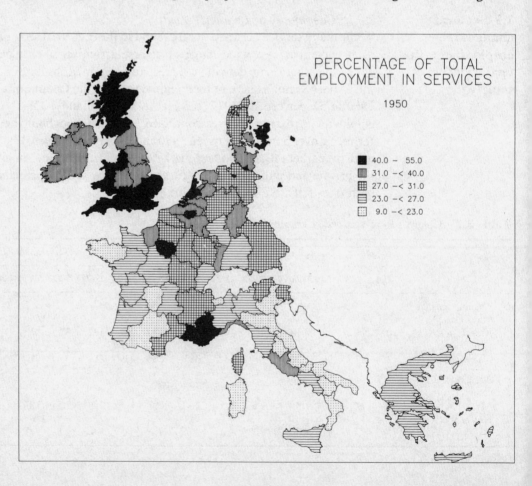

administrative capitals (see Figure 3.32). In the next decade, all regions except Ireland experienced absolute growth in service sector employment, though the spatial pattern of increases varied between countries. In some, the greatest absolute increases tended to be in those regions with the greatest concentrations of such employment in 1950: for example, the regions containing Copenhagen, London and Paris, major centres of population and concentrations of decision-making power. In contrast, in Germany increases were distributed much more evenly between regions, with Italy occupying an intermediate position with growth concentrated absolutely in the regions of Milan (Lombardia) and Rome (Lazio), major urban centres of economic and political power, respectively, within the Italian territory.

In terms of growth rates, the outstanding feature is the high rate for virtually all German regions, in part reflecting the German federal administrative structure (see Parker, 1979: 11–12), with most Italian regions having lower but fairly closely grouped rates (see Figure 3.33). Indeed, in general regional growth rates varied much more between than within countries, in part because of nationally applicable standards and criteria for public service provision, the major exceptions to this pattern being the exceptionally high rate of East Anglia within the UK, while Wallonia, the north of the Netherlands and several French peripheral regions had rather lower rates than their respective national averages.

Thus by 1960 all regions had increased their share of employment in services, the pattern of regional differences remaining very much as in 1950, if anything these having narrowed with a range of from 13 per cent in Molise to 58 per cent in Hamburg. In the 1960s, regional growth rates displayed less variation than in the 1950s (see Figure 3.34), though at national level some quite marked changes did occur. Especially in German regions, but also in most of those of the UK and north-west Italy, growth rates fell but remained quite tightly clustered. In contrast, in all Belgian, Danish and Dutch regions

Figure 3.33

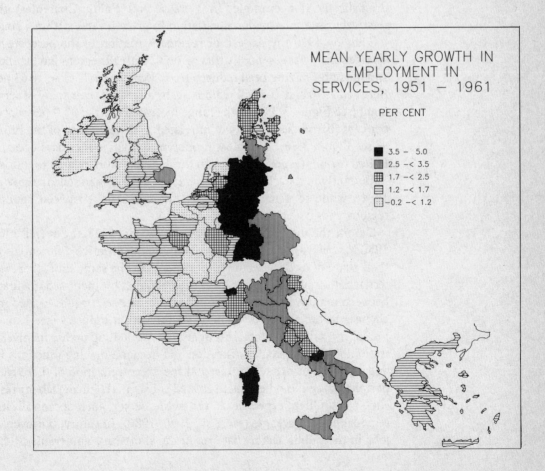

MEAN YEARLY GROWTH IN
EMPLOYMENT IN
SERVICES, 1951 – 1961

PER CENT

3.5 – 5.0
2.5 – < 3.5
1.7 – < 2.5
1.2 – < 1.7
−0.2 – < 1.2

Figure 3.34

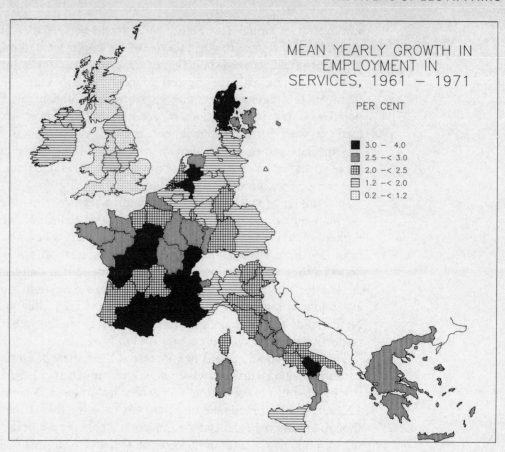

MEAN YEARLY GROWTH IN
EMPLOYMENT IN
SERVICES, 1961 – 1971

PER CENT

- 3.0 – 4.0
- 2.5 –< 3.0
- 2.0 –< 2.5
- 1.2 –< 2.0
- 0.2 –< 1.2

and in most French regions growth rates rose relative to the 1950s, in some cases quite dramatically (for example, in Corsica and Poitou-Charentes) though again with relatively little inter-regional variation in growth rates within a single country.

Thus by 1970 the pattern of regional variation in the percentage employed in the service sector was essentially that of 1950, with all regions having increased their shares and the range having been reduced from 26 per cent (Molise) to 63 per cent (Hamburg). Between 1970 and 1977 all regions again increased their share of service sector employment (see Figure 3.35) but the range increased a little: 37.9 per cent (Piemonte) to 76.3 per cent (Brussels, a figure not unrelated to the existence of the European Community – see Figure 3.36). The most pronounced relative increases occurred in German and Italian regions (especially those in the Mezzogiorno, related to tourist growth but more importantly to the 'clientilistic' character of the Italian state in the south – see Pugliese, 1984), while in general there was more variation between countries than between regions within a country.

Despite the slight widening between 1970 and 1977, the overall effect of changes since 1950 has been a considerable narrowing of quantitative differentials between regions in their share of tertiary sector employment. At the same time, there is evidence that this tertiarization of society has been accompanied by increased qualitative differentiation between regions in terms of the type of service sector jobs located in them, paralleling changes in the spatial division of labour within industry (see Lipietz, 1981). Both in public and private sectors, this quantitative levelling up has involved increased concentration of high-level administration and decision-making functions in national capitals and other major urban centres, and the decentralization of more routine operations to peripheral regions where there existed substantial (female) labour reserves to undertake such tasks. Often, especially in the public sector, such decentralization formed part of regional policy packages (see Yuill et al., 1980). In future, however, it is precisely such jobs in the public sector that are, in the short run, vulnerable to the effects of public

Figure 3.35

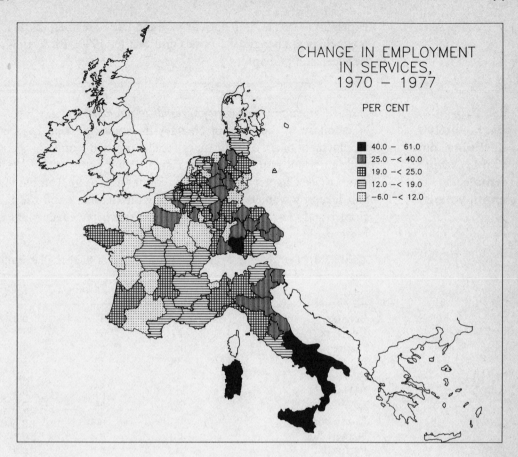

CHANGE IN EMPLOYMENT
IN SERVICES,
1970 – 1977

PER CENT

- 40.0 – 61.0
- 25.0 –< 40.0
- 19.0 –< 25.0
- 12.0 –< 19.0
- –6.0 –< 12.0

Figure 3.36

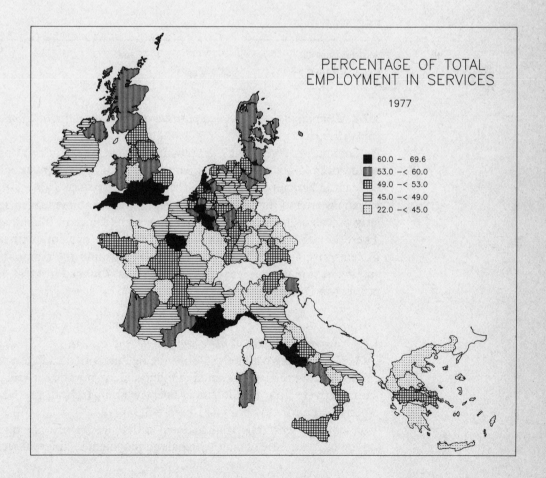

PERCENTAGE OF TOTAL
EMPLOYMENT IN SERVICES

1977

- 60.0 – 69.6
- 53.0 –< 60.0
- 49.0 –< 53.0
- 45.0 –< 49.0
- 22.0 –< 45.0

expenditure cuts and, in both private and public sectors, in the long run to the effects of technological change (see Hines and Searle, 1979; Bird, 1980; Counter Information Services, n.d.; Chapter 6).

3.7 Pro-portionately declining male and growing female employment

3.7.1 Community and national trends in total employment

A corollary of the sectoral changes in labour markets has been the rising share of employment taken by women, especially married women − a change which in turn has had important ramifications on consumption patterns and lifestyles within the Community (see Chapter 5). By 1977 over one-third of total employment in the Community was taken by women (see Table 3.3) with Denmark and the UK, followed closely by France and Germany, being the countries where female wage employment was most marked.

Table 3.3 Female employment as a percentage of total civilian employment, 1960–77

	1960	1965	1970	1977
Belgium	n.a.	31	n.a.	35
Denmark	31	34	39	42
France	n.a.	n.a.	36	38
FR Germany	38	37	37	38
Greece	32[1]	n.a.	27[2]	n.a.
Ireland	n.a.	27[3]	n.a.	27[4]
Italy	30	28	27	31
Luxembourg	n.a.	n.a.	n.a.	29
Netherlands	n.a.	n.a.	n.a.	25
Portugal	n.a.	n.a.	n.a.	39
Spain	n.a.	n.a.	n.a.	29
UK	34	34	36	39
EEC Nine	n.a.	n.a.	34	36

Sources: Eurostat, 1980a: Table 11/3; OECD, 1978 and 1979

Notes: 1 = 1960 2 = 1971 3 = 1966 4 = 1973

3.7.2 Community and national patterns of the sectoral distribution of male and female employment

At Community level female employment is most heavily concentrated in the service sector, over 45 per cent of jobs there being taken by women, as compared to almost 32 per cent in agriculture and 23 per cent in industry (see Table 3.4). There are national variations around this pattern, however. Female employment in agriculture is particularly prevalent in Germany and of minor significance in Ireland and the Netherlands. There is rather less variation in industrial employment, with all countries except Luxembourg and the Netherlands clustered around the Community average, and in employment in the service sector, which in 1977 ranged from 33 per cent in Italy to 52 per cent in Denmark.

3.7.3 Regional patterns of male and female employment

By 1977, reflecting national patterns, the regions with the highest proportions of female employment were mainly located in France, Germany and the UK. Conversely, regions with relatively little female employment were in Ireland, the Netherlands and Italy, especially the Mezzogiorno (see Figure 3.37).

To some extent reflecting national differences, there are quite striking regional variations in the ratio of male to female employment in different sectors of the economy.

Table 3.4 Female employment as a percentage of total employment by sector, 1977

	% of total employment which is female in:		
	Agriculture	*Industry*	*Services*
Belgium	22.2	19.1	40.2
Denmark	19.5	21.8	52.0
France	33.9	25.0	49.0
FR Germany	49.0	24.2	46.0
Ireland	8.4	19.8	39.3
Italy	29.5	22.7	33.7
Luxembourg	24.7	9.9	44.1
Netherlands	7.8	10.4	36.2
UK	17.6	24.0	50.8
EEC Nine	31.6	23.2	45.2

Source: Eurostat, 1978: Table 16

In agriculture, female employment was particularly concentrated in the south and east of Germany, with north-west France and parts of the Mezzogiorno also emerging as areas of relatively high female employment in agriculture. In contrast, in Ireland, the Celtic fringes of the UK and much of the Netherlands, agricultural employment was predominantly male. Such differences are generally related to the varying proportions of wage labour and family labour in agriculture (see Figures 3.21–3.23). Moreover, in the specific case of the Mezzogiorno, the high level of female employment in agriculture can be related to the growth of male out-migration (see Chapter 2), a symptom of a broader set of social changes whereby women have of necessity had to move from their traditional place in the social structure, 'in the shadows' (Cornelissen, 1976), and work in the fields as men have migrated to work elsewhere.

Figure 3.37

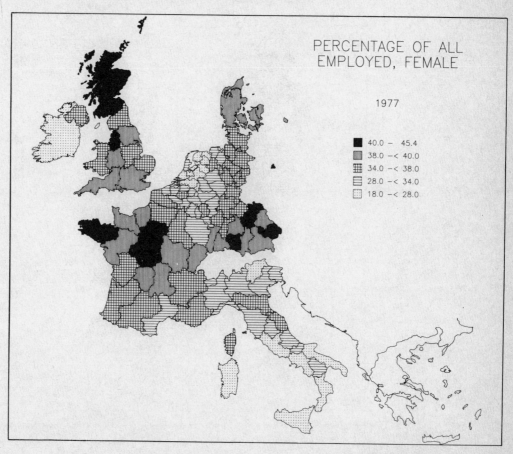

Figure 3.38

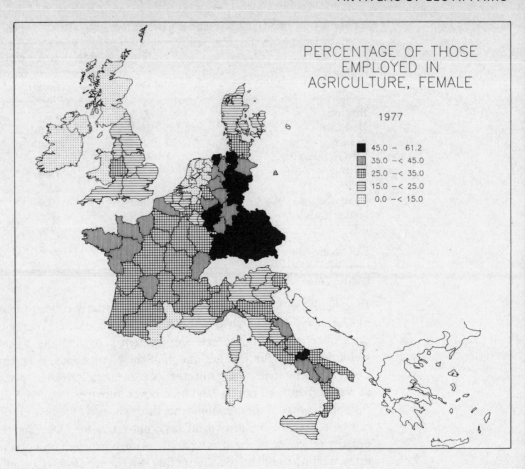

PERCENTAGE OF THOSE
EMPLOYED IN
AGRICULTURE, FEMALE

1977

45.0 – 61.2
35.0 –< 45.0
25.0 –< 35.0
15.0 –< 25.0
0.0 –< 15.0

Figure 3.39

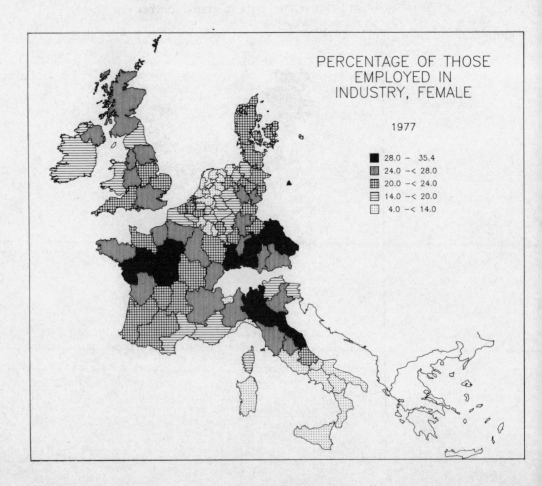

PERCENTAGE OF THOSE
EMPLOYED IN
INDUSTRY, FEMALE

1977

28.0 – 35.4
24.0 –< 28.0
20.0 –< 24.0
14.0 –< 20.0
4.0 –< 14.0

Figure 3.40

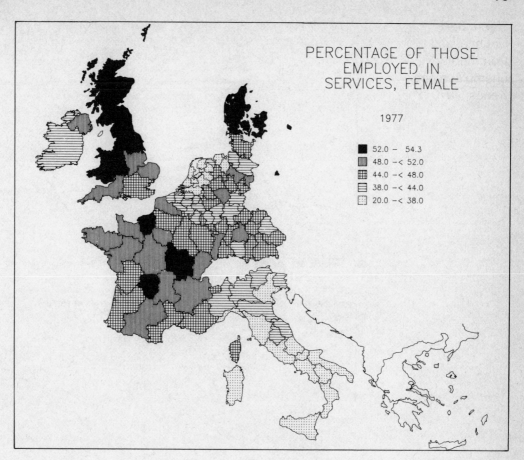

PERCENTAGE OF THOSE
EMPLOYED IN
SERVICES, FEMALE

1977

- 52.0 – 54.3
- 48.0 –< 52.0
- 44.0 –< 48.0
- 38.0 –< 44.0
- 20.0 –< 38.0

Much of south-east Germany also had relatively high proportions of female manufacturing employment, along with areas in central and western France and northern and central Italy – in general, these are rural areas that have been industrialized relatively recently. Over much of the Netherlands and the Mezzogiorno, in contrast, manufacturing employment was dominated by males.

In the service sector, there were many regions where women took almost, or even slightly more than, half of all service sector employment: notably Denmark and much of the UK and France. Women occupied relatively few of the available service sector jobs in the Netherlands and in many Italian regions, usually those in the Mezzogiorno (see Figures 3.38–3.40).

3.8 The growing crisis of unemployment

3.8.1 Community and national trends

During the 1960s, unemployment fell to historically low levels in all member countries of the Community. Overall, the period can reasonably be regarded as one of full employment. In the Nine, registered unemployment fell from 2.5 million in 1960 to 2.1 million in 1970; or from a rate of 2.5 per cent to one of 2.0 per cent (Eurostat, 1980). National levels fluctuated around this Community trend but did not seriously deviate from it.

In contrast, in the 1970s unemployment began to grow in total in the Community due to changes in patterns of labour supply and demand (see Chapter 2 and sections 3.2 to 3.7 above). At the same time, unemployment trends increasingly began to diverge between countries (see Figure 3.41). Thus by the end of the decade registered unemployment in the Community was almost 6 million, a rate of 5.5 per cent. Of the individual countries, only Germany, Luxembourg and the Netherlands had lower rates and of these only in Germany was there any definite evidence to suggest a trend of falling unemployment in the later 1970s – which reflected to a considerable degree an

Figure 3.41
National and
Community
unemployment
trends, 1970—9

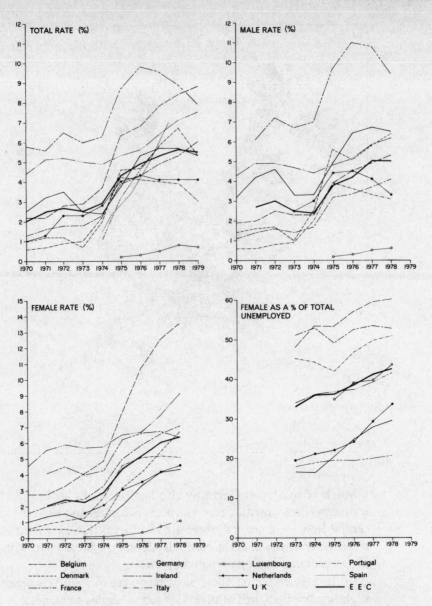

embargo on the recruitment of foreign migrant labourers (see Chapter 2) – and this, in fact, was sharply reversed in the early 1980s. By May 1983 registered unemployment in the Community of Nine (excluding Greece) had risen to 12.3 million and was expected to rise further.

Furthermore, as the overall level of unemployment has risen the structure of the unemployed has altered as the proportions of long-term unemployed, young people and women have all risen. Long-term unemployment has risen as a result of falling labour demand and has become generalized over all age groups, whereas previously it tended to be associated with older workers who were made redundant. Rising youth unemployment reflects demographic changes and the mass arrival on the labour market of young people at a time of falling or static demand for labour, a situation that can only get worse as another 10 million young people join the labour force in the 1980s. There are, nevertheless, marked national variations in the severity of the youth unemployment problem: at one extreme, almost 50 per cent of all registered unemployed in Italy are aged twenty-five years or less while at the other extreme, in Denmark, less than 25 per cent are. The increase in female unemployment reflects the increased incorporation of women into the wage labour force in the preceding years coupled with changes in eec pattern of labour demand in the later 1970s. While registered male unemployment approximately

Figure 3.42

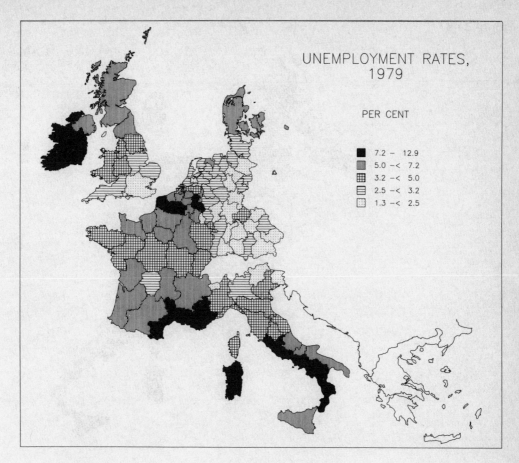

UNEMPLOYMENT RATES,
1979

PER CENT

■	7.2 – 12.9
▦	5.0 –< 7.2
▦	3.2 –< 5.0
▤	2.5 –< 3.2
▱	1.3 –< 2.5

doubled in the 1970s, registered female unemployment more than quadrupled from 600,000 in 1970 to 2.6 million in 1978 (see also OECD, 1976). By 1978 a majority of the registered unemployed in Belgium and Germany were female whereas in Ireland only 20 per cent were, the period after 1974 witnessing a widening of national differences in this respect.

3.8.2 Regional trends

While national levels of unemployment were generally low in the 1960s, nevertheless there were problem regions with unemployment rates well above the average – typically these were either agricultural regions or those affected by the decline of coal mining (see also Chapter 4). To some extent, the regional map of unemployment towards the end of the 1970s displayed evidence of the continuation of this familiar pattern, with high rates in the Mezzogiorno, Ireland, northern England, Northern Ireland and Scotland (see Figure 3.42). It also, however, displays symptoms of the emergence of new problem regions in addition to the old ones as the recession affected more and more sectors of manufacturing and high unemployment became a generalized phenomenon. For example, by the end of the 1970s the effects of restructuring the iron and steel industry were expressed in high unemployment rates in north-east and central France and southern Belgium and by the 1980s had appeared in a similar fashion in the North and East Midlands of England and Wales and were beginning to emerge in the Ruhr in Germany.

What seems crucial in the context of the changing map of unemployment is regional economic structure, in the sense that if one examines rates of change of unemployment prior to and after 1975, those regions that were initially most vulnerable to recession

Figure 3.43

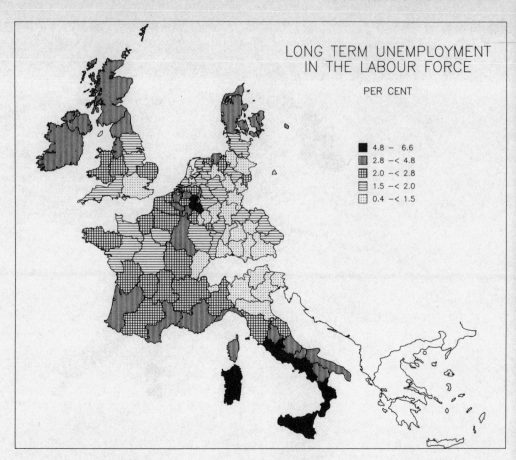

also had the greatest ability to respond to crisis, while the less industrialized and declining industrial regions reacted more sluggishly to the onset of crisis but were subsequently less able to adapt to it (Commission of the European Communities, 1978: 30). As a result, regional unemployment differences first narrowed but then expanded in the course of the 1970s.

By the end of the 1970s there was a reasonable correlation between regions with high levels of total and long-term unemployed (see Figure 3.43). Regions with the highest shares of long-term unemployment are concentrated in the Mezzogiorno and parts of central Italy, southern Belgium, Corsica, Ireland and Northern Ireland, all regions of high total unemployment. In contrast, in other cases this relationship did not hold: for example Piemonte had a low overall unemployment rate but within this a considerable concentration of long-term unemployed while Provence-Alpes-Côte d'Azur had high overall but low long-term unemployment.

There is a fair degree of correspondence between regional and national patterns of both youth and female long-term unemployment (see Figures 3.44, which maps the percentage of the labour force aged 14–24 registered as unemployed, and 3.45). The severity of the former problem in Italy is emphasized by the fact that in all regions except Umbria more than 50 per cent of the unemployed were young people while in Lazio, Val d'Aosta and Veneto this rose to over 70 per cent; in many French regions it also exceeded 50 per cent. Female long-term unemployment is particularly high (over 50 per cent or even 60 per cent of total unemployment) in many Belgian, Danish and French regions, as well as in some in Germany and Italy. In contrast, in the Netherlands and UK it is relatively and uniformly low. Furthermore, between 1977 and 1979 the position of regions characterized by high female and/or youth long-term unemployment in the former year generally deteriorated (Commission of the European Communities, 1981a: 32).

Figure 3.44

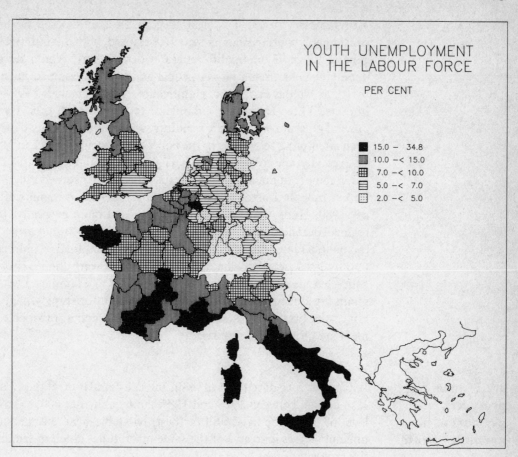

YOUTH UNEMPLOYMENT
IN THE LABOUR FORCE

PER CENT

15.0 — 34.8
10.0 —< 15.0
7.0 —< 10.0
5.0 —< 7.0
2.0 —< 5.0

Figure 3.45

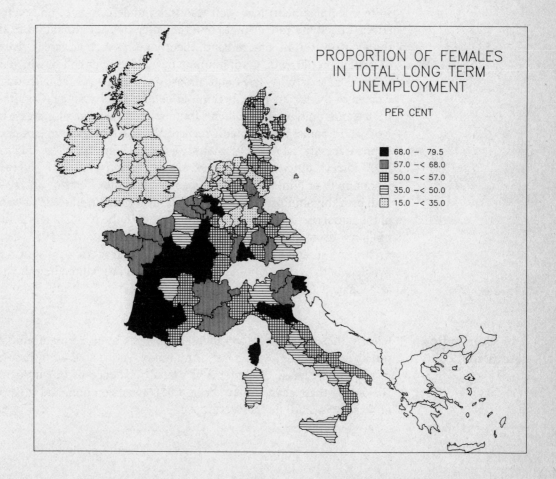

PROPORTION OF FEMALES
IN TOTAL LONG TERM
UNEMPLOYMENT

PER CENT

68.0 — 79.5
57.0 —< 68.0
50.0 —< 57.0
35.0 —< 50.0
15.0 —< 35.0

In summary, then, it is clear that the problems posed by unemployment became considerably more serious as the 1970s elapsed, both quantitatively and qualitatively. In general unemployment differences widened, both regionally and nationally, while unemployment among young people and women assumed much greater political and social, as well as economic, significance. These changes have had a variety of major impacts. Three examples will suffice to demonstrate this. Firstly, they have led to upward pressure on public expenditure at a time when many national governments have been attempting to cut this in the belief that it would reduce inflation rates (see Chapter 4). Secondly, the collapse of regional economies and sharp rises in unemployment have led in some (but not all) regions to sustained civil disorder and violence on the streets – for example, in Lorraine and the Nord-Pas-de-Calais regions of France (see Carney *et al.*, 1980; Hudson and Sadler, 1983b) – and more generally to pressures for greater regional autonomy to counter the effects of high unemployment, thus threatening both the political integrity of existing nation states and further political unification at Community level (see also Chapter 6). Thirdly, beneath the mass of aggregate statistics is concealed the decimation of many individuals' and families' lives under the pressures of mounting unemployment, especially long-term unemployment (see Hudson, 1982b). Given the breadth and depth of these consequences, prospects for future unemployment are of immense significance.

3.9 Future prospects: permanent mass unemployment?

In Chapter 2 we noted that the working-age population of the Community would rise by 12.3 million between 1975 and 1985 and by a further 600,000 by 1995. Given that the level of labour demand will (at best) be stable over this period, this would suggest unemployment increases of the same magnitude, much of which are already visible in the problem of youth unemployment.

Such a simple equation of the relevant population age group to the labour force (and so to unemployment) may well lead to an underestimate, however, for it ignores the effects of activity rate changes and the entry to or continuation in the labour force of those outside the 14–65 age band. Incorporating such variables gives a higher estimate of labour force growth – 16.3 million by 1995 – over half of which is accounted for by rising female activity rates and almost another 20 per cent through the addition of women to the labour force because of demographic change (Commission of the European Communities, 1978). Such a forecast presumes a great increase in part-time female work and assumes (undoubtedly incorrectly) that low levels of labour demand would not depress activity rates. Nevertheless, even allowing for these qualifications, the most likely forecast outcome would seem to be a rise in the range of 12.0 to 16.0 million in the Community of Nine – to which one must add the effects of unemployment in Greece and, probably, in Portugal and Spain. This forecast rise needs to be seen in the context of the actual rise in registered unemployment in the Nine, in less than eight years, of 7.7 million – from 4.6 million in 1975 to 12.3 million in May 1983. Coping with this and preventing serious fissures in the existing social fabric will continue to pose a major problem both to the Community as a whole and to national governments within it (see also Chapter 6).

3.10 Concluding comments

Clearly there have been considerable changes in patterns of employment, both sectorally and spatially, within the Community. Associated with these have been changes in the overall level, character and spatial incidence of unemployment. Some of the reasons for these changes have been briefly touched upon, and in the next chapter some of these points are further developed.

ECONOMIC PERFORMANCE AND RESOURCES

4.1 Introduction

In this chapter we concentrate upon the resource base and economic performance of the Community and its constituent nations and regions. First of all, variations in rates of economic growth (in terms of gross domestic product (GDP)*) and associated variables such as labour productivity and fixed capital investment, together with the uses of GDP, are examined. Then the resource issue, especially that of energy, is examined. Following this, inflation rates and other monetary variables are discussed. Finally, the balance of payments and aggregate trade flows are analysed.

4.2 Gross domestic product*

4.2.1 Community and national trends

Historians of future generations may well examine the later 1970s in the European Community and consider themselves faced with a puzzling paradox. For by 1979 the Community had emerged as a major world economic power with a GDP in 1978 of $2253.2 billion, in excess of those of the other major capitalist world economic nations of the USA ($2112.4 billion) and Japan ($973.9 billion), although on a per capita basis GDP was higher in the USA than the EEC ($9,687 as compared to $8,674) and the gap between the EEC and Japan ($8,476) had virtually disappeared. Yet the Community was deeply conscious of being in the midst of a major economic crisis, substantially deepened although not simply caused by the series of crude oil price rises which began dramatically in November 1973, with another sharp round of increases in 1979 (although falling by 1983 in response to the same recession they allegedly caused). Despite this, while there were some manifest signs of economic problems, notably the combination of rising inflation (see section 4.10 below) and unemployment (see Chapter 3) which undoubtedly contributed to this perception of crisis, nevertheless GDP per capita continued to grow at over 2 per cent per annum between 1974 and 1978 in the Community and annual rates of real GDP growth recovered to between 5.6 per cent and 2.3 per cent between 1976 and 1978, after falling sharply in the years following 1973 and, indeed, becoming negative in 1975. While these did represent a marked deceleration from the sustained average annual growth rates of the period 1950–73 of about 4.5 per cent, they still constituted a considerable expansion in GDP, although at a slower rate than in the USA and Japan in this period.

Of individual member countries in 1978, FR Germany had by far the largest GDP, followed by France, the UK and Italy – between them, these four countries accounted

---

* There are a number of ways of defining and measuring GDP at any point in time: principally at market prices and at factor cost, but also from purchasing parities. The former definitions are more appropriate for considering production, the latter for consumption (see Chapter 5). There are further major problems, however, in constructing a time series of real (i.e. volume) increases in GDP since observed increases reflect the combined effect of inflation and volume changes, problems that are compounded when considering international temporal comparisons by variations in currency exchange rates. As different sources employ different definitions and/or different base years for standardizing to constant prices and/or different denominators into which to translate national currencies, the construction of a consistent time series for the whole post-war period would itself be a major research project. In the next section, data are used which relate to gross value added (GVA); this is broadly synonymous with GDP.

for 85 per cent of total Community GDP, virtually the same share as in 1950 (see Figure 4.1). There have, however, been marked changes in the relative size of national economies and in GDP per capita, for while all countries have experienced real growth in GDP, growth rates have varied considerably around the Community mean. Thus in 1950 the UK was by far the largest single economy of the current member countries, followed by France and Germany – the latter still recovering from the devastation of the Second World War – although Belgium, Denmark and Luxembourg all had greater GDP per capita than the UK (see Figure 4.2, which shows GDP per capita relative to the EC average (100) for each year). In the 1950s, reflecting the scale and pace of the post-war reconstruction effort, the German economy grew appreciably faster than those of the remaining member countries (although there is less divergence between countries in terms of growth rates of GDP per capita than in terms of total GDP: see Figures 4.3 and 4.4), so that by 1960 it was only marginally smaller than that of the UK. Moreover, the differences in GDP per capita had generally narrowed considerably, as compared to 1950. In the 1960s, partly influenced by the creation of the Common Market, national growth rates (both of total GDP and GDP per capita) converged more closely around a higher Community average, the main exception to this trend among the major economies being the UK, at that time outside the Community. By 1970, Germany had the largest share of Community GDP and the highest per capita GDP of the major countries while the relative position of the UK declined sharply.

In general, GDP growth rates fell in the 1970s as compared to the 1960s but it is important to make a distinction between the periods before and after 1974. In the former period, the pattern of the 1960s was basically reproduced: growth rates in some countries (generally the economically stronger ones) fell a little, those in others (generally the weaker ones) increased, so that while the overall Community growth rate fell back a little, there was a closer convergence of national rates around this (see Figure 4.3). Furthermore, this tendency was perhaps even more marked in terms of growth rates of

Figure 4.1

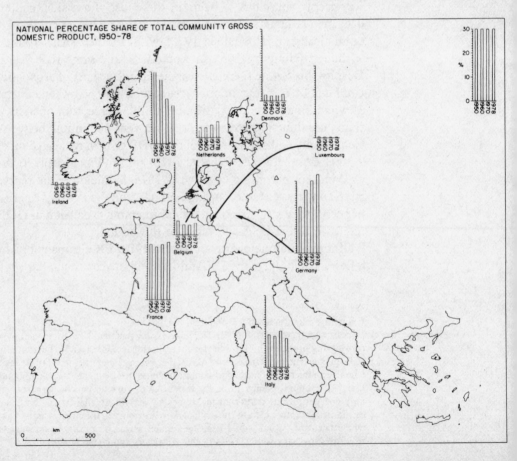

NATIONAL PERCENTAGE SHARE OF TOTAL COMMUNITY GROSS DOMESTIC PRODUCT, 1950–78

GDP per capita, which increased in Belgium, France, Ireland, Luxembourg and the UK in the period 1969–73 as compared to that of 1960–70 (see Figure 4.4), though in this case the overall EEC rate remained unchanged.

After 1973, though, not only did the average Community growth rate fall but national growth rates began to diverge and it was this increasingly uneven national development at a time of slower growth that came to be seen as a major political threat to the continuation and further development of the Community. Of the member countries, Ireland continued to grow most strongly throughout the 1970s. While the stronger economies were initially affected more severely by recession, they exhibited a greater capacity for adaptation and recovery so that growth rates, although declining somewhat compared to the early 1970s, were around 3 per cent per annum in the late 1970s, both in terms of GDP and GDP per capita: Germany and France fall in this category. Next, occupying an intermediate position with per capita growth rates around 2.5 per cent per annum by the late 1970s, were Belgium, Luxembourg and the Netherlands. The remaining countries – Denmark, Italy and the UK – recovered rather more weakly and falteringly from the mid-1970s slump, especially the UK which by 1980 was deep in a further bout of recession. One manifestation of these differences was that the French and German shares of Community GDP rose further while those of Italy and the UK (and indeed Ireland) fell further, and in terms of per capita GDP this pattern was basically repeated, although the Netherlands, Denmark (in particular) and Belgium retained above-average per capita GDP in 1979 (see Figure 4.2). However, by the start of the 1980s the Community's economy was again in the grip of a deep and generalized recession.

The reasons for these spatial and temporal variations will be touched upon again later. For the moment, there is one further point to be made and this concerns the impact of the accession of Greece and possible accession of Spain and Portugal to the Community.

Figure 4.2

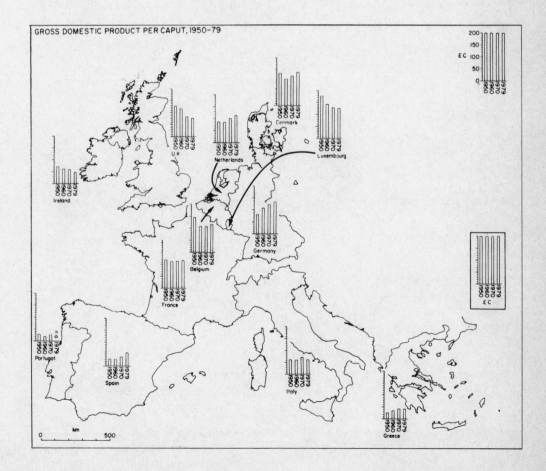

GROSS DOMESTIC PRODUCT PER CAPUT, 1950–79

Figure 4.3

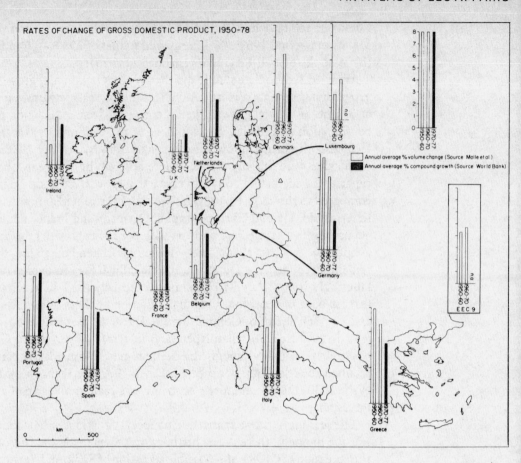

RATES OF CHANGE OF GROSS DOMESTIC PRODUCT, 1950-78

Figure 4.4

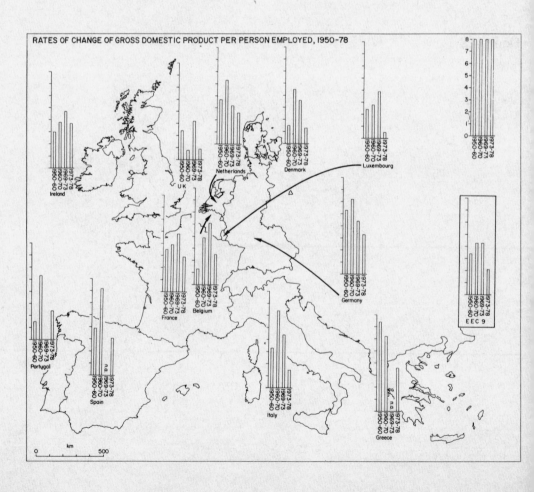

RATES OF CHANGE OF GROSS DOMESTIC PRODUCT PER PERSON EMPLOYED, 1950-78

For despite the generally higher growth rates achieved by these countries in the 1960s, most notably by Spain, and their attaining above Community average growth rates in the 1970s, their overall economic impact on the Community will range from marginal to slight (although this is not to say that this would be unimportant in all branches or sectors). In 1978, for example, the addition of Greece would have increased Community GDP by 1.61 per cent, that of Portugal by 0.94 per cent, and even that of Spain by only 7.54 per cent; together 10.1 per cent. This emphasizes that the arguments for the enlargement of the EEC into the Mediterranean area are political (or political-economic) rather than narrowly economic, for in fact not only would Greece, Portugal and Spain do little to increase the Community's overall economic power and in fact would lower average GDP in the Community, but also in a time of general economic crisis would add significantly to the problems of agriculture (see Chapters 1 and 3), some branches of industry (see Chapter 3), and to those of regional disparities within the Community (see Chapter 6).

4.2.2 Regional trends

The regional distribution of GDP per capita for 1950 is shown in Figure 4.5; comparable data for 1960, 1970 and 1977 are shown in Figures 4.6–4.8. While the regional pattern of GDP per capita in 1950 had evolved into a rather different one by 1970, to a considerable degree the pattern of regional variations in GDP per capita mirrors that of national variations; essentially there is more variation between countries than between regions within countries. This correspondence between regional and national trends is further revealed by analysing rates of change of GDP and GDP per capita in the periods 1950–60 and 1960–70, for while GDP per capita increased in all regions it did so at different rates, though regions with similar growth rates tended to be clustered within

Figure 4.5

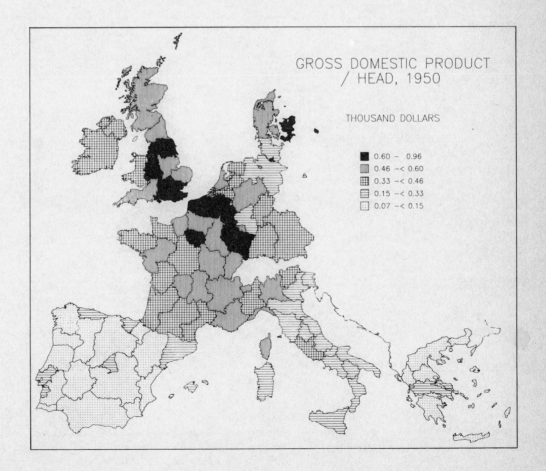

Figure 4.6

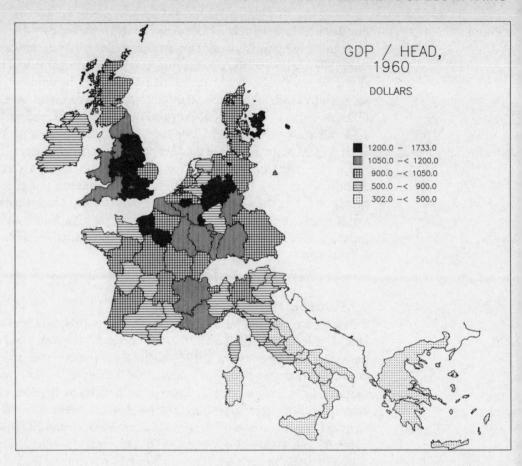

Figure 4.7

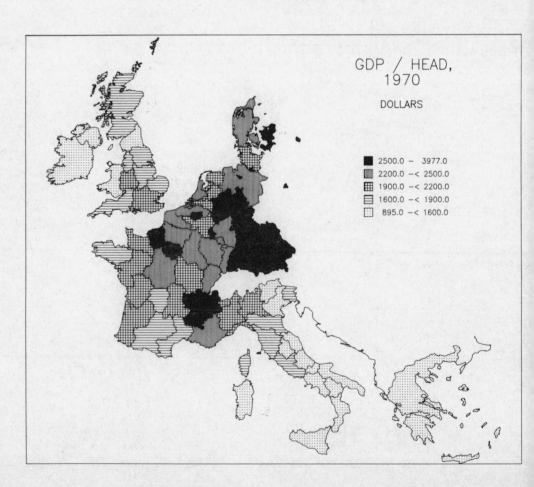

Figure 4.8

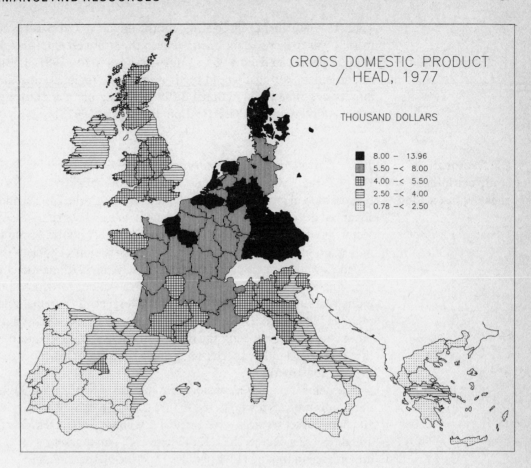

particular countries. Nevertheless, it has been argued that inter-regional differences in GDP per capita narrowed in the 1960s (Commission of the European Communities, 1981a: 41).

In contrast, between 1970 and 1977 regional disparities increased, and as in the preceding years these regional changes can again be related to national changes, though in this case the changes tended to produce divergence rather than convergence. For what is clear is the relative deterioration in the position of Italian and UK regions (and also Ireland) and the relative strengthening of the position of many German regions, some Dutch regions, the Antwerp region of Belgium and the Danish regions other than Copenhagen. In fact, the regions of the Community may be neatly dichotomized in terms of levels of GDP per capita in 1977, and growth rates between 1970 and 1977, largely along national lines. The first group with above Community average levels and rates consists of: Germany (except Luneburg), the Netherlands (except Friesland), France (except a group in the west and south – Basse Normandie, Pays de la Loire, Brittany, Poitou-Charentes, Aquitaine, Midi-Pyrénées, Limousin and Languedoc-Roussillon), Val d'Aosta in Italy, Luxembourg and all Danish regions (with the exception of Greenland). In the second group are those exceptions noted above, together with Ireland, all UK regions and the remaining regions in Italy (which have less than Community average levels of GDP per capita and, except for Basilicata, below average growth rates (Commission of the European Communities, 1981a: 46)).

Overall, regional disparities in terms of GDP per capita increased sharply in the 1970s; whereas the ratio of the ten strongest to the ten weakest regions on this indicator was 2.88 to 1 in 1970, by 1977 it was 3.95 to 1; moreover this was considerably greater than in 1960 (Commission of the European Communities, 1981a: 46). This is not to say that there were not considerable continuing inter-regional disparities within countries, but these were fairly constant in magnitude in the 1970s and the overall widening at Community level was principally due to increasingly uneven national development.

There is a further point to stress for the impact of Greek accession to the Community in 1981 was to increase the ratio between the strongest and weakest ten regions in terms of GDP per capita from 3.95 to 1 in 1977 to 5.0 to 1 in 1981. The addition of Spain and, in particular, Portugal would further aggravate regional inequalities within the Community at a time when national differences in growth are already leading to widening regional differentiation (see Hudson and Lewis, 1982b).

4.3 Sectoral composition of gross value added

4.3.1 Community and national trends, 1970–7

By 1970 there was considerable homogeneity between member states in the sectoral composition of gross value added (GVA). By 1970, the EEC economy had evolved to an advanced degree of capitalist development: over 50 per cent of GVA arose in the service sector, predominantly in market services (roughly equivalent to the private sector), an indication of the extent to which the 'tertiarization of society' was reflected in value added as well as in employment. Conversely, in 1970 manufacturing contributed less than one-third of GVA, an indication of the extent to which, relatively speaking, de-industrialization had progressed in this respect. The remaining sectors contributed relatively little to GVA – less than 5 per cent in the case of agriculture and fuel and power products, reflecting the decline of these sectors (the former over a long period, the latter over a rather shorter one), and a little more than 5 per cent in the case of building and construction.

In general there was a considerable convergence of national figures around those for the Community as a whole (see Figure 4.9): in terms of the service sector, both market and non-market services were particularly important in Denmark (44.2 per cent) and, to a slightly lesser degree, the UK (43 per cent); non-market services were of above average importance in Ireland (15.1 per cent) and the Netherlands (13.4 per cent) while market

Figure 4.9

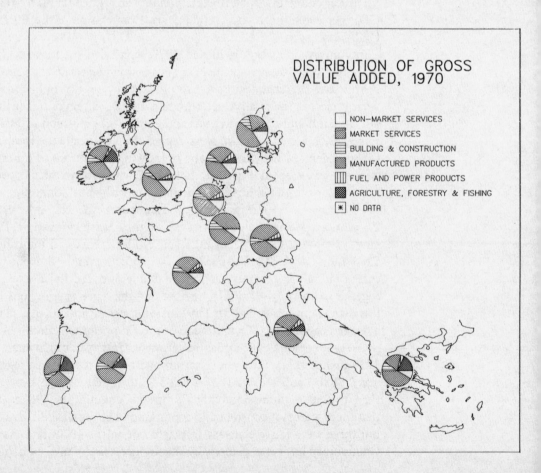

services were of below average importance in Germany (35.7 per cent) and Ireland (33.3 per cent). There was much greater variation in the shares of value added contributed by manufacturing, ranging from 20.3 per cent in Denmark to 37.8 per cent in Germany and 40 per cent in Luxembourg; except for Ireland (24.2 per cent), the remaining member countries clustered fairly closely around the Community average, however. The greatest variation, though, was in terms of agriculture's share of GVA, varying from 2.2 per cent in the UK to 15.1 per cent in Ireland, with all member countries except Belgium, Germany and the UK exceeding the Community average.

Of the three Mediterranean countries – Greece, Portugal and Spain – the latter had a sectoral distribution of GVA quite similar to that of the Community as a whole but the former two most closely resembled the Community's least developed member, Ireland, in having about 18 per cent of their GVA originating in agriculture, Greece having a particularly small manufacturing sector, Portugal a weakly developed market services sector.

Over the next three years, GVA in each sector at Community level grew in such a way as to broadly reproduce in 1973 the sectoral pattern of 1970. The share of the service sector rose a little, that of manufacturing fell, but essentially the pattern at this scale was one of stability. Broadly, this trend held also at national level, but there were one or two important changes: the share of fuel and power products in GVA increased in the Netherlands, reflecting natural gas developments; and manufacturing's share of GVA fell in the UK and Germany while the share of market services rose in the former and the share of non-market services rose in the latter by way of compensation. In the three Mediterranean countries, the predominant aspect was again the stability between 1970 and 1973.

After 1973, however, quite marked changes took place, both at Community and national level. At Community level, the value of agricultural output declined between 1973 and 1977 at a rate of 0.5 per cent per annum; only in the Netherlands did it continue to grow, with growth rates falling almost to zero in the UK and Germany and output actually declining elsewhere, most severely in Belgium (−1.9 per cent p.a.) and France (−1.7 per cent). Consequently, by 1977 the share of agriculture in Community GVA had fallen to 4.1 per cent, while in each individual country it also had a smaller share in 1977 than in 1973 (see Figures 4.10 and 4.11). Despite, or perhaps because of this agriculture remained pre-eminent in Community policy concerns (see Chapter 1).

Fuel and power products, in contrast to the change between 1970 and 1973, increased their share of GVA at Community level after 1973, although the annual growth rate of GVA fell from 4.1 per cent to 3.4 per cent. This mainly reflected a continuing sharply rising share in the Netherlands (despite a lower growth rate after 1973 as compared to before) and the UK (where the growth rate more than doubled between 1973 and 1977 as compared to 1970–3) – in both cases, countries with substantial indigenous energy resources in North Sea oil and gas, exploited at an accelerating rate in response to the energy crisis. In other countries, though, some of which, like the UK, had considerable coal reserves, the growth rate of fuel and power products declined and in the case of FR Germany became negative, so that in these countries the share of these products in GVA either was stable or declined between 1973 and 1977. These changes are indicative of the lack of any coherent policy response in the sphere of energy, despite the problems posed by rising oil prices (see also Chapter 1).

In manufacturing the growth rate of GVA at Community level fell sharply after 1973 and this sector's share of GVA had fallen further by 1977. This process was especially marked in Luxembourg and the UK where GVA in manufacturing fell absolutely between 1973 and 1977, though in fact it fell absolutely in *all* countries of the Community (and Portugal) between 1974 and 1975, and in Greece between 1975 and 1976. In contrast to the other EEC countries, however, the capacity of the manufacturing sector to recover from this setback was much less marked in the UK and Luxembourg

Figure 4.10

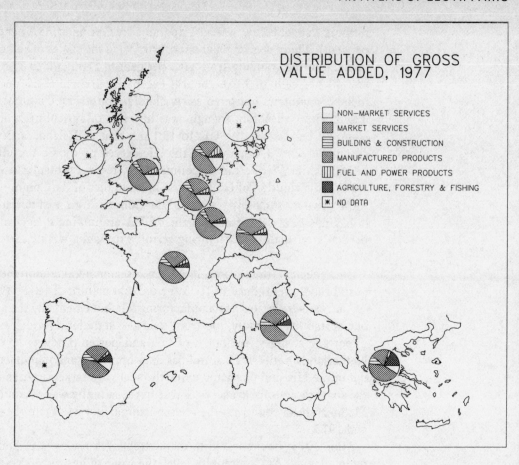

Figure 4.11

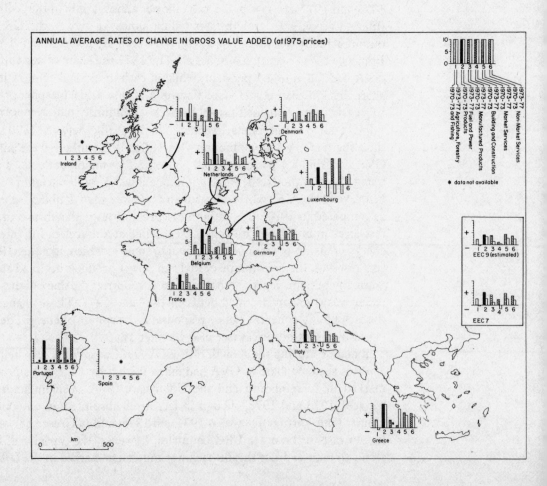

(the latter because of the central role of iron and steel production in its manufacturing sector, this being an industry particularly severely affected by recession). Thus, in all countries of the Community (except Italy) and in Spain, manufacturing's share of GVA fell between 1973 and 1977, in some cases (Belgium, Luxembourg and the Netherlands) quite sharply. Nevertheless, the relatively strong performance of the manufacturing sector in Greece, Italy, Portugal and Spain in part reflects a locational switch in manufacturing investment from the rest of the Community to them (Paine, 1980). At the same time, it continued to offer export markets to those industries within the Community, particularly those of FR Germany, producing machinery for these new manufacturing developments.

The recession also had a severe effect upon the construction sector, the value of construction output falling in six of the nine members of the Community, and increasing only marginally at Community level, apparently largely as a result of the increased rate of growth of GVA after 1973 in Belgium.

In the market service sector, growth rates at both Community and national levels generally fell after as compared to before 1973 (and in the case of Luxembourg GVA in this sector fell absolutely). Despite this, growth rates remained above those in manufacturing and as a result market services increased their share of GVA somewhat between 1973 and 1977, though less dramatically than non-market services. These latter grew at a rate only slightly below that of the 1970–3 period at Community level; at national level, growth rates increased after 1973 in Denmark, Luxembourg and the Netherlands, and only fell sharply in the UK. These differences largely reflect central government attitudes to public expenditure in response to recession, as do the overall rates of growth in non-market services, and macro-economic priorities. The effect of the recession – at least up to 1973 – was to accelerate the 'tertiarization' and deindustrialization of the Community's economy in terms of the sources of GVA; by 1977, market and non-market services accounted for almost 55 per cent of GVA, manufacturing for less than 30 per cent. There was, however, no obvious systematic correlation between the overall health and strength of national economies and the magnitude of the manufacturing sector's contribution to GVA – for while Germany had the highest proportion (34 per cent, down from almost 38 per cent in 1970), Italy had the second highest (almost 31 per cent, up from less than 29 per cent in 1970). This raises questions as to the type of manufacturing and the specialization of national economies in the international division of labour, for whereas Italian manufacturing tended to develop sectoral specialization based on cheap labour, in FR Germany the tendency has been towards increasingly sophisticated, high value added production, based on heavy fixed capital investment. Likewise, endowment with substantial oil and gas resources and a rising share of these in GVA was no guarantee of overall economic well-being. Rather the contrary, for oil and gas reserves seemed to create rather than solve economic problems in the Netherlands and UK, particularly in terms of the international competitiveness of manufacturing: their national currencies appreciated in value against those of other major industrialized countries and their manufactured exports rose in price while that of manufactured imports to them fell because of these currency movements.

4.3.2 Regional patterns, 1976–7

There is considerable regional variation in the contribution of different sectors to regional GDP, more so than at national level, and more than in the case of employment at regional level (compare Figures 4.12–4.14 with 3.20, 3.30, 3.36). The regions where agriculture makes the largest contribution to GDP are located on the physical periphery of the Community; nevertheless, there is a considerable qualitative difference between the capital-intensive, mechanized, market-orientated agriculture of regions in Denmark

Figure 4.12

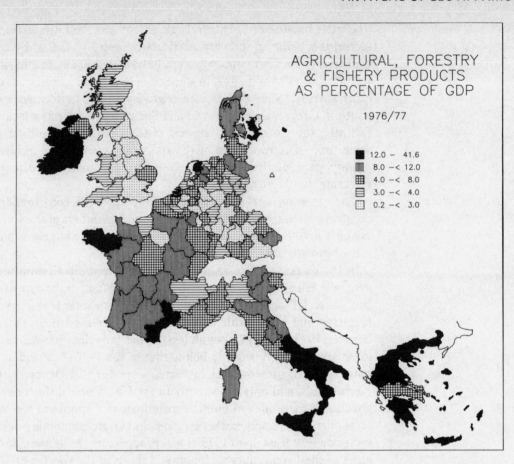

AGRICULTURAL, FORESTRY
& FISHERY PRODUCTS
AS PERCENTAGE OF GDP

1976/77

■	12.0 – 41.6
	8.0 –< 12.0
	4.0 –< 8.0
	3.0 –< 4.0
	0.2 –< 3.0

Figure 4.13

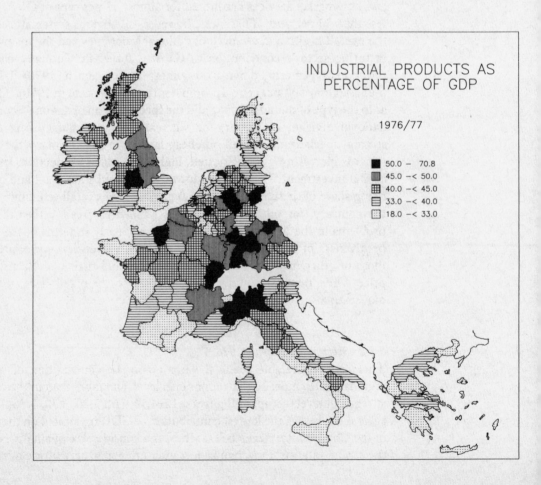

INDUSTRIAL PRODUCTS AS
PERCENTAGE OF GDP

1976/77

■	50.0 – 70.8
	45.0 –< 50.0
	40.0 –< 45.0
	33.0 –< 40.0
	18.0 –< 33.0

Figure 4.14

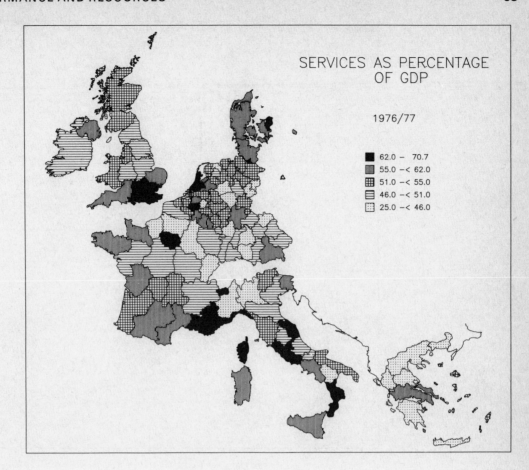

and the Netherlands and those in Greece, the Italian Mezzogiorno, Languedoc-Roussillon and Brittany in France, the Alpine and other upland areas of France, FR Germany, Italy and Ireland, based much more on small-scale, labour-intensive subsistence production.

These regions tend to be ones in which industrial products contribute a relatively small share of GDP. Those with the highest concentrations of GDP from industrial products tend to be concentrated in Germany, together with 'traditional' industrial core regions in other countries, such as Lombardy and Piemonte in Italy and the West Midlands of England. Not all regions with high proportions of GDP from industry are of this type, however: for example, Groningen in the Netherlands owes its position in this category to the extraction of natural gas there.

Regions with a relatively large share of GDP arising from the service sector are of two main types. First, those regions containing national political capitals or major commercial centres (Amsterdam, Brussels, Copenhagen, Hamburg, London, Paris, Rome and Rotterdam) or regions where tourism is an important element in the economy (such as Calabria, Provence-Alpes-Côte d'Azur, Sardinia and Val d'Aosta: for example see Pearce, 1981).

4.4 Labour productivity by sector: Community and national trends

Examination of the growth rates in labour productivity (see Figure 4.15), along with those of output and employment, reveals some interesting inter-sectoral differences, both at the level of the Community (of seven, for which data are available) and individual countries.

The first point is that at Community level, rates of increase in labour productivity declined in all sectors after 1973, this decline being most marked in agriculture, building

Figure 4.15

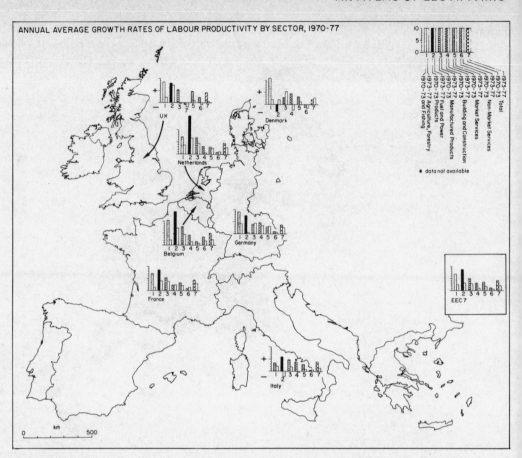

ANNUAL AVERAGE GROWTH RATES OF LABOUR PRODUCTIVITY BY SECTOR, 1970-77

and construction, fuel and power products, and less so in manufacturing and services; however, the ranking of sectors in terms of rates of productivity increase remains unchanged before and after 1973. This fall reflects a variety of factors: for example lower levels of investment in new plant, machinery and technology (see section 4.5 below); demand falling more rapidly than labour forces; and so on. If the growth rates in labour productivity are compared with those in value added (see Figure 4.11) then an important distinction emerges. Both before and after 1973, labour productivity increased more rapidly than GVA, or increased while the latter fell, in the agriculture, fuel and power, manufacturing and construction sectors; thus these were sectors characterized, at Community level, by falling labour demand or by labour demand growing more slowly than gross output, which after 1973 was often only growing slowly (see Chapter 3). In contrast, in the service sector, output consistently grew more rapidly than labour productivity, a tendency particularly marked in the non-market (public) service sector; thus the service sector was characterized by considerable employment growth (see Chapter 3).

At national level, a rather more complicated pattern emerges. Particularly marked is the decline in the rates of increase of labour productivity in agriculture; with the exception of Germany and Italy, these fell by a factor of four or five. As GVA was generally falling, though, agricultural employment continued to fall (see Chapter 3). A similar pattern of sharp falls in labour productivity is also observable in fuel and power products in most countries except Denmark (where productivity rose) and the UK, where it fell a little but moved up to first place in the ranking of countries on this measure. Likewise, in construction, labour productivity fell sharply (except in France and to a lesser extent FR Germany), falling absolutely in Denmark, Italy and the UK.

A much greater differentiation at national level emerged in labour productivity trends in manufacturing and in many ways this contains the clue to the increasingly uneven development of national economies in the Community after 1973. For in Denmark and

Germany labour productivity actually rose between 1973 and 1977, as compared to 1970–3, to 5.5 per cent and 4.5 per cent, while in Belgium, France and the Netherlands it declined but still attained annual rates of increase of around 4.0 to 4.5 per cent p.a. In contrast in Italy the rate of increase fell sharply to less than 2 per cent while in the UK labour productivity actually fell in absolute terms. Given the importance of the manufacturing sector to overall national economic performance (notwithstanding its falling share of GVA), these different labour productivity responses to recession go some considerable way towards indicating the reasons for increasing divergence of national economies in the European Community.

To some extent, this pattern of changes in productivity was repeated in the service sector. In the market service sector the growth rate of productivity fell particularly sharply, to less than 1 per cent p.a. in Belgium, Italy and the UK and to just above 1 per cent in Denmark; in contrast it rose a little in Germany to over 3 per cent and in France and the Netherlands comfortably exceeded 2 per cent. In the non-market sector, labour productivity fell absolutely in Denmark and the UK and the growth rate increased only in France: in general, though, productivity growth rates only ranged from 0.5 per cent to 1.5 per cent p.a., markedly less than those of GVA.

4.5 The uses of GDP

At Community level, some significant changes occurred in the use of GDP in the 1970s (see Figure 4.16). For while the proportion of GDP taken up by private consumption remained fairly stable at around 60 to 61 per cent, public expenditure (collective consumption of general government) rose from 14.3 per cent in 1970 to 16.3 per cent in 1979, while gross fixed capital formation fell from 22.9 per cent to 20.9 per cent over the same period. There is some evidence to suggest that while the expansion of public expenditure was accelerated by the general recession of the 1970s and the costs of

Figure 4.16

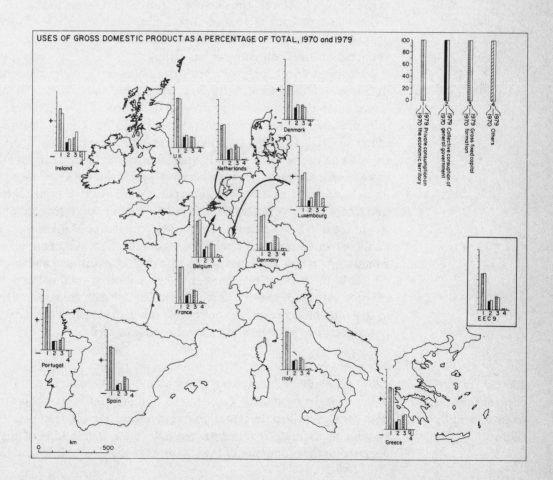

USES OF GROSS DOMESTIC PRODUCT AS A PERCENTAGE OF TOTAL, 1970 and 1979

financing expanding unemployment, it had begun before the start of the recession, and the fall in investment was very much a consequence of and then in its turn a cause of recession, the decline being concentrated after 1974. While the Community compares favourably with the USA (17.3 per cent in 1970 and 18.1 per cent in 1979) on this crucial indicator, it lags far behind Japan (35.4 per cent in 1970 and 31.7 per cent in 1979).

Considerable variations occurred at national level in the allocation of GDP in 1970 though by 1979 these had been in some cases substantially reduced. In 1970 the proportion of GDP allocated to private consumption varied within the Community from 51.8 per cent in Luxembourg to 71.0 per cent in Ireland, with the three Mediterranean countries having similar levels to Ireland. By 1979, however, the range within the Community had been reduced to a minimum of 55.8 per cent in Denmark and a maximum of 63.1 per cent in Ireland, although in Greece, Portugal and Spain, especially the latter two, the share of private consumption was still over 70 per cent.

In contrast, the variation in terms of shares of GDP taken by public expenditure changed much less. In 1970 this ranged from 10 per cent in Luxembourg to 20 per cent in Denmark, with only Spain of the three Mediterranean countries recording a lower share (8.5 per cent) than Luxembourg. By 1979 the range was from 13.7 per cent in FR Germany to 25.1 per cent in Denmark, with again only Spain falling below the lowest national level of member states. The provision of public facilities and some indicators of private consumption levels are discussed in Chapter 5.

The greatest variation – and in some ways the most important indicator of the resilience of national economies to conditions of recession – occurred in gross fixed capital formation. In 1970 there was relatively little national variation within the Community – from 18.6 per cent in the UK to 25.7 per cent in the Netherlands; of the three Mediterranean countries only Portugal (17.6 per cent) fell below the UK's level of investment. By 1979, though, the range was from 17.8 per cent in the UK to 32.4 per cent in Ireland and, perhaps of greater importance, while the share of investment was rising again by 1979 in Germany and the Netherlands, as well as in Ireland, in the remaining countries of the Community it was falling.

While there are some broad correlations between overall economic performance and the shares of GDP allocated to public expenditure and fixed capital formation, it is by no means obvious that a high proportion of GDP allocated to public expenditure automatically precludes national prosperity; indeed, it is the countries with some of the highest shares of GDP allocated to public expenditure (Denmark and the Netherlands) that enjoy some of the highest living standards in the Community while, conversely, the three Mediterranean states have very low proportions of GDP directed to public expenditure but are hardly economic superpowers or havens of high general living standards (see Chapter 5). Nevertheless, the poor economic performance of Italy and the UK would seem to bear some relation to their low shares of investment and high shares of public expenditure; conversely, the strength of the German economy in particular would seem to bear some relation to high capital investment and low total public expenditure. Without examining further the allocation of total national public expenditure between various purposes (for which comparable data are not available) it is impossible to draw definite conclusions on its role other than that there is no simple correlation between its overall level and national economic virility.

4.6 Gross fixed capital formation: in total and by sector

4.6.1 Community and national trends
While considering total investment as a share of GDP offers some useful insights, it is both desirable (given the central role of investment in the economic growth process) and possible to examine investment trends in more detail. One of the key changes that occurred in the economies of the countries of the Community and in those of the three

Figure 4.17

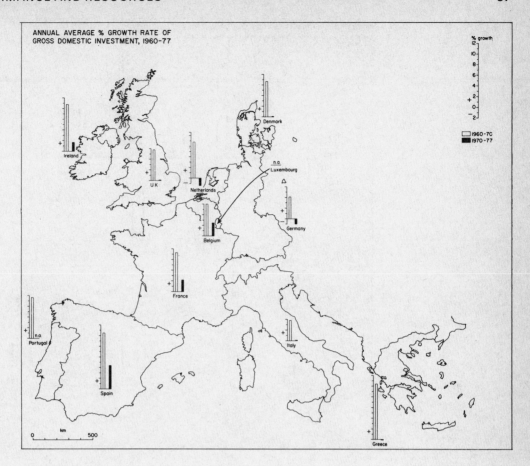

Mediterranean applicants was the sharp decline in the growth rate of domestic investment in the 1970s as compared with the 1960s (see Figure 4.17) – although this masks
considerable variations in overall and per capita levels and the sectoral distribution of
investment, issues that can be examined in the 1970s.

By 1970, there was quite a clear differentiation of countries into two groups around
the mean EEC Nine average per capita investment (see Figure 4.18): Denmark, Germany, Luxembourg, the Netherlands, France and Belgium (in that order) all exceeded
this average while Italy, the UK, Ireland, Greece, Spain and Portugal all fell below it.
The effects of the post-1973 recession were to reduce these differences a little, most of
the countries in the former group having a rather lower per capita level in 1975 than in
1970, most of those in the latter a rather higher level. After 1975, however, international
differences tended to widen again. Investment per capita recovered quite strongly in the
countries in the first group (particularly Germany) while to some extent the second
group became more differentiated. Ireland recorded the greatest relative increase of any
of the twelve countries considered between 1975 and 1979 (+47 per cent), taking it to the
top of this second group. Elsewhere, increases were more modest. By 1979 per capita
investment in Italy was still below the level of 1970 while in Spain the 1979 level was
below that of 1975 though above that of 1970. Thus the separation of the current and
applicant members of the Community into two divisions on this key indicator of investment was not simply reproduced but enhanced between 1970 and 1979; only Ireland
suggested that, after 1975, it might be bridging the gap in per capita terms, although in
terms of total investment it remained dwarfed by Germany, France, the UK and Italy.
Furthermore, since Ireland, Italy and the UK have a below Community average GDP
and the latter two a below average share of GDP in investment, this suggests that the
gap between the productive capacity of these three and the remaining six members
widened in the 1970s.

Figure 4.18

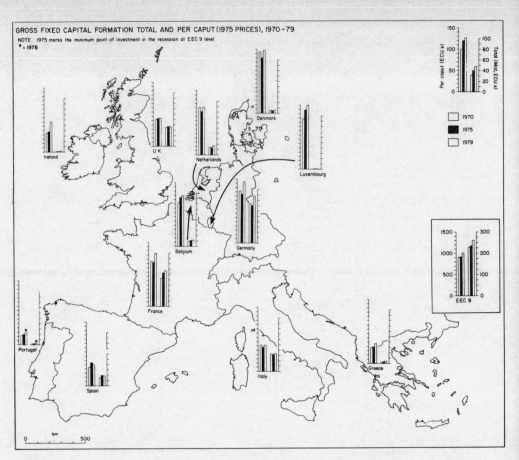

GROSS FIXED CAPITAL FORMATION TOTAL AND PER CAPUT (1975 PRICES), 1970-79
NOTE 1975 marks the minimum point of investment in the recession at EEC 9 level
* = 1978

As to the sectoral distribution of investment, this has displayed much less national variation than investment per capita. By 1970, the dominant feature at Community level was that over 60 per cent of gross fixed capital formation was in services, with less than 25 per cent in manufacturing and 7 per cent in fuel and power products (see Figure 4.19). In 1970 there was in fact relatively little variation around the Community average; only in Ireland (14.7 per cent) did the share of agriculture, forestry and fishing greatly deviate from the Community average of 4.1 per cent; Luxembourg (38.5 per cent) was the only member country to deviate markedly from the Community average for manufacturing (23.0 per cent), though Portugal (31.2 per cent) and Greece (14.2 per cent) also differed somewhat from this; of member countries, Luxembourg (37.4 per cent) was also the only major departure from the Community average for market services (49.5 per cent), and Ireland the major one for non-market services (7.2 per cent as compared to a Community average of 15.7 per cent), although Greece (28.2 per cent) recorded a very high share for the latter. The main effects of the recession on this pattern in 1975 were to reduce the share of manufacturing (the exceptions being Greece, Ireland, Italy and Portugal) and building and construction (again with the exception of Ireland and the UK) and increase the shares of services, fuel and power products (especially in the UK, associated with North Sea oil, though not in Ireland) and agriculture (with the major exception of Ireland). This sectoral pattern of 1975 was broadly reproduced at Community level in 1978 (see Figure 4.20), with one or two major exceptions. In Ireland, the share of agriculture rose to 19.0 per cent, exceeding the 1975 level and suggesting that this was mainly responsible for its overall improvement in per capita terms.

Thus by the end of the 1970s gross fixed capital formation in the Community was dominated by the service sector which had increased to 70 per cent of the total (56 per cent to market and 14 per cent to non-market services) while the share of manufacturing had fallen to 17.5 per cent – further evidence of the relative deindustrialization and

Figure 4.19

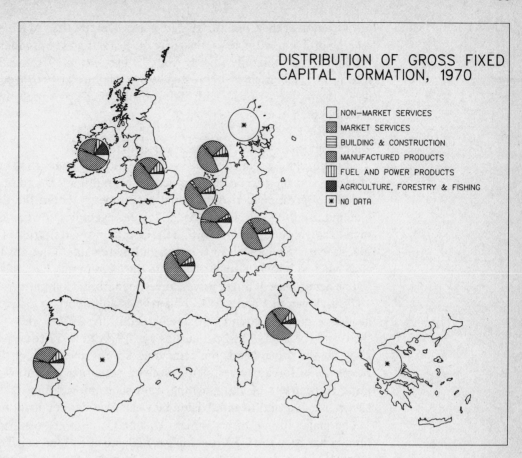

DISTRIBUTION OF GROSS FIXED
CAPITAL FORMATION, 1970

NON—MARKET SERVICES
MARKET SERVICES
BUILDING & CONSTRUCTION
MANUFACTURED PRODUCTS
FUEL AND POWER PRODUCTS
AGRICULTURE, FORESTRY & FISHING
NO DATA

Figure 4.20

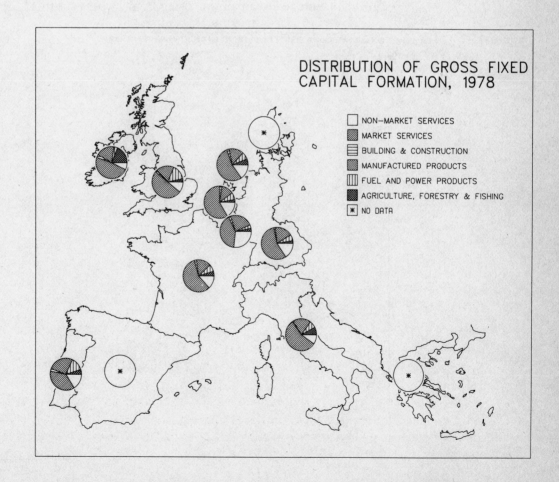

DISTRIBUTION OF GROSS FIXED
CAPITAL FORMATION, 1978

NON—MARKET SERVICES
MARKET SERVICES
BUILDING & CONSTRUCTION
MANUFACTURED PRODUCTS
FUEL AND POWER PRODUCTS
AGRICULTURE, FORESTRY & FISHING
NO DATA

tertiarization of the Community's economy. Despite the sudden emergence of a serious 'energy problem' after 1975, the share of fuel and power products in total fixed capital formation had risen only slightly from 7.1 per cent in 1970 to 8.3 per cent in 1975 and has, in fact, fallen since 1975, suggesting a failure at both Community and national levels to grapple seriously with the problems of energy supply and energy policies (see section 4.8).

4.6.2 *Foreign investment: national patterns and trends*

This issue, closely related to the increasing internationalization of production as well as of trade, and the increasing significance of multinational companies, is one that has become of great concern to national governments within the Community and to the Community itself (see Hamilton, 1976): for example, to what extent is the decline of manufacturing employment within the Community a reflection of the extra-Community investment strategies of EEC-based multinationals? What are the costs and benefits associated with inward-investment into the Community by USA-based multinationals?

The net balance of direct private investment from Community countries for 1970 and 1977 is shown in Figure 4.21. This reveals an important differentiation between two groups of member countries that emerged in the 1970s: while Germany, the Netherlands and the UK all had net outflows in 1970, by 1977 these had increased considerably; on the other hand, the remaining six members, which in 1970 had been net recipients of foreign investment, received yet larger net inflows in 1977. Bearing in mind the dangers of extrapolating from such information, these figures are at least suggestive of a significant division between member countries in this respect.

The major source of investment by non-Community companies within the Community has been the USA (see Figure 4.22; see also Hood and Young, 1976). Accumulated US direct investment grew globally from $12.8 billion in 1950 to $133.2 billion in 1975 with Europe's share of this rising from 15 per cent to 37 per cent, this increase

Figure 4.21

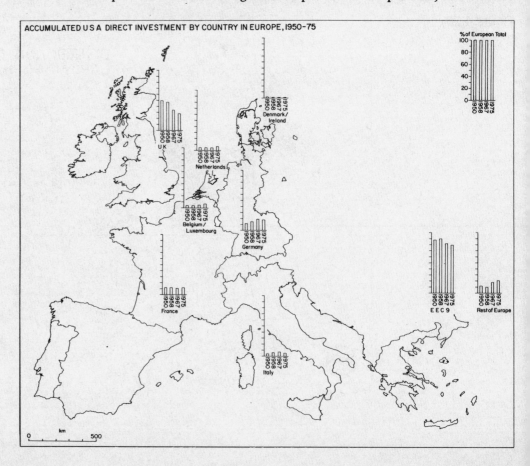

being concentrated between 1958 and 1967, at least in part in response to the formation of the Community. For while the Community's share of US direct investment in Europe fell from a peak of 90 per cent in 1958 to 79 per cent in 1975, this reflected a sharp fall in the UK's share (from 47 per cent in 1958 to 28 per cent in 1975) and a tendency for the shares of other Community members to rise, particularly that of Germany (see for example, Stubenitsky, 1973). While at first generally welcomed as a stimulus to economic growth and technological advance, the increasing penetration of US multinational investment, particularly into key sectors of energy and manufacturing, became increasingly a cause for concern as fears of external control and a potential challenge to sovereignty within the Community came to the fore (see for example, Firn, 1975).

4.6.3 Regional trends

At regional level, it is only possible to examine patterns of industrial investment per capita in relation to each national average (equal to 100); nevertheless it is a revealing one (see Figure 4.23). Apart from some predominantly urban regions, where service activities are particularly prominent, regions with above average GDP also tended to have above average industrial investment per capita in the 1970s. Notwithstanding this, though, the highest levels of investment tended to be found in peripheral, often maritime, regions. This reflects the concentration of major investments in sectors such as chemicals and iron and steel production in such regions (see also Arcangeli *et al.*, 1981; Hudson, 1983a), often in relation to regional policies and the spatial concentrations of public expenditure on infrastructure. Such investments were frequently justified in terms of the employment creation goals of regional policy – although the forecast employment growth, without exception, failed to materialize (Bleitrach and Chenu, 1982; Hudson, 1982a).

Figure 4.22

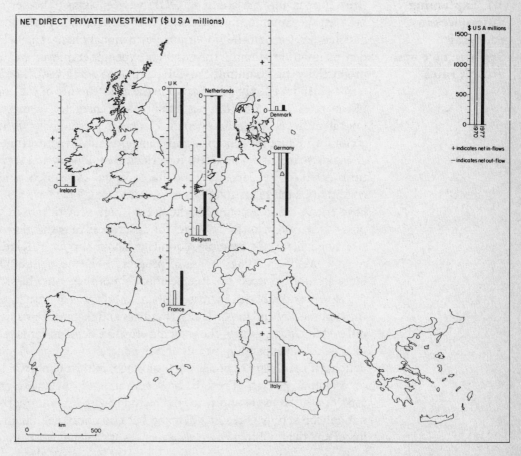

Figure 4.23

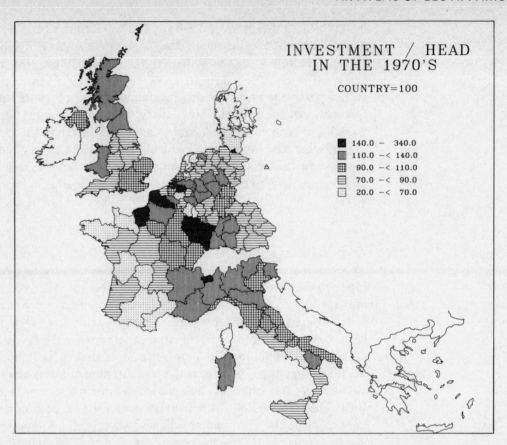

INVESTMENT / HEAD
IN THE 1970'S

COUNTRY=100

■	140.0 — 340.0
▨	110.0 —< 140.0
▦	90.0 —< 110.0
▤	70.0 —< 90.0
▦	20.0 —< 70.0

4.7 Explaining differences in economic performance and growth rates

Broadly speaking, variations in GDP between areas (whether regions or countries or between the Community itself and other areas, although the focus here will be on the national level, given the importance of national changes in relation to regional ones) depend upon variations in the numbers of people employed and on differences in labour productivity (that is output or GDP per person employed). The level of employment in terms of labour supply depends upon the age structure of the population, upon participation rates and upon the net balance and character of migration (see Chapter 2). Overall differences depend upon differences in productivity within sectors and upon the sectoral structure of economies and changes in this structure (one expression of which is changing shares of employment in agriculture, industry and services; see Chapter 3); in turn, productivity depends upon fixed capital investment and upon labour market conditions, such as resistance to new technology. There are a number of studies which have attempted to account for the overall high growth rate in western Europe in the post-war period prior to 1973 and for differences in national growth rates. Often these stress one factor (for example, abundant labour supply – Kindleberger, 1967; investment – Madison, 1964; technical progress – Denison, 1967) whereas it is probably more accurate to stress the interrelationship of these variables.

There is no doubt that increased labour supply was of great importance both overall in the Community and in particular countries and regions. For a variety of reasons, which differed for each country, the growing effective demand for labour up to 1973 could be satisfied by an expanding supply which generally exceeded demand and meant that (at national if not always regional level) shortages in the quantity of labour were not a brake on economic growth. There is, however, another qualitative rather than quantitative aspect to the issue of supply, for the maintenance of labour market flexibility depended not only on supply exceeding demand but also upon the militancy or docility of labour forces and their willingness to accept or resist changed work practices, new technology, etc. Often workers were in a weak position on the market; many were migrant workers, many others were being introduced to factory work for the first time with no tradition of trade union membership or organization, and in some countries, especially FR Germany and Italy (and to a lesser extent France) union organization was initially very weak, having been smashed during the Fascist period. This resulted in relatively low wage levels and few barriers either to introducing technological change or to changing working practices using existing technologies and so gaining substantial labour productivity increases. In other countries, such as Belgium and the UK, trade unions remained more powerful and combatative and as such these countries were less attractive destinations for new capital investment.

More generally, capital investment as a share of the value of output (GDP) and of manufacturing output was at much higher levels than in the inter-war years (Aldcroft, 1978), generally around 15–20 per cent, except for the UK and Denmark. Generally, countries with high investment ratios experienced faster growth (for example FR Germany and the Netherlands) and vice versa (for example Belgium and the UK), although the relationship is a far from perfect one. The similarity in investment ratios is an important factor in relation to the narrowing of growth rate differentials in the 1960s.

One might also reasonably expect labour productivity and fixed capital formation to be positively related. Indeed, Denison's (1967) results suggest this as countries with the greatest productivity gains tended to be those with the largest increases in the quantities of both fixed capital and labour (that is, FR Germany, Italy, France and the Netherlands). There is an intuitively plausible explanation of why this should have been so, for these were countries whose industrial capacity was most destroyed by the war and was afterwards replaced by the then current technology, and/or were countries where large areas were industrialized for the first time in the 1950s or 1960s. The key to national growth differences probably lies in the degree to which the 'new' science-based industries of the third technological revolution, characterized by rapid technical progress and productivity increases, came to be represented in various national economies, initially in those industries producing the machinery and raw materials for other consumer goods' industries and heavily associated in the 1950s and 1960s with the penetration of US multinational capital into the Community (Stubenitsky, 1973) – something which began to be seen as a major threat to national and Community sovereignty. This new technology and investment diffused at varying speeds to different countries, and those which initially presented particularly favourable (profitable) environments were those which then and subsequently experienced higher growth rates as productivity gains arising from these new science-based industries spread and were generalized throughout their economies. Nevertheless, by the early 1970s the dominant tendency was of convergence of national growth rates.

After 1973, however, a rather different balance of forces influenced national growth rates. The basically favourable configuration of circumstances of the pre-1973 period (leading to growth) was replaced by an altogether less favourable one. Why this change occurred is a subject of considerable debate. Some attribute it essentially to events internal to the Community – inflation, public spending and market imperfections impeding structural change (Commission of the European Communities, 1981b: 21–7). Others attribute it more to events outside the Community, notably the oil price rises of 1973–4 (Begg et al., 1981: 13–22); still others to the internal contradictions of capitalism (Mandel, 1975a; 1978). Whatever its causes, the effects of recession were felt severely within the Community and the differential ability of national and regional economies to respond to the new economic climate, itself a product of recent economic history, led to widening disparities within the Community.

Within the Community the aggregate growth of labour demand slowed down. This found expression in the cessation of net in-migration of international migrant labourers and subsequently when such flows did begin again, they did so at much lower levels.

Considerable reduction of inter-regional migration within the Community from peripheral to core regions also occurred, resulting in rising unemployment and falling GDP per capita in the former. Within countries, though, employment rate differences account for between one-half and two-thirds of inter-regional GDP differences. The main factor at Community level in accounting for both increasing national and regional differences in GDP was labour productivity (which in turn reflected differences in investment), with differences in the proportion of the population in employment exercising a weaker countervailing influence. These productivity differences reflected the structure of national economies – both the sectoral structure and differences in productivity within a sector in different countries. Thus, although the causes remained in dispute, the expressions of recession within the Community were only too apparent, posing major challenges in terms of devising policies to cope effectively with them (see also Chapter 6).

4.8 The energy crisis and transport: Community and national trends

In some ways the single most traumatic event for the Community in the 1970s was the first oil price rise of November 1973, although the second major round of price increases in 1979 also had a severe impact. By the early 1970s domestic energy consumption in the Community far outstripped production (respectively 809.4 and 319.2 million tonnes of oil-equivalent in 1970). This partly reflected the run-down of the production of high-cost coal within the Community from the late 1950s in response to the availability on the world market of large amounts of cheap oil (see Minshull, 1978: 19–22). Nevertheless, in 1970 some 70 per cent of primary energy sources produced in the Community was coal (see Figure 4.24), a reflection of the general absence of alternatives within it, even though such other sources as hydro-electric power and natural gas were important in some countries, notably Italy and the Netherlands. Thus the Community had become more and more dependent on energy imports in general – these accounting at their maximum for 63.9 per cent of total consumption in 1979 – and on imports of oil in particular (although a considerable amount of oil was in demand as a raw material for petrochemicals production as well as for fuel). While both in absolute and per capita terms the Community consumed less energy than the USA in 1973, energy consumption was higher than in Japan, which was even more reliant upon energy imports than the EEC.

Plate 2   The nuclear option: Chinon power station, France

Plate 3   Part of the non-nuclear alternative? Tagebau Fortuna, open-cast lignite workings to the east of Aachen, FR Germany

One reaction to the rise in the price of oil was a fall in net imports to the Community (see Figure 4.25) but, on the other hand, net consumption, having fallen between 1973 and 1975, then rose to a new peak in 1979, both in absolute and per capita terms, while net production continued to rise from 1973 to 1979. Energy consumption followed a similar pattern in Japan and the USA, while domestic production in the USA in 1979 was still below the levels of 1973 and that in Japan continued to decline gently from 1973. Thus it would appear that the Community adjusted more positively and strongly

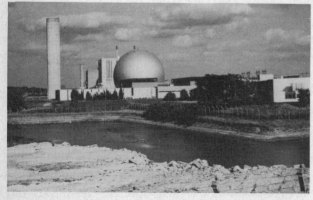

2

3

Figure 4.24

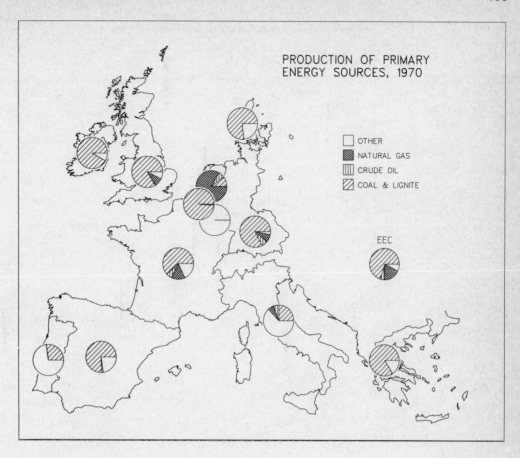

PRODUCTION OF PRIMARY
ENERGY SOURCES, 1970

OTHER
NATURAL GAS
CRUDE OIL
COAL & LIGNITE

EEC

Figure 4.25

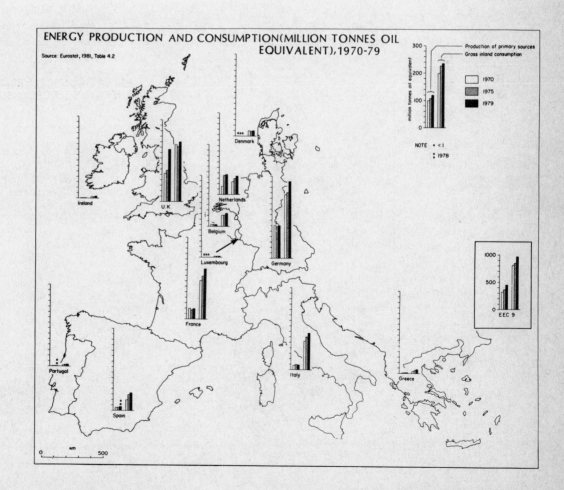

ENERGY PRODUCTION AND CONSUMPTION(MILLION TONNES OIL
EQUIVALENT),1970-79

Source: Eurostat, 1981, Table 4.2

Production of primary sources
Gross inland consumption

1970
1975
1979

NOTE * < 1
: 1978

Denmark

Ireland

U.K.

Netherlands

Belgium

Luxembourg

Germany

France

Portugal

Spain

Italy

Greece

EEC 9

0   500

Figure 4.26

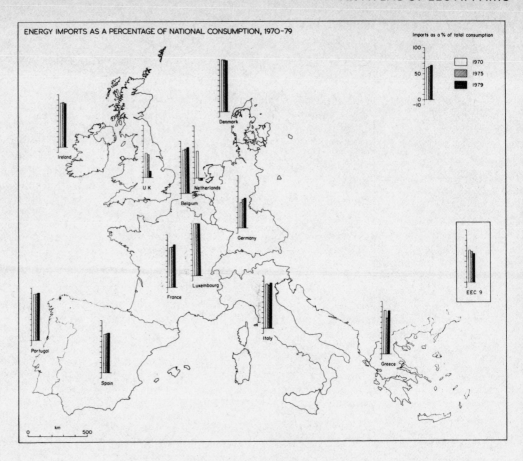

ENERGY IMPORTS AS A PERCENTAGE OF NATIONAL CONSUMPTION, 1970-79

Figure 4.27

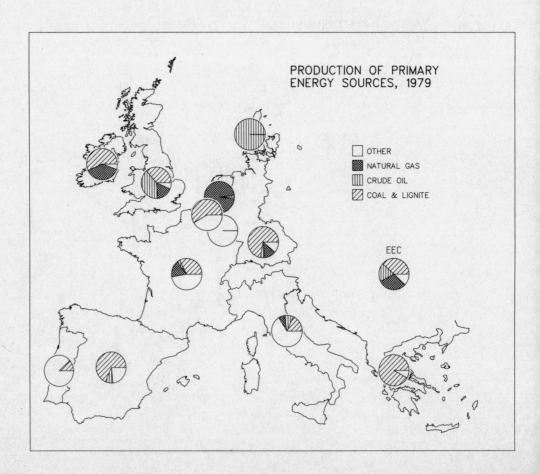

PRODUCTION OF PRIMARY ENERGY SOURCES, 1979

to the new situation on world energy markets, more so than the other two major industrial powers.

This, however, is to some extent illusory, as becomes clear if consumption, production and energy trade trends are examined within individual countries (see Figure 4.26). The seemingly virile response of the Community after 1973 is in fact wholly accounted for by the continuing expansion of natural gas production in the Netherlands, the expansion of UK oil production from the North Sea after 1976, and the increase in nuclear power production, most notably in France (see Figures 4.24 and 4.27). Despite the energy crisis, domestic coal production continued to decline in all producer countries in the Community with a tendency to switch from deep to open-cast mining; and for the member countries other than the Netherlands and the UK reliance on net energy imports tended, if anything, to increase after 1973 (and this was also true of Greece, Portugal and Spain). Thus while the spatial pattern of energy trade may have changed somewhat, the extreme dependence of most Community countries on net energy imports remained at very high levels, a condition that the Mediterranean enlargement would further exacerbate. Increasing consumption, therefore, reflected continuing oil imports despite substantial price rises and was symptomatic more of a failure to adjust social and economic structures to the changed conditions on the world energy market (unlike Japan) rather than of a successful solution having been found to the energy problem.

The rapid evolution of a coherent Community energy policy remains a pressing priority – the more so as in the late 1970s the Commission were forecasting total consumption in the order of 1400 million tonnes oil-equivalent by 1990 (*Financial Times*, 7 July 1979), an increase approaching 50 per cent of the consumption levels of the late 1970s. Of this increase, about 40 per cent was forecast to be met by nuclear power, between 5 per cent and 17 per cent by increased domestic oil production, between 6 per cent and 22 per cent by increased oil imports and about 20 per cent by increased natural gas imports; the remainder was to come from smaller relative increases of coal imports and production. These forecasts imply a number of potential risks and dangers, one of which is the continuing dependence of the Community on oil and gas imports, which increasingly might have to be sought from countries such as the USSR and might therefore pose military and political risks to the Community (for example, see Alting von Gesau, 1975). On the other hand, the expansion of nuclear power production within the Community has already encountered significant opposition in several member countries (for example, see Ardagh, 1982).

Perhaps solutions will have to be found in other directions, for example, policies to cut energy demand. Existing dwellings could be modified to conserve energy via higher standards of insulation, and new ones built with this objective in mind. The emphasis in transport might be switched from policies which foster relatively energy-inefficient modes to those which promote energy-efficient ones: from personal movement by car to bus or rail (see section 5.7.1), from long-distance freight movement by road to rail or inland waterway. For example, since 1970 there has been a considerable modal switch from rail to road freight transport in all member countries (see Figure 4.28): in 1970, approximately 40 per cent of freight tonne/kms was moved by rail but by 1978 this had fallen to less than 30 per cent. Such modal switches, which would have other benefits such as reducing environmental pollution and reducing inequalities in personal mobility, imply quite dramatic changes in societal attitudes and lifestyles and in transport policy. This would also be true of more general planning policies which could aim to minimize movement, leading to marked changes in urban form and settlement structures, although of necessity these would have to operate over a longer time period than policies aimed simply at securing modal switches.

Figure 4.28

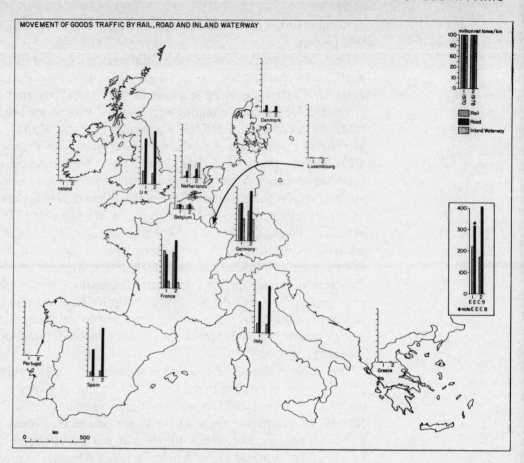

MOVEMENT OF GOODS TRAFFIC BY RAIL, ROAD AND INLAND WATERWAY

Figure 4.29

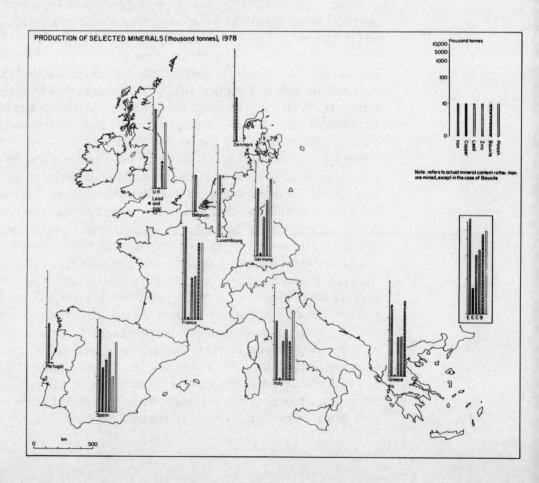

PRODUCTION OF SELECTED MINERALS (thousand tonnes), 1978

4.9 Other mineral resources: international and national comparisons

As with energy, the Community is comparatively badly endowed with other mineral resources, both absolutely and, in so far as one can draw international comparisons given the problems of resource definition and data availability, in comparison to other countries (see Figure 4.29). For example, the Community's iron ore resources are about 25 per cent of those of the USA and less than 10 per cent of those of the USSR; moreover, the Community's iron ore resources, which are heavily concentrated in France, are generally of low quality (about 30 per cent metal content). The entry of Spain to the Community would raise iron ore reserves by about 25 per cent. Indeed, Spanish entry would also add relatively greatly to Community mineral reserves in other respects though the absolute amounts are generally small, a reflection of the paucity of current Community mineral resources; the same point can be made concerning Greece's entry which more than doubled the Community's bauxite reserves and added relatively large amounts to its resources of lead and zinc. Overall, however, the Community, whether of ten or twelve members, remains one with relatively small reserves of many key minerals and none of others which are vital to a modern, industrial economy, thus helping to account for the Community extending its trading links into the Third World and other non-Community areas to try and secure supplies of such key materials (see section 1.4.6).

4.10 Inflation, money supply and central government borrowing: national trends

At both national and Community level, concern with monetary issues became increasingly central to macro-economic policies as the 1970s progressed and the low annual inflation rates of the 1960s were increasingly replaced by double-digit ones. In the 1960s and the initial years of the 1970s, the countries of the Community generally experienced relatively low annual inflation rates (see Figure 4.30) and the money supply also grew comparatively slowly. Similarly, the current Mediterranean applicant countries also

Figure 4.30

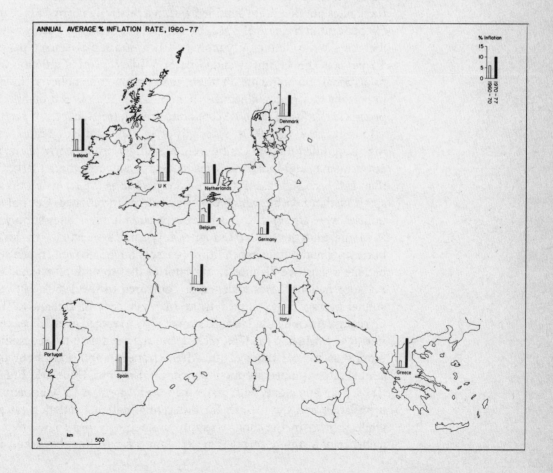

Figure 4.31

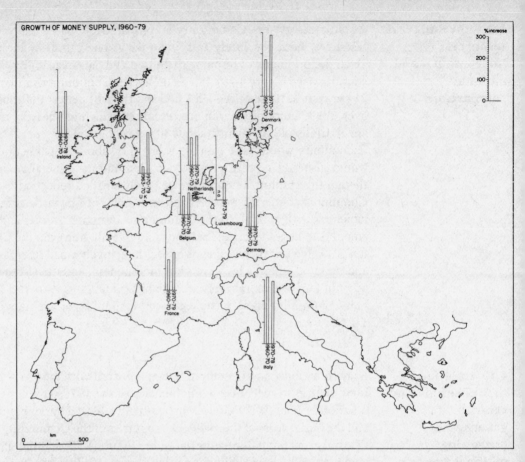

GROWTH OF MONEY SUPPLY, 1960-79

experienced modest inflation rates. There were, nevertheless, national variations in these rates but they were confined within a relatively narrow range in the 1960s – from 6.3 per cent in the case of Spain to 3.0 per cent in that of Portugal, with the current ten members of the Community more tightly grouped between 6.0 per cent (Denmark) and 3.2 per cent (FR Germany and Greece). While control of inflation was of some concern to national governments in their macro-economic policies, in general it was less important as a policy objective than – say – the pursuit of full employment or the promotion of faster national economic growth (see Chapter 4, section 7).

In contrast, in the 1970s, especially after 1973 as inflation rates rose sharply, combating rising inflation came to figure increasingly prominently in the policies of national governments, and indeed policies tended to converge more markedly around this goal than had been the case in the previous decade as the recession drastically reduced the space available within which policies could be formulated. Central to these converging policies were attempts to check the expansion in the money supply which rose sharply as compared to the 1960s (see Figure 4.31), and, associated with this, to cut government borrowing and public expenditure (see section 4.5 above). In one sense, inflation rates became a sensitive diagnostic indicator of the strength of national economies, and the range of national rates widened as compared to the 1960s: between 1970 and 1977 annual average rates ranged from 14.7 per cent in Ireland to 5.9 per cent in FR Germany. As well as in Ireland, annual rates averaged over 13 per cent in Greece, Italy, Portugal, Spain and the UK, picking out the weak national economies within the Community as well as those of the Mediterranean applicants. Four other countries had annual rates grouped around 9 per cent – Belgium, Denmark, France and the Netherlands. Standing alone, with easily the lowest rate, was FR Germany. Clearly the causes of inflation and the reasons for differential national inflation rates are complex, and while growth in the money supply undoubtedly has some effect, there is no clear evidence of a simple correlation, let alone a causal link, between them.

Figure 4.32

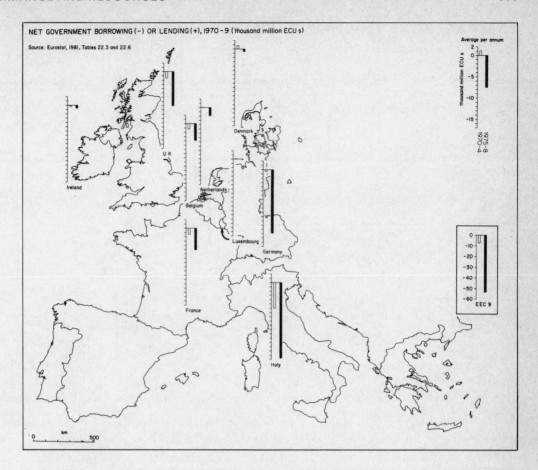

Contrary to the wishes and intentions of national governments in their anti-inflation policies, the effects of the recession after 1973 were in many ways to increase pressures for government expenditure – and hence for increased taxation and borrowing. For example, the increased price of oil altered the terms of trade and led to balance of payments problems, given dependence on oil imports, and to problems of domestic unemployment, all of which tended to push up public expenditure (see section 4.5 above) and net government borrowing, both absolutely and as a share of GDP (see Figure 4.32). With the exception of Luxembourg, net government borrowing rose significantly after 1974 (perhaps most strikingly of all in FR Germany), and several countries – Denmark, France and the Netherlands – which were net lenders in the early 1970s were net borrowers in succeeding years. Thus, between 1975 and 1978, net government borrowing as a share of GDP ranged from 1.6 per cent in France to 9.9 per cent in Italy, which may be compared to the range between 1970 and 1974, from the borrowing of 5.0 per cent in Italy to the lending of 3.6 per cent in Denmark. By the second half of the 1970s, national governments in Italy, Ireland and, to a lesser degree, in Belgium, had become increasingly tied by relations of dependency on external sources of finance to help meet their borrowing requirements.

A further symptom of the effects of recession on government financing was to push up taxation as a share of GDP (see Figure 4.33). In 1970 tax receipts were equivalent to 34.6 per cent of GDP in the Community of Nine, ranging from 27.5 per cent in Italy to 40.5 per cent in the Netherlands; in 1979 the comparable figures were 38.8 per cent, 33.4 per cent and 47.4 per cent respectively. While the balance of this increase varied between the private individual and the business sector in different countries, the overall result was to squeeze both corporate profitability and consumer real incomes, in turn further depressing effective demand.

Figure 4.33

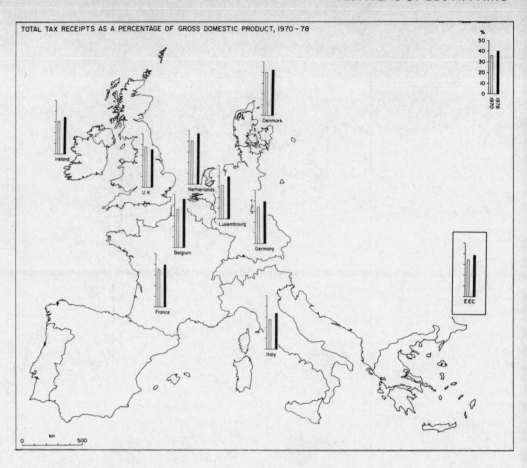

TOTAL TAX RECEIPTS AS A PERCENTAGE OF GROSS DOMESTIC PRODUCT, 1970 - 78

Figure 4.34

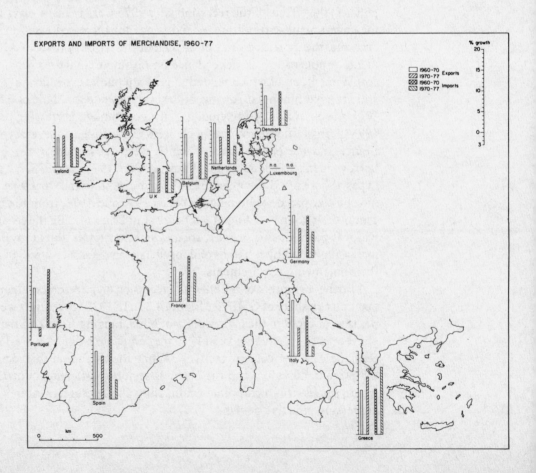

EXPORTS AND IMPORTS OF MERCHANDISE, 1960-77

**4.11 Trade
patterns and the
balance of
payments:
national patterns**

A major consequence of the formation of the Common Market was the reduction or abolition of tariffs within it on commodities traded between member countries, and the creation of a common, external tariff wall around it. At the same time the Community has entered into a variety of trade agreements with non-member countries to secure agricultural products and energy and industrial raw materials which it lacks (see Chapter 1). Given this, it would be reasonable to expect the share of each member country's trade with other members, and with non-member countries formally tied to the Community by trade agreements, to have increased, and this has been the case.

It is another question, however, as to what extent this increase was caused by the formation of the Community and to what extent it would have occurred in any case – a question that cannot be answered with precision. Nevertheless, the growing overall importance of multinational companies with operations in many countries has itself contributed significantly to the growth of international trade – many inter-country movements are intra-company ones, for example. What is undeniable is the considerable increase in trade that took place in the decade of the 1960s (see Figure 4.34): annual average growth rates for exports ranged from 13.5 per cent in Italy to 4.8 per cent in the UK, those of imports from 18.4 per cent in Spain to 5.0 per cent in the UK. The greatest discrepancies between import and export growth occurred in Portugal and Spain, economies then being opened to the currents of world trade following prolonged periods of protectionist policies (see Hudson and Lewis, 1984b). In the 1970s, especially after 1973, both export and import growth rates generally fell: between 1970 and 1977, only Greece recorded increases in both of these while export growth rates grew in Ireland and the UK.

Nevertheless, irrespective of the degree to which changing trade patterns depended upon the formation of the Common Market *per se*, by the end of the 1970s trade with the remaining Community members was the most important single element in each member country's overall trading pattern (see Figures 4.35 and 4.36). There were, though,

Figure 4.35

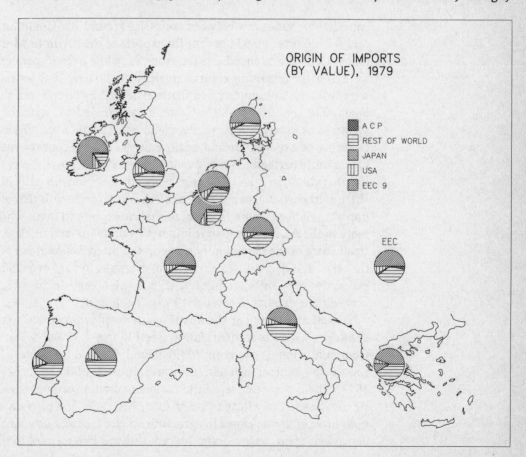

ORIGIN OF IMPORTS
(BY VALUE), 1979

ACP
REST OF WORLD
JAPAN
USA
EEC 9

EEC

Figure 4.36

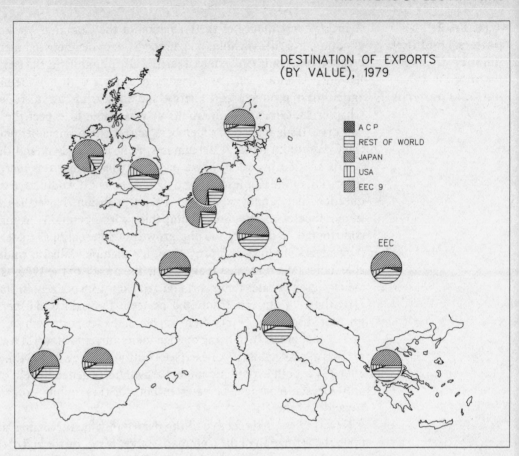

DESTINATION OF EXPORTS
(BY VALUE), 1979

ACP
REST OF WORLD
JAPAN
USA
EEC 9

considerable variations between countries around the Community averages of 50 per cent for imports and 53 per cent for exports in the extent to which their trade was with fellow Community members: for example, while over 75 per cent of Ireland's imports were from the remaining eight countries in 1979, only 40.8 per cent of the UK's imports were from the Community – a figure exceeded by Greece and Portugal, though not by Spain. The significance of the Community's trade links with the ACP countries is also shown to be in terms of particular commodities rather than the overall volume of trade. In terms of exports, Ireland again emerges as the country most integrated with its Community partners, 77.6 per cent of its exports being to them, followed closely by the Benelux countries, the UK again being the least so with 41.8 per cent. Comparing its share of imports and exports to the USA and Japan reveals that overall, the Community imports relatively more from them than it exports to them while it exports relatively more to the ACP states than it imports from them; nevertheless, though this trade is a small share of the Community's imports, it often constitutes a very high proportion of the various ACP countries' exports: for example, in 1978 over 75 per cent of Cameroon's exports were to the Community, with many other African states sending over 40 per cent of their exports (Eurostat, 1980b: Table 110).

As well as examining the spatial pattern of imports and exports, it is possible to consider their sectoral distribution (see Figures 4.37 and 4.38). Almost 40 per cent of Community imports were (in 1979) of food, fuel and raw materials, with roughly half of these being mineral fuels and lubricants, imports of the latter having risen sharply after 1973. There was relatively little national variation around these Community average figures, particularly in the case of food, beverages and tobacco, although Italy (with a high share of its workforce in agriculture – see Chapter 3) emerged as the country most dependent upon food imports. Indeed, this was also the case in terms of dependence on

Figure 4.37

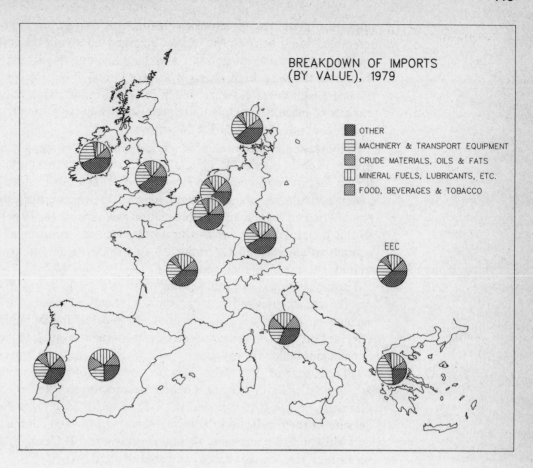

BREAKDOWN OF IMPORTS
(BY VALUE), 1979

OTHER
MACHINERY & TRANSPORT EQUIPMENT
CRUDE MATERIALS, OILS & FATS
MINERAL FUELS, LUBRICANTS, ETC.
FOOD, BEVERAGES & TOBACCO

EEC

Figure 4.38

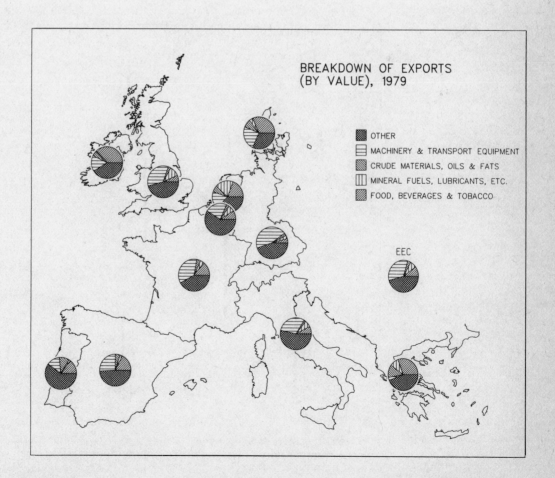

BREAKDOWN OF EXPORTS
(BY VALUE), 1979

OTHER
MACHINERY & TRANSPORT EQUIPMENT
CRUDE MATERIALS, OILS & FATS
MINERAL FUELS, LUBRICANTS, ETC.
FOOD, BEVERAGES & TOBACCO

EEC

imports of fuels and raw materials, and in this respect both Portugal and Spain most resembled Italy; in contrast, Ireland emerged as having the lowest share of its total imports in these two categories. As to the remaining import patterns, the outstanding feature is the very high share of Greece's total import bill in the machinery and transport equipment category; much of Greek industrial development depends upon imports of machinery while there are also considerable imports of motor vehicles to Greece (in both cases from FR Germany).

In contrast, manufactured products are a much more significant component of Community exports, almost 80 per cent overall, attaining a maximum of almost 90 per cent for FR Germany and falling to less than 60 per cent for Denmark, Greece and Ireland (where agricultural products account for over 30 per cent of exports) and for the Netherlands (where mineral fuels, notably natural gas, account for 19 per cent of total exports). Within the broad groupings of manufactured goods, exports of machinery and transport equipment are particularly important in FR Germany and are also above the Community average in France and the UK.

These changing sectoral and spatial patterns of trade, as well as changes in the growth rates of total exports and imports, can be summarized in terms of changes in the current account balance of payments position. In general, the combined direct and indirect effects of the 1973 oil price rises on trade patterns was either to increase existing balance of payments deficits or to convert surpluses to deficits (see Figure 4.39). For example, in 1970 only four of the current member countries of the Community recorded current account deficits – Denmark, Greece, Ireland and the Netherlands. By 1977 only FR Germany, the Netherlands and the UK recorded surpluses, the latter two primarily because of their indigenous energy reserves. In marked contrast to the general trend, and without significant oil or natural gas reserves, FR Germany significantly increased its current account surplus as compared to 1970.

Figure 4.39

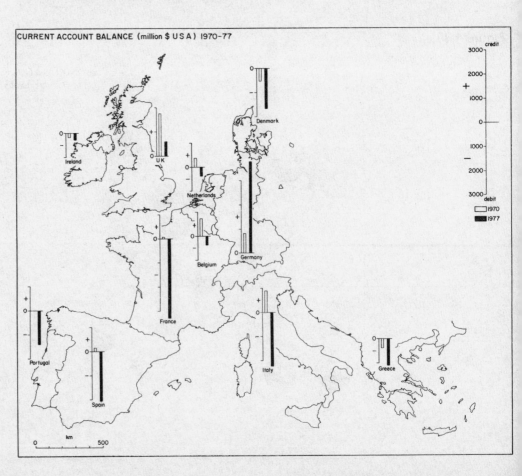

4.12 Concluding comments

The 1970s saw a marked deceleration in the rate of growth of the Community's economy, particularly so in some national and regional cases. This undoubtedly posed serious problems which will probably persist throughout the 1980s, given the Community's continuing dependence on imported oil and, indeed, on other key raw materials upon which a modern industrial sector depends. Even so, both in aggregate and per capita terms, the Community remains a major economic power on the world stage and is likely to continue in this role. Past growth to present levels of economic performance has provided a basis for, on average, a high material standard of living. It is to a consideration of lifestyles and living conditions that we now turn.

5 SOCIAL CONDITIONS, CONSUMPTION PATTERNS AND LIFESTYLES

5.1 Introduction

The issues discussed in previous chapters, dealing with demographic, labour market and economic changes, clearly have considerable implications for people's living conditions and lifestyles; for example, the incidence of unemployment, especially long-term unemployment, brings with it often traumatic changes in levels and styles of living (for example, see Hudson, 1982b). In this chapter, the issues of spatial variations in living conditions are explored more fully, although examination of these is rather more difficult than those of (say) employment structure. These difficulties arise for two main reasons (see also Commission of the European Communities, 1981a: 88). Firstly there tends to be less reliable data available on variables that relate to consumption and lifestyles, especially at regional level, not least because such variables are more likely to be influenced by cultural and social differences, posing problems of comparable common definitions. Secondly, where such data are available, there are considerable problems in accounting for differences between areas on variables such as education, health or housing, as these can be influenced to a considerable degree by differing cultural norms, by differences in legislatively established minimum standards, and by varying definitions as well as, in the case of housing, by climatic variations. Nevertheless, bearing these qualifications in mind, it is possible to examine the extent to which living conditions and lifestyles vary outside the workplace over the European Community.

5.2 Public and private consumption: national patterns and trends

This forms a useful starting point in that this issue has already been touched upon (see section 4.5) in terms of the share of GDP taken by these two categories of consumption. One might reasonably expect some correlation between overall rates of economic growth (see section 4.2) and growth rates of public and private consumption.

Indeed, an examination of consumption growth rates in the 1960s and 1970s (see Figure 5.1) reveals the extent to which, in aggregate, the recession of the latter decade slowed the growth in consumption and altered the balance between private and public: growth rates in the 1970s exceeded those of the 1960s in FR Germany, Greece, Ireland, Spain and the UK in terms of public consumption, and only in Belgium in terms of private.

As well as this general slowing down in growth, especially of private consumption, there are interesting national variations in both decades. The highest annual growth rates of public consumption in the 1960s (over 5 per cent) were found in Belgium, Denmark, Greece, Portugal and Spain − the high rates in the latter three being attributable to a process of development from very meagre levels of provision of public services, infrastructure, etc. With the exception of the UK, which already had a quite fully developed public sector by 1960, growth rates in public consumption in the remaining member states were between 3 per cent and 4 per cent. The pattern in the 1970s was rather more complicated, depending on national governments' responses to recession.

In terms of private consumption, annual growth rates in the 1960s exceeded 5 per cent in France, Greece, Italy, the Netherlands, Portugal and Spain, and with the exception of the UK (2.3 per cent), exceeded 3.5 per cent in the remaining member states of the

Figure 5.1

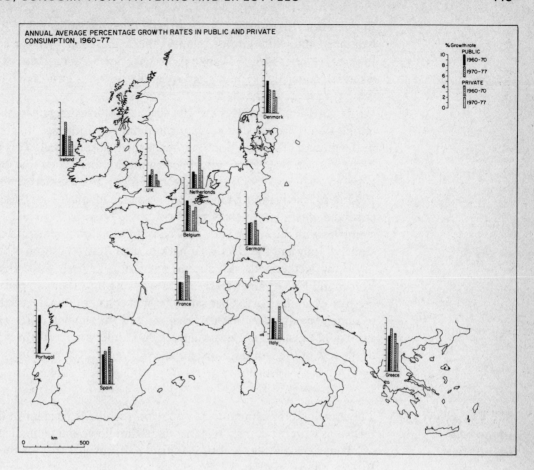

Figure 5.2

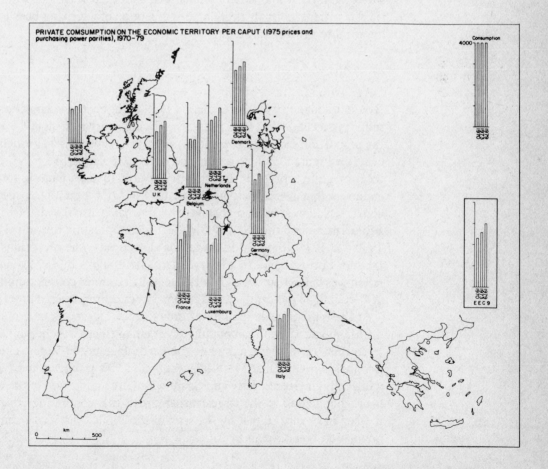

Community. In contrast, these growth rates generally fell in the 1970s (except in Belgium), and while Greece retained the highest rate (5.3 per cent) and the UK the lowest (1.1 per cent), the ranking of countries between these extremes altered somewhat: for example, Belgium's and Ireland's positions improved while those of Italy and the Netherlands declined.

It is worth emphasizing, however, that at least in aggregate (without considering their implications for particular groups or individuals), these figures point to a slowing down in the growth of consumption, rather than an absolute fall. This point is amplified by Figure 5.2. In real terms, private consumption per capita rose by almost 30 per cent between 1970 and 1979, this increase tending to be concentrated between 1970 and 1973. While consumption increased in all nine member countries, some marked differences did emerge in the ranking of countries between 1970 and 1979. While the three countries with the lowest per capita consumption levels remained the same in both years (Ireland, Italy and the UK), Denmark slipped from a position of first in 1970 to fifth in 1979; the Netherlands also slipped from fifth to sixth while Belgium, Luxembourg, France and FR Germany all rose in the ranking by one or two places so that by 1979 FR Germany had the highest per capita level of consumption. Nevertheless, it is important to remember that despite these changes and the slowing in the rate of growth of consumption, consumption levels in the Community are greatly in excess of those in much of the rest of the world (for example, see Brandt (Report), 1980).

5.3 The growth of the urban population

The growing proportion of the population which is resident in urban areas is closely related to patterns of inter-regional migration flows and sectoral changes in the pattern of labour demand (see sections 2.4.2 and 3.4), changes that are themselves interrelated. In fact, the proportion of the population designated as urban is a reasonably good surrogate for a whole variety of changes associated with the switch from a traditional rural to a modern urban lifestyle, the perception of which has been a key factor influencing rural to urban movement.

5.3.1 National trends

By 1960, a majority of the population in all of the current member countries of the Community, except Greece and Ireland, was living in urban areas and even in these two cases the proportion exceeded 40 per cent; Portugal, however, had a much lower share, 27 per cent (see Figure 5.3). The proportion of the population living in urban areas continued to grow quite rapidly during the 1960s, growth rates tending to be highest in those countries that were least urbanized in 1960 (for example, Greece and Spain) and, conversely, lowest in those that were most urbanized at that date (for example Denmark, FR Germany and the UK). While the urban population continued to increase between 1970 and 1975, it tended to do so at a slower pace, the exceptions to this trend being Ireland, Portugal and, to a lesser extent, Italy. Thus by 1975 a majority of the population was defined as urban in all the countries under consideration with the exception of Portugal (28 per cent), ranging from 55 per cent in Ireland to 90 per cent in the UK.

At the same time as the rate of growth in the urban population fell, a rather more diffuse spread of the urban population began to emerge, as the percentage of those living in smaller towns increased while the percentage in the largest cities declined as their population decentralized into adjacent areas. This trend was most evident in Denmark while only in Greece, Italy and Spain was there an increase in the concentration of the urban population in the largest urban areas; this continuing concentration was most marked in Greece so that by the start of the 1980s over 30 per cent of the total Greek population was resident in Athens.

Figure 5.3

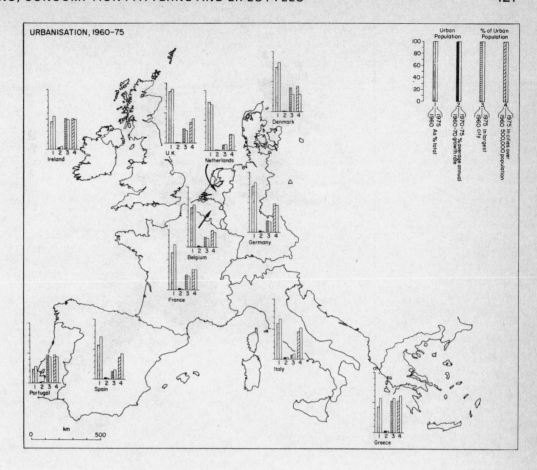

5.3.2 Regional trends

By 1960, many regions of the Community had considerable proportions of their populations resident in urban areas (see Figure 5.4). The highest concentrations tended to be found in heavily industrialized regions (such as the West Midlands or the Ruhr) and/or regions containing capital cities (such as the South-East of England and Paris). Conversely, regions with a relatively low proportion of their populations resident in urban areas tended to be those in which agriculture remained more important within the regional economy (for example, much of south and west France and the south-east of Germany); a major exception to this general trend is the relatively high proportion of the population living in urban areas in much of central and southern Italy, which is attributable in part to the historical evolution of settlement patterns there with the population concentrated in hill-top urban settlements (for example, see Bethemont and Pelletier, 1983: 194–5).

Between 1960 and 1970, the urban population generally grew in all regions of the Community, with the exception of a few in Belgium and Germany (see Figure 5.6). The outstanding feature of this period was the high rates of growth in virtually all French regions outside Paris. More generally, growth rates tended to be inversely related to the concentrations of urban population in 1960. Thus by 1970 the pattern of regional differences in the urban proportion of the population differed little from that in 1960.

In the 1970s, a rather different pattern of changes developed. In many more regions, especially in Belgium, England and FR Germany, the share of the population living in urban areas declined; these tended to be regions that in 1970 were heavily urbanized and reflected population decentralization in response to the changing perceptions of the advantages of life in major urban areas (see Figure 5.7). Elsewhere, growth rates remained positive but generally fell relative to those of the 1960s, and in the few regions where

Figure 5.4

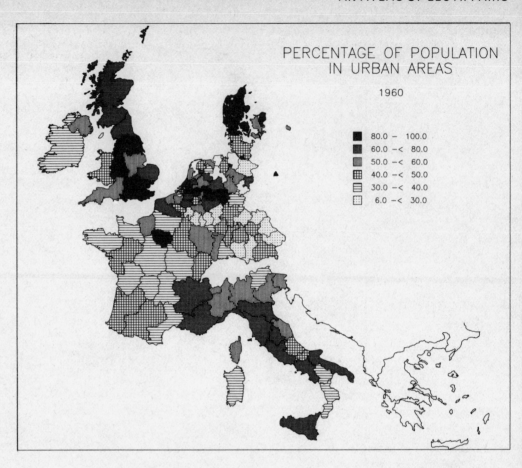

Figure 5.5

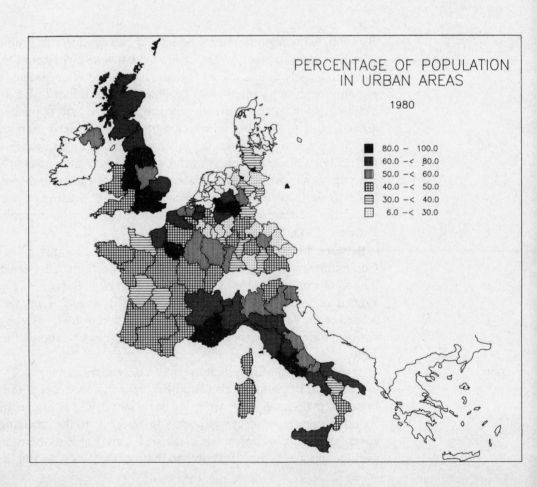

Figure 5.6

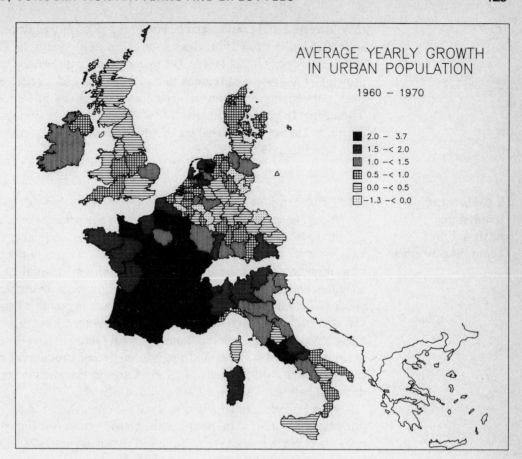

Figure 5.7

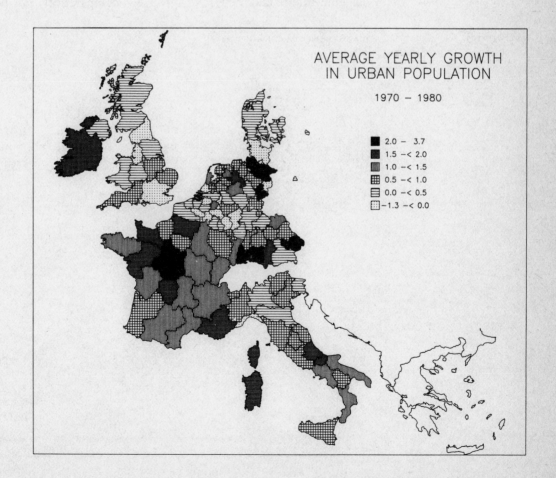

they increased, this could often be attributed to decentralization from major urbanized regions to smaller towns in adjacent ones (for example, in the Centre region of France and those regions in northern Germany which experienced rapid urban population growth) or to growth in regions that in 1970 had had a relatively small proportion of their populations resident in urban areas (such as Niederbayern, Schwaben and Tubingen). In general, though, by 1980 the pattern of regional variation in the proportion of the population that was living in urban areas was essentially similar to that of 1970 (see Figure 5.5).

5.4 Housing conditions: national and regional patterns

5.4.1 The age of the housing stock

At national level, there are wide variations in the percentage of the housing stock built prior to 1949, ranging from 30.9 per cent in Italy to 62.3 per cent in Belgium (see Figure 5.9). To some extent, these variations reflect differences in the timing of the economic transformation of economies, the switch from agricultural to industrial and service activities, and the associated rural to urban migrations; these changes did not occur over much of Italy until the post-war period whereas in countries such as Belgium and the UK they occurred much earlier, often in the nineteenth century. Furthermore, the relatively low percentages of older housing in FR Germany and the Netherlands reflect the destruction of urban areas and the post-war reconstruction of new housing units: for example, almost 40 per cent of all dwellings in Germany were destroyed or severely damaged between 1939 and 1945 (Wild, 1981: 97).

Regional differences largely echo national ones, there tending to be more inter- than intra-national variation in the age of the housing stock (see Figure 5.8). The highest proportions of older houses are to be found either in rural, predominantly agriculturally-based regions (notably in Denmark and France) or in older industrial ones (concentrated in Belgium, France and the UK). Conversely, comparatively low percentages of older

Figure 5.8

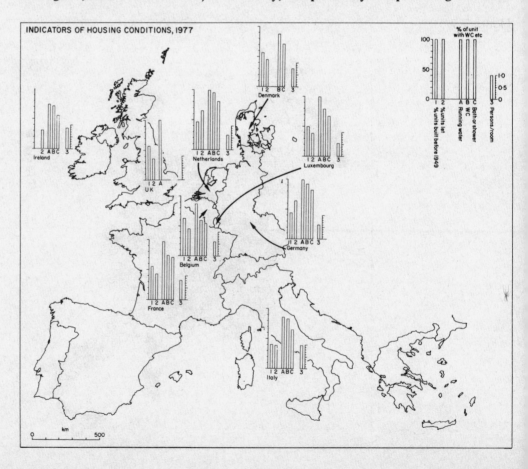

Plate 4   Modern high-rise housing: Brøndby, suburbs of Copenhagen   Plate 5   Modern low-rise housing: Albertslund, suburbs of Copenhagen

4   5

housing units are to be found over much of Italy, reflecting the relatively recent expansion of urban areas there, and in parts of the Netherlands and FR Germany, the latter centred on the Ruhr – in contrast to most other major countries in the Community, new housing units to replace war-time losses were built on central sites that had been bombed rather than in the suburbs (Wild, 1981: 79).

Figure 5.9

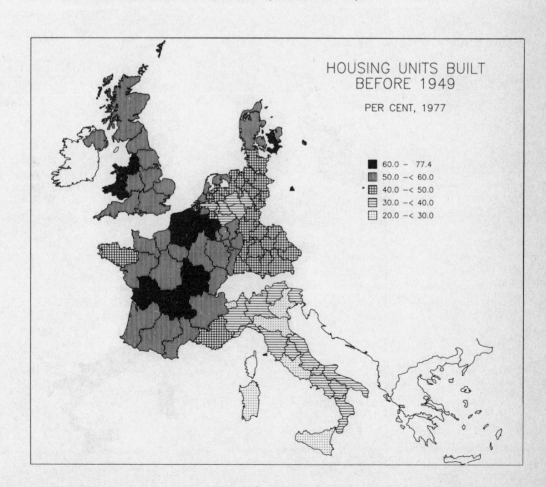

HOUSING UNITS BUILT BEFORE 1949

PER CENT, 1977

■ 60.0 – 77.4
▥ 50.0 –< 60.0
▦ 40.0 –< 50.0
▤ 30.0 –< 40.0
▦ 20.0 –< 30.0

5.4.2 *Number of persons per room*

This represents a reasonably sensitive and useful measure of living conditions, although it takes no account of varying room sizes. There are considerable variations at national level – at one extreme Belgium, FR Germany and Luxembourg have about 0.6 persons per room, while at the other extreme France, Ireland and Italy have about 0.9, a pattern that tends to suggest more favourable living conditions in the core countries of the Community with less favourable ones towards the periphery (Figure 5.8).

This is a pattern that is broadly reproduced at regional level, with greater variation between than within countries (see Figure 5.10). The most overcrowded housing is to be found in the Mezzogiorno and in Lombardy – the latter containing Milan, the destination of many southern migrants (see section 2.4.2) and an area that has considerable planning problems as a result (see Arcangeli, 1982). Densities of persons per room also tend to be high over most of the rest of Italy and France. The lowest room densities are to be found in Denmark, England, central and northern FR Germany and the south-east of Belgium.

5.4.3 *Rented housing*

It is worth noting at the outset that these data do not differentiate between housing units let by private companies or individuals, and those let by the public sector. Even so, they reveal considerable national variations, with rented housing being particularly concentrated in FR Germany and the Netherlands (over 64 per cent). Elsewhere, with the exception of Ireland (31.2 per cent) the remaining countries have about 40 per cent to 50 per cent of their housing stock in this category (see Figure 5.8).

At regional level there is considerably more variation, both between and within

Figure 5.10

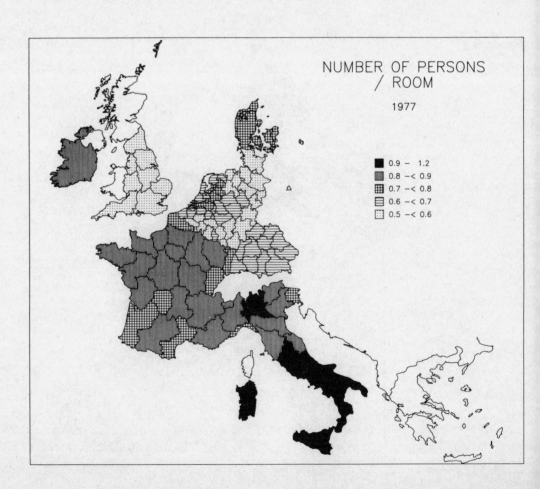

NUMBER OF PERSONS
/ ROOM

1977

■ 0.9 – 1.2
▨ 0.8 –< 0.9
▦ 0.7 –< 0.8
▤ 0.6 –< 0.7
▨ 0.5 –< 0.6

Figure 5.11

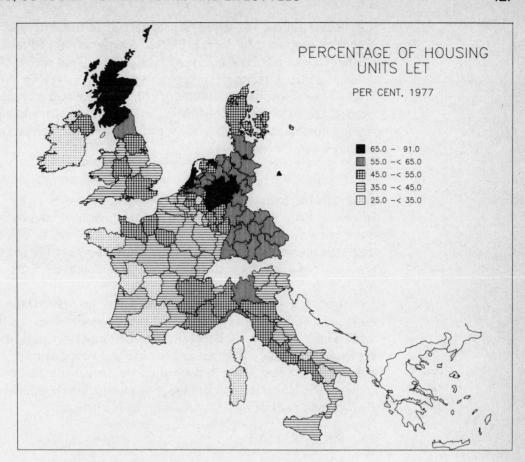

PERCENTAGE OF HOUSING
UNITS LET

PER CENT, 1977

65.0 – 91.0
55.0 –< 65.0
45.0 –< 55.0
35.0 –< 45.0
25.0 –< 35.0

countries (see Figure 5.11). For example, within the UK, Scotland, with its traditional reliance upon public-sector rented housing, emerges in the highest category while in East Anglia, the East Midlands, the North-West, the South-West and Wales, the figure is below 45 per cent. In FR Germany, very high percentages of rented housing are found in Bremen, Hamburg and the regions around the Ruhr, where much of the working-class housing is still rented directly from major industrial companies (Wild, 1981: 102). The regions with the lowest percentages of rented housing tend to be rural, agricultural ones – notably parts of south and west France, Ireland and Italy, often areas where farming is organized in small, family owned units (see section 2.4).

5.4.4   Housing units with running water

While in many countries of the Community the supply of running water to houses is virtually universal, it is salutary to recall that this is not the case in Ireland, Italy and, perhaps more surprisingly, Belgium, where quite high proportions of housing units lack this basic amenity (see Figure 5.8).

At regional level, rather more differentiation between areas is apparent. While this confirms the relatively disadvantaged position of many people living in dwellings in Ireland, central, north-eastern and southern Italy, and northern Belgium, it also reveals that the French regions of Bretagne and Basse Normandie are also characterized by a relatively high proportion of dwellings without running water (see Figure 5.12).

5.4.5   Housing units with WCs

There is considerable variation between member countries in the provision of WCs; at one extreme over 90 per cent of dwelling units in FR Germany have one whereas, at the other extreme, less than 60 per cent of those in Belgium do so (see Figure 5.8).

At regional level, the largest concentrations of dwellings lacking this amenity are found in Belgium and in the French regions of Nord-Pas-de-Calais and Poitou-Charentes, with relatively high percentages of dwellings without WCs over most of the remaining French regions, northern and parts of central Italy, and Ireland (see Figure 5.13). These constitute a mixture of old, industrialized and urbanized regions with relatively many apartments (with shared WCs) and relatively poor rural agricultural regions, combined with the rather specific Belgian and French cultural preferences in sanitary arrangements.

5.4.6   Housing units with baths or showers

In general there is a reasonable correlation at national level between the incidence of dwellings with WCs and those with baths or showers, though with generally fewer dwellings possessing the latter amenities. FR Germany (82 per cent) has the greatest proportion of dwellings with baths or showers, Belgium (55 per cent) the smallest (see Figure 5.8).

At regional level a rather different pattern emerges, related more to the regional distribution of dwellings with running water than to that of dwellings with WCs (see Figure 5.14). Thus the regions with the lowest proportion of dwellings having baths or showers are found in southern Belgium and the Italian Mezzogiorno, while comparatively low proportions are also found in parts of central, north and west France, and Ireland. In contrast, the most favoured dwellings in terms of these amenities are to be found in England and parts of FR Germany and the Netherlands.

 Figure 5.12

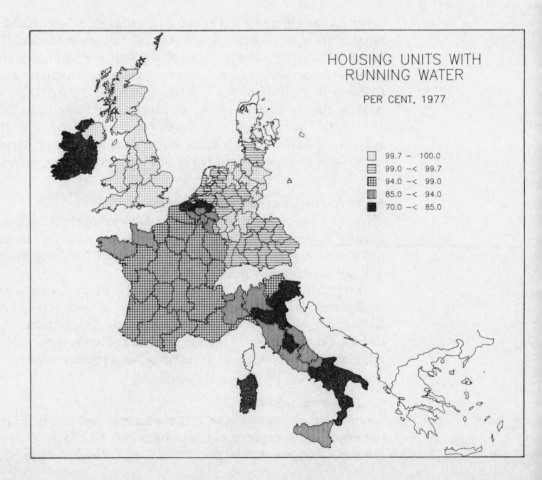

Figure 5.13

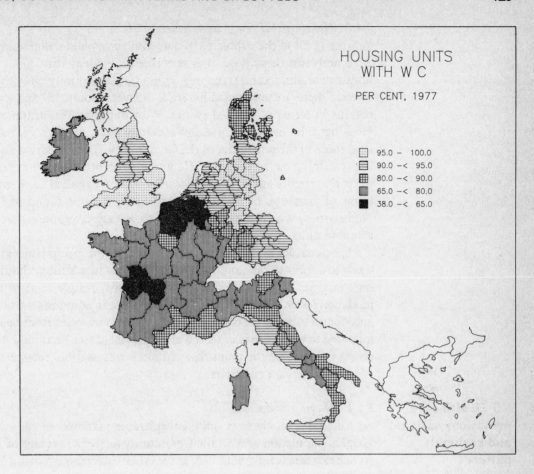

HOUSING UNITS
WITH W C

PER CENT, 1977

95.0 – 100.0
90.0 –< 95.0
80.0 –< 90.0
65.0 –< 80.0
38.0 –< 65.0

Figure 5.14

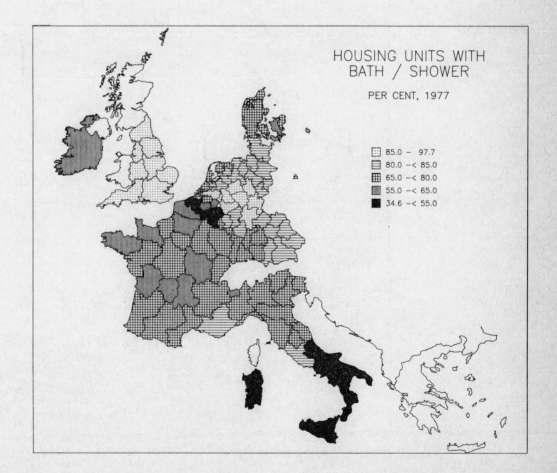

HOUSING UNITS WITH
BATH / SHOWER

PER CENT, 1977

85.0 – 97.7
80.0 –< 85.0
65.0 –< 80.0
55.0 –< 65.0
34.6 –< 55.0

5.4.7 Housing conditions: an overview

Bearing in mind the problems of data availability and comparability and the interpretative problems these pose, it is nevertheless evident that there are wide variations in housing conditions and standards within the Community, at both national and regional levels. There are marked differences between countries and even more so between regions in terms of room densities – an important indicator of housing conditions. Housing units in France, Ireland and Italy have, on average, more persons per room than those in the remainder of the Community. The latter two also compare badly with the remaining countries of the Community on other indicators of housing quality but so, perhaps more surprisingly, does Belgium. In general the better quality housing, in terms of provision of these basic amenities, is to be found in FR Germany and the Netherlands, which both have a comparatively large percentage of newer, post-war dwelling units.

At regional level the pattern of poorer housing being concentrated in poorer areas tends to appear as one might have anticipated. In addition, though, in many relatively high-income, high population density regions, people tend to live in rented accommodation (often apartments) at high densities, in some cases from choice and a preference for an urban style of living but in many more cases from necessity, as people have migrated to urban areas in search of employment (see sections 2.4.2 and 5.3). This only serves to reinforce the point that caution is necessary in interpreting such spatial variations in housing conditions.

5.5 Health care provision: national and regional patterns

5.5.1 Number of doctors

At national level there is quite considerable variation in the number of doctors per 100,000 population around the Community (of Nine) average of 141 (see Figure 5.15). At one extreme is Italy with 246, at the other Luxembourg with 115. Levels of provision

Figure 5.15

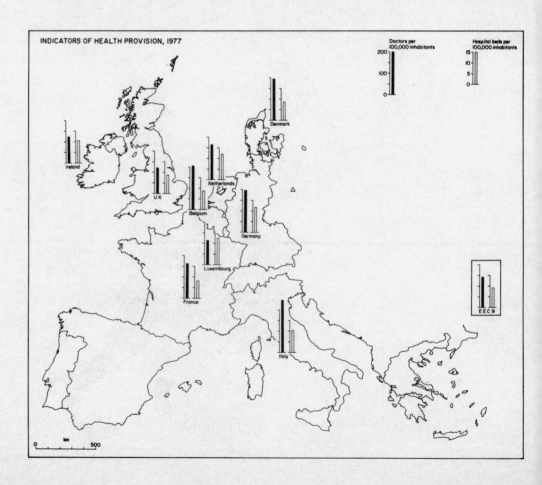

INDICATORS OF HEALTH PROVISION, 1977

are also relatively high in Belgium, FR Germany and the Netherlands while, in addition to Luxembourg, they are below the EEC average in Ireland and the UK. In general, though, there seems no clear relationship between levels of provision and rates of economic growth (see section 4.2). There are, however, differences at national level in methods of financing health care which influence people's access to and consultation of doctors (for example, see Ardagh, 1977: 455–6).

At regional level the pattern of variation is equally complex and variable. The regions of the Nine with the highest levels of provision are Lazio and Liguria in Italy, Hamburg and West Berlin in FR Germany and, in Belgium, Brabant (see Figure 5.16); the reasons for this grouping are by no means clear. Within individual countries there are equally puzzling patterns: for example, within France the regions with the highest levels of provision are Ile de France (including Paris) and Languedoc-Roussillon, while northern France, like much of the UK, has some of the lowest regional rates in the Community. Overall, one is forced reluctantly to the conclusion that the reasons governing the spatial variation in the numbers of doctors per capita are complex and by no means obvious. Nevertheless, while difficult to account for, the point remains that, prima facie, there is evidence of considerable regional variation on what is for many people an important indicator of access to medical care and, more generally, of quality of life.

5.5.2 Provision of hospital beds

It is important to note that these data make no distinction between privately and publicly provided hospital accommodation, the balance of which varies between member countries and which is of considerable importance in shaping people's access to hospital beds. Even so, there are marked variations in the numbers of hospital beds per 100,000

Figure 5.16

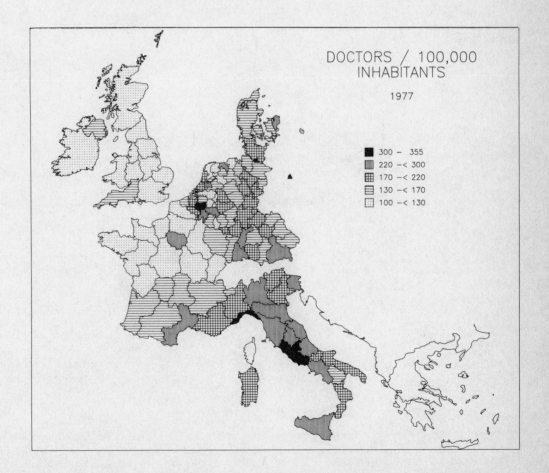

population in the member countries of the Community (see Figure 5.15). The highest levels of provision occur in Luxembourg, the Netherlands and FR Germany (12.4, 12.1 and 11.8 respectively), the lowest in France, Denmark, the UK and Belgium (which, at 8.2, 8.6, 8.7 and 8.9 are all below the Community average of 9.3). This pattern differs somewhat from that of the number of doctors per 100,000 people and while there is some tendency towards greater provision of beds in those countries which have stronger national economies, and vice versa, it is by no means a perfect correlation.

At regional level there is greater variation, both within individual countries and across the Community as a whole. The sharpest inter-regional contrasts within one country are found in Italy: Friuli-Venezia-Giulia, Liguria and Marche have some of the highest levels of provision in the Community, while Basilicata, Calabria, Molise and Sardinia have some of the lowest. The remaining regions with high levels of provision are to be found in FR Germany and the Netherlands while the greatest concentrations of regions with low levels of hospital bed provision are found in central and northern France, with a few others mainly in Belgium, Denmark and England.

5.5.3 Health care provision: an overview

One might reasonably expect that there would be some relationship between levels of health care provision and either the absolute amount or the share of a country's resources and wealth (as measured by GDP) devoted to them. To some extent there is evidence to support this view. The proportion of GDP devoted to health care varies considerably between member countries: over 10 per cent in FR Germany; over 8 per cent in the Netherlands; 7.2 per cent in France; about 6 per cent in Belgium, Denmark, Ireland and

Figure 5.17

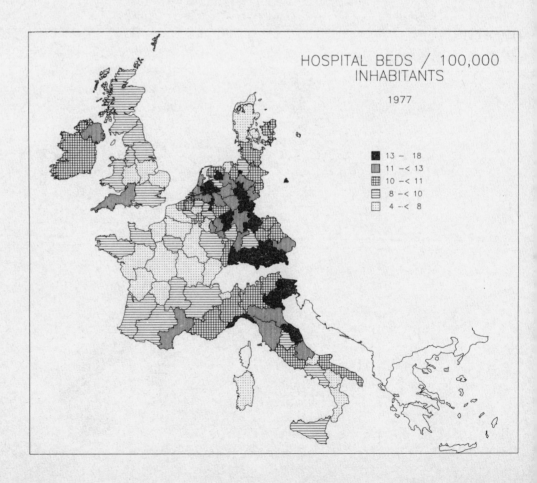

HOSPITAL BEDS / 100,000 INHABITANTS

1977

■ 13 – 18
▨ 11 –< 13
▦ 10 –< 11
▤ 8 –< 10
▥ 4 –< 8

the UK; less than 5 per cent in Italy (*Financial Times*, 14 January 1982). In general, these percentages have grown over the post-war period.

Spatial variations, both national and regional, in the provision of medical care are not necessarily related in a simple manner to the volume of resources devoted to it. It also depends upon how those resources are used. For example, the balance of resources allocated between curative and preventive medicine varies between areas, so that low levels of provision of doctors or hospital beds per capita do not necessarily imply low standards of health care. In addition, there is no systematic, consistent relationship between health care indicators themselves; for example, high levels of doctors per capita are found with high, medium and low levels of provision of hospital beds. Moreover, the need for health care — even bearing in mind the problems associated with the culturally specific definition of need — varies between areas for a whole range of reasons, ranging from climate to economic and occupational structure.

Thus while good health undoubtedly plays a crucial role in ensuring human happiness, it is difficult to assess the degree to which provision of resources for health care contributes to this, for there is little evidence to suggest any consistent relationship between health provision and patterns of illness and mortality (see section 2.3). For example, there is evidence of some regions with a high level of doctors per capita also having high infant mortality rates.

To put the point in a rather different way, there is clearly a need for caution in interpreting spatial variation in such indicators of health provision as reliable surrogates for health conditions or, even more ambitiously, for overall welfare. Fuller understanding of these variations in levels of health care provision will require sophisticated analyses to relate them not simply to differences in economic development but also to such variables as the age and occupational structures of the population, the balance between preventive and curative medicine, and between privately and publicly provided medical care in different areas (for example, see Maynard, 1975; Drury, 1983).

5.6 Educational provision: national patterns

While education is provided both privately via the market and publicly via governments, the latter tends to predominate within the Community. Government expenditure on education has increased considerably in member countries: in France, for example, it grew six-fold in real terms between 1952 and 1968 (Ardagh, 1977: 465). Government expenditure on education currently varies considerably between member countries, both relatively and absolutely (see Figure 5.18): relatively from 7.3 per cent of GDP in Denmark and the Netherlands to 4.7 per cent in Luxembourg, and absolutely (per head of population aged 5–24 years) from 1372 EUAs (European Units of Account) in Denmark to 354 in Ireland. While these differences to some extent reflect government choices as to the allocation of resources, they also reflect the volume of resources available to be distributed; Ireland, for example, devotes a relatively large share of GDP to education yet has the lowest per capita level of expenditure, while FR Germany devotes a smaller share of GDP but attains a level of per capita expenditure almost three times that of Ireland.

As well as reflecting these variations in economic performance, expenditure on education also reflects the age distribution of the population. The numbers of pupils in schools and their varying national distribution between the first two levels of education (primary and secondary: see Figure 5.19) closely reflect the age distribution of the population in different countries (see section 2.5). Full-time attendance at school between the ages of 6 years (except in the cases of the UK and Denmark: 5 and 7 respectively) and 14 (in Belgium and Italy) to 16 (Denmark, France and the UK) is compulsory.

Variation in the proportions of pupils and students in the third level of education, beginning at the age of 18 or 19, while related to varying age distributions, also reflects other factors, as participation rates depend more upon individual choices and the

Figure 5.18

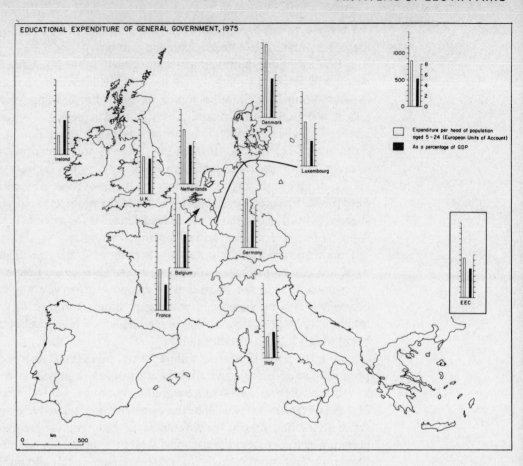

Figure 5.19

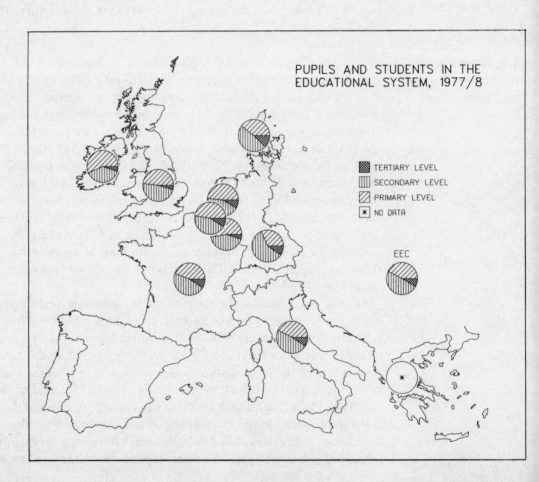

constraints (for example of income and available places) within which they are made. Particularly striking here is the high proportion (12.3 per cent) in Denmark while FR Germany, Italy, Belgium, France and the Netherlands also exceed the Community average share of 8.1 per cent, while Ireland, Luxembourg and the UK, with less than 5 per cent, fall well below it. In so far as access to tertiary education influences the opportunities open to individuals, these data suggest considerable inequalities in opportunity within the Community.

5.7 Other indicators of lifestyles

5.7.1 Private car ownership: national and regional patterns

Car ownership levels represent a reasonable index of aggregate differences in mobility although it is important to remember that a majority of people, even in households with a car, remain dependent on other forms of transport (for example, see Hillman *et al.*, 1973). Moreover, the private car is both inefficient in use of energy and generates a variety of undesirable environmental effects (Independent Commission on Transport, 1974; Organization for Economic Co-operation and Development, 1973).

Private car ownership has risen dramatically in the post-1945 period: for example, in 1956 there were only 3.7 cars per 100 people in FR Germany, less than half the UK figure at that time (Wild, 1981: 98). To a considerable extent, contemporary per capita car ownership levels vary nationally with the level of economic development and disposable incomes: hence the highest rates are to be found in Luxembourg (almost 40 cars per 100 inhabitants), followed by FR Germany (32.6), but with all the remaining Community members except Greece (6.6) and Ireland (18.0) exceeding 25 cars per 100 inhabitants (see Figure 5.20). In fact the last two, together with Portugal and Spain, are quite markedly differentiated from the remaining members of the Community in this

Figure 5.20

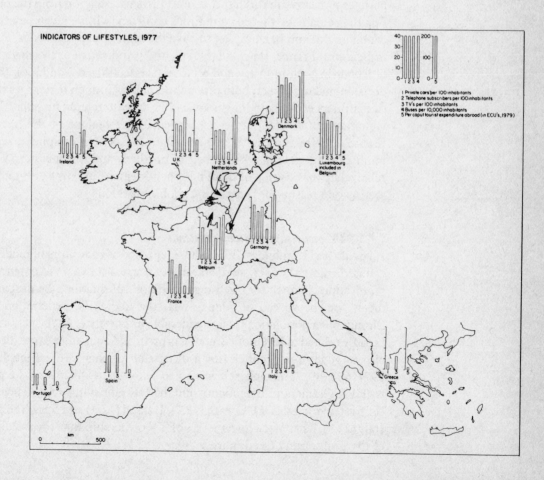

respect. While there is a general relationship between economic development and car ownership levels, other factors are also relevant in influencing the latter, notably government policies towards transport and the price of petrol. Indeed the question of appropriate transport policies in an era of scarce and expensive fuel is a pressing one (see sections 1.4.3 and 1.4.4).

That this is so becomes clear if one examines regional variations in car ownership levels, for these are often highest in essentially poor, peripheral agricultural regions, such as those of western France, where car ownership is a necessity rather than a luxury in order to be able to get access to shops and services in areas deprived of public transport (see Figure 5.21). The greatest regional variations within countries are to be found in France and Italy with comparatively little variation in Belgium, the Netherlands and the UK.

5.7.2 Telephone subscription: national and regional trends

While vital to the conduct of modern business and government, the telephone has also helped radically to transform patterns of personal communication; no longer does the ability to communicate verbally depend upon physical proximity. To this extent, per capita differences in the number of telephones point to important differences in lifestyles, and at national level these differences are considerable, roughly correlated with the strength of national economies. The highest subscription levels are in Denmark (38.4 per 100 inhabitants) and Luxembourg (32.9), the lowest in Ireland (10.9), Italy (18.0) and France (18.8): see Figure 5.20.

By and large, there is much greater variation between countries than between regions within countries; nevertheless, at Community level there is variation at the regional scale (see Figure 5.22). The regions with the highest telephone subscription levels comprise all those in Denmark, North and South Holland, Luxembourg and West Berlin, perhaps indicative in this last case of its physical isolation from the rest of FR Germany. For the remainder there is a definite tendency within given countries for the region containing the political capital to have the highest national levels. Such a pattern holds in Belgium, France, Italy and the UK and is indicative of the changing spatial division of labour in both industry and services (see sections 3.5 and 3.6), the concentration of decision-making power, both private and public, in such regions, as well as the comparative affluence of their inhabitants. The lowest telephone subscription rates in the Community (of Nine) are concentrated in the regions of the Mezzogiorno, western France and Ireland (north and south) − the poorer peripheral regions of the Community − but also in a broad belt of northern and north-eastern France. Indeed, the relatively poor position of these peripheral regions in terms of communications is often seen as one reason for them being problem regions.

5.7.3 TV ownership: national patterns

Like cars and telephones, TVs can be regarded as indicators of modernization that have diffused unevenly over the Community's space. Given the potency of TV as a communication channel, for the transmission of information, the propagation of advertisements, or the spread of propaganda, the degree of penetration of TV ownership throughout a population is of considerable importance. At the national scale at least, it is broadly related to levels of economic growth and consumer expenditure, and to a degree also to government policy (for a discussion of this in the French case, see Ardagh, 1977: 630–49). The highest levels are to be found in Denmark (34.8 per 100 inhabitants) with FR Germany, Luxembourg and the UK all having over 30 per 100 inhabitants. In contrast, Portugal (7.6), Greece (12.7), Ireland (17.4) and Spain (18.5), and, to a degree, Italy (22.5), have much lower levels of TV ownership than the remaining member states of the Community (see Figure 5.20).

Figure 5.21

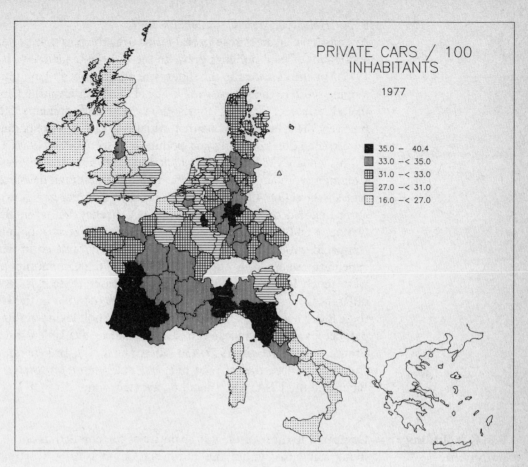

Figure 5.22

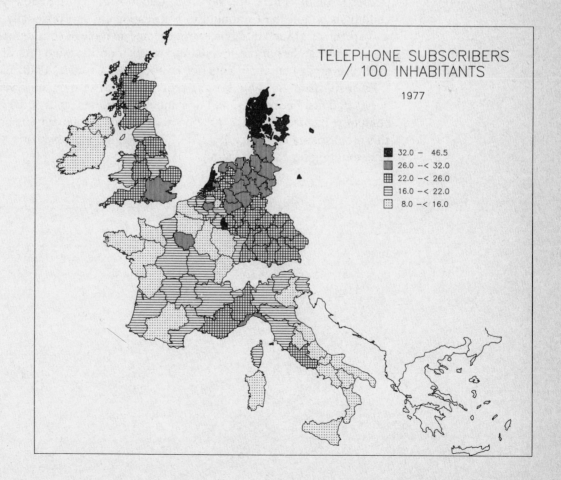

5.7.4 Holidaying abroad: national patterns

As consumer incomes rose in real terms over the post-war period and as the incidence and length of paid holidays grew, so too did the tendency to holiday abroad (Young, 1973). In the case of the inhabitants of the European Community, this often meant moving south to the sun, sea and sands of the Mediterranean (Ilberry, 1981: 119–24) – though the very scale of tourist flows and developments often tended to destroy precisely those environments that initially attracted tourists (for example, unplanned, unrestricted hotel building and pollution – see Gonen, 1981; UN, 1981).

This tendency to holiday abroad developed to differing degrees in the countries of the Community, in large part influenced by the differential development of national economies (see section 4.2 and Figure 5.20). By 1979, per capita expenditures on holidays abroad exceeded 200 ECUs (European Currency Units) in Belgium, Denmark, FR Germany and the Netherlands. Given the much greater population of FR Germany compared with these other three countries, it dominated in terms of absolute tourist expenditures abroad. In the other countries of the Community per capita expenditures were much lower, and although in some cases these can be explained in terms of differences in average consumer real incomes (notably in the UK), in other countries these lower levels reflect a cultural tradition of holidaying within one's own country, in part because Mediterranean sun, sea and sand are available within them (for example, in France – see Ardagh, 1977: 430–50 – and Italy). In general, the inhabitants of the Community nevertheless tend to spend much more on foreign tourism than those of Japan and the USA, who spend, on average, about 30 ECUs per head on this.

5.8 Concluding comments

Compared to those of the vast majority of the population of the Third World, average living standards within the European Community are extremely high (see Brandt (Report), 1980). There are, however, undoubtedly considerable variations in living conditions within the Community, both nationally and regionally and between rural and urban areas. Such differences can become an issue of considerable political importance as those at the bottom seek to improve their position and protest against the quality of their everyday environments (for example, see Castells, 1978; Pickvance, 1976).

Even so, there are quite serious problems of describing such variations, especially across national boundaries, and of combining different individual indicators to give a composite picture of spatial variation in living conditions (for one proposed solution to this problem, see Ilberry, 1981: 131–46). Much more problematic, though, is the issue of accounting for these variations.

6 THE COMMUNITY IN THE YEAR 2000? ISSUES FOR THE REST OF THE TWENTIETH CENTURY

6.1 Introduction

Several years ago Galtung (1973) posed the question of whether the European Community was an emerging superpower. From the evidence presented in the preceding chapters, there are reasonable grounds for arguing that it has indeed attained such a status, particularly as regards the size and sophistication of its economy. Yet equally many problems remain in the Community, some of which we have touched on in these chapters. By way of conclusion, we seek here to identify some half dozen related issues which will continue to pose major challenges to the Community in the years to come: the future of the Community itself is inextricably bound up with whether and in what ways it responds to these.

6.2 Continuing deindustrialization?

The accelerating relocation of manufacturing industry from the Community not only to Mediterranean Europe and North Africa and to other parts of the Third World but also to the USA increasingly emerged as a major problem in the 1970s. This was linked with the growing significance of multinational companies in the world economy, responding to declining profitability in what was (for them) a rational manner by switching production to more profitable locations outside the Community; attempts by national governments in peripheral and semi-peripheral countries to encourage industrialization as part of their national development strategies also played a part in bringing about such locational switches. To date, these changes have mainly been concentrated in a few sectors such as textiles and clothing, electronic engineering and bulk iron and steel production, but in the future will probably come to encompass a much broader spectrum of industries, including some that have become central to the European economy – notably basic chemicals (see for example Laurençin *et al.*, 1977; Merrett, 1981; Hudson, 1983b). Given that it would be neither feasible nor desirable for Community producers to attempt to compete with the lower production costs (especially as regards labour) of such areas, notwithstanding the probable further extension of the Community southwards into the Mediterranean region, this implies the need for co-ordinated industrial policies at national and Community level to bring about changes in the structure of the Community's manufacturing base towards high value added, more technically sophisticated products (what has been referred to as the 'German model': see Schlupp, 1980). Such policies are currently notable by their absence (for example, see Tsoukalis, 1981: 168–72).

6.3 Permanent mass unemployment?

By the mid-1980s, registered unemployment in the Community may well be in excess of 15 million people. Moreover, even if a 'successful' industrial policy were evolved and implemented by then to restructure the Community's manufacturing base so as to enable it to remain profitable and internationally competitive, there is no guarantee that this would reduce the unemployment total. Indeed, as more automated, efficient production technologies are substituted for older, more labour-intensive ones, it might further increase it (see Godet and Ruyssen, 1981). Similarly the increases in service sector employment of the last two decades will probably be checked and then reversed by a combination of public expenditure restraints in the short run and the effects of the micro-chip in the medium run. Put another way then, whatever happens to the economy, it seems only reasonable to assume continuing mass unemployment in the absence of significant new policy initiatives designed specifically to deal with it. In particular, new policy initiatives are urgently needed to cope with the problems of the greatly increased numbers of long-term unemployed and those of youth unemployment, that is, of a large proportion of a generation leaving school and heading straight for the dole queues.

Are such policies likely? At present, the available evidence does not point to this. Cosmetic job creation schemes to disguise the real impact of youth unemployment and talk of job-sharing, an increase in part-time working and so on do not get to grips with the essential problems of unemployment. But if this is so, how can the economic, social and political consequences of persistent high unemployment be contained? Will unemployment in itself pose a major threat to the continuation, to say nothing of the further development, of the Community, particularly given its uneven incidence between ethnic groups and social classes, between countries and regions?

6.4 An ageing population: what are the implications?

In addition to coping with the costs of mass unemployment, the Community is faced with a major challenge in the rising numbers of people of retirement age within its population and, within this group, of a growing number of elderly people. These pressures will be particularly felt in FR Germany and, to a lesser extent, in Denmark and the UK. Will the resources be made available to offer a decent standard of living to these people in an era of slow − or even nil − growth and recession? Or will retirement pensions be cut in real terms to protect other national government public spending programmes? What will be the implications in terms of changing patterns of housing needs and, for those who require it, residential care? What role can the Community itself take in devising policies to cope with this growing number of retired people?

6.5 The energy problem: can it be solved?

The era of cheap energy is past; for the foreseeable future, the trend in real energy costs will be upwards while the prospect of physical shortages of oil cannot be ruled out over the medium term. How can the Community adjust to this situation, both in its total energy demands and in the proportions of these met from different primary sources? Is the present policy response − of reducing dependence on imported oil and reducing further Community coal production while increasing output of natural gas and nuclear energy − the most appropriate one? Energy remains perhaps *the* central issue in so far as successfully tackling it has manifold implications for the economy and for people's styles and standards of living within the Community. For example, can the spatial arrangement of houses, jobs, shops and services, transport patterns and housing designs be changed so as to be more in tune with a high-cost energy environment? Put another way, over what time period is such a transformation feasible, bearing in mind the massive fixed capital investment in the built environment and spatial structure? Can lifestyles be reoriented towards the minimization of the use of fossil fuel resources rather than maximizing their use, as often appears the case today? At the same time, will these changes occur in such a way as to increase or to reduce differences in the quality of different people's lives? What contribution can Community policies make in bringing about desired changes?

6.6 The crisis of the Community budget and the CAP

If the Community is to design and implement successful new energy, industrial, social and regional policies, then, in the absence of a sharp increase in the Community's total budget, resources will have to be diverted to these areas. At present, it is difficult to see how this could be achieved as there are problems in funding the budget to sustain the Community's present level of expenditure, while some 65 to 70 per cent of that total is directed to the CAP. The second Mediterranean enlargement of the Community will itself make greater demands upon the CAP in the short term although adding further pressure for reform in the medium term. Therefore, reform of the CAP is a pre-condition for the Community being able to develop effective new policies to deal with pressing problems in other areas. Recognizing this does not necessarily make such reform probable, however; the need for fundamental change in the CAP has been recognized for several years (see, for example, Commission of the European Communities, 1975 and 1980) but without as yet being translated into meaningful action. It remains to be seen whether the switch from an appointed Assembly to an elected European Parliament will change this. Nevertheless, the importance of a sensible reform of the CAP to the future evolution of the Community cannot be over-stressed.

6.7 The Mediterranean enlargement

As has been suggested above, the enlargement to include Portugal and Spain as well as Greece will pose a fresh set of problems for the Community and its member states, both old and new. Some of these will be economic, notably those in agriculture and some sectors of industry; associated with these will be pressures to transfer Community funds to these less developed economies, with the implications that transfers to problematic national and regional economies within the current Community will have to be reduced as a result. Consequently political tensions within the Community may well be heightened. Furthermore, such political problems may extend beyond the Community's immediate territory: for example, one effect of enlargement will be self-sufficiency in many Mediterranean agricultural products and a consequent reduction in the need for imports from non-Community areas in the Mediterranean. But what will be the impact on relations between the Community and the Arab League if it is proposed to cut − say − Tunisia's agricultural exports to the Community?

6.8 Synthesis: the challenge of national and regional uneven development?

In a sense, this serves to summarize many of the most crucial of the preceding points. For as the Community enlarges from nine to ten and then twelve members, the scale of social and economic differences between countries and regions within it will increase. Moreover, in the probable continuing recession of the 1980s, the differential ability of national and regional economies to respond to changing economic circumstances will further enhance these disparities and regions may cease to be simply peripheral but rather will become effectively excluded from the economic system; in Kielstra's (1984) terminology, they will become 'relict spaces'. These increasing differentials may well lead to challenges to the political authority of national governments and the Community itself. One response may be increased separatist pressures from regionalist and nationalist movements; there are already several well-established in the present Community and the addition of Spain in particular would add further to them. The recent referendum in Greenland which produced overwhelming support for withdrawal from the Community may be a 'one-off' case because of Greenland's unique position, but equally it could be the beginning of a more general trend.

What then does the future hold? The disintegration of the Community as member states withdraw from it? A further devolution and decentralization to regions (see Hudson and Lewis, 1982a), creating a new balance between regional, national and Community political forces? For the Community, the challenge is a clear one: to devise new policies to combat uneven development or to risk its own possible disintegration as the 'logic of unity' (Parker, 1975) becomes increasingly debatable. To do so will involve not simply stronger regional policies *per se* but also new policies in agriculture, energy, industry, etc., each of which will need to recognize explicitly the regional and, more generally, spatial dimension. Without such a radical reorientation, the Community will become even more remote from the lives of most people resident within it and be seen by them as increasingly irrelevant, with all that this implies for its own further development.

APPENDIX: THE TECHNICAL BASIS
OF THE ATLAS

Introduction

Considerable effort has been devoted by the Regional Statistics Section of the Statistical Office of the European Community (SOEC) to the harmonization of demographic, socio-economic and related statistics of the EEC: without it, this Atlas would not have been possible in its present form. The bulk of their latest available figures (Eurostat, 1980c) pertain to 1978; hence the statistics (even if, in some cases, being based on estimates) are extremely up to date by the standards of many others. In recent years, SOEC have also devoted effort to the dissemination of certain of their statistics (Le Cour, 1980; Mesnage, 1980). Indeed, some statistics – such as CRONOS, the economic time series – are available on-line by dialling EURONET. Until very recently, however, the only mapping carried out by SOEC was of a crude and manually produced nature.

Such statistics are of fundamental importance to research and education on a variety of aspects of the European Community – and even for comparison of countries therein with others outside. What is particularly valuable is that these statistics are for sub-national geographical units. The current level of geographical disaggregation used is the so-called EEC level II regions, totalling 112 areas for the Community prior to the membership of Greece in 1981. The authoritative definition of these units is given on the EEC map at 1:3 million scale produced for the EEC Commission by Professor Kormoss of the College of Europe in Bruges (though some modifications of boundaries have occurred since the compilation of the map).

The objectives of this Atlas are simple: to describe, in maps and words, recent trends and current problems in important aspects of economic, social and political life in the Community. Wherever possible, we portray data not only at national level but also at the level II regional scale; while the nation state remains the principal focus of political authority in the Community and the only meaningful level for considering some issues, the degree of variability between regions is often as great as those between countries. It is worth noting that data for Greenland – until recently the Community's largest areal unit – is absent from the maps in the atlas, a reflection of its marginal status in terms of population and levels of socio-economic development. Data for Greece are included in the maps wherever available. All the regional and many of the national maps were produced by computer mapping procedures, which this Appendix describes.

Mapping the data by computer

Map symbolism

Two forms of map symbolism were selected *ab initio*. The first (and most frequently used) was choropleth mapping, in which tones of different intensity indicate the value of the attribute being mapped. Clearly such symbolism is not appropriate for mapping absolute numbers (or even, according to Williams (1976) and others, for mapping many ratios whose denominators are not the area of ground).

The second form of symbolism used was proportional point symbols, located centrally within each area wherever possible. Considerable benefit was gained from the automated hidden area suppression for overlapping symbols carried out by software written by Rase (1980).

These symbolisms were chosen because they 'map' – in the computer sense – directly to the areas for which the data are summarized. It is known that large but real discontinuities and 'cliffs' exist in the data and thus no use was made of any smoothing function in manipulating the data to produce interpolated surfaces or of contour type mapping.

Encoding zone boundaries

The boundaries of all the 112 EEC level II regions − the most detailed areas for which harmonized statistics are currently made available − are required for both choropleth mapping and to compute a suitable central point for the point symbol for each region. Those boundaries were digitized by now traditional methods, using a Ferranti-Cetic manually guided digitizer and working from the Kormoss map of the EEC. Boundaries were encoded as bounding segments and labelled with a hierarchical code. Hence in GIMMS 3 (Waugh, 1978; Lane, 1981), a typical boundary segment defining the boundary between two British regions − Scotland and northern England − would consist of:

/CUSCOTLA/CUNORTHE/BU48/BU39/AU1/AU1	*label*
$X_1 Y_1$	*co-ordinate*
$X_2 Y_2$	*co-ordinate*
$\cdot$ $\cdot$	*co-ordinate*
$\cdot$ $\cdot$	
$\cdot$ $\cdot$	
$X_n Y_n$	

The strings CUSCOTLA and CUNORTHE define the boundary as separating Scotland and northern England, while BU48 and BU39 indicate that it also separates the 48th and 39th EEC level I region while AU1 and AU1 (optional) indicate that it is internal to a national state. The second letter of each string is a country identifier (U = United Kingdom) while the first letter (C = level II, B = level I and A = nation state or level O) serves as the level in the EEC hierarchy at which a unit exists.

Use of the GIMMS mapping package ensured that, during the creation of polygons from these bounding segments, considerable flexibility in specifying areas of interest was possible, e.g. if exclusion of all regions whose labels did not begin with B was specified, a map of only the level I boundaries would be created. Selection based on the second letter of the string provided a means of mapping only data for a nominated country.

Because certain data were not available for all level II regions (see below), *ad hoc* aggregations of polygons were sometimes created so as to permit the mapping of these areas at level I or for whatever larger areal unit the data were available. This ability of GIMMS to regenerate a variety of polygon files from the 'nuts and bolts' of the boundary segments was an essential requirement for the mapping project.

Encoding the attribute values

Around 300 variables − many of them breakdowns of major variables (such as 'total population' broken down into different age groups) − were encoded by manual means mainly from the Eurostat volumes published in 1978 and 1980, i.e. pertaining mostly to the periods 1977 and 1978/9, but with some variables encoded for earlier moments (e.g. 'birth rates in 1961'). In addition, some variables indicating change over time were also included. Broadly speaking, the variables on file include population characteristics, employment and unemployment data, vital statistics (i.e. on births and deaths), migration data, measures of economic performance (such as GDP) and resources (such as production of energy), plus description of social conditions, consumption patterns and lifestyles.

The manual encoding of these attributes of the level II regions was tedious but unavoidable: though Eurostat statistics are computer set, SOEC was then (and still is) unable to supply a magnetic tape of the data in an industry-standard format: it is hoped that this will be rectified in the near future, facilitating routine mapping. All data were initially coded onto punch-card forms; subsequently, it was found easier to enlarge photographically pages of the Eurostat volumes and use these as punching documents, given the high quality of staff in the University of Durham Data Preparation Unit. Each record was identified by the Eurostat level II region name and all records were written to disk file. The data were checked by a variety of means, including visual inspection of listings and statistical summaries.

Where some data values were not available for a particular level II region, negative values were inserted as 'missing data flags' (though the value of these had to be chosen to be extreme since some change variables could have negative values). In some cases, the missing data were available for the larger level I region or for some *ad hoc* grouping of the level II regions: in these cases, the data were kept on a separate file and 'patched in' when necessary — the procedure necessitating considerable operational skill and good record keeping.

Data manipulation

Various simple manipulations of the attribute data, such as combining variables, were routinely carried out as necessary. Indeed, all data were validated and statistically described prior to generation of the maps, using the interactive statistical package MIDAS. Hence the conventional flow line was as follows:

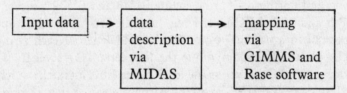

All transfers between programs were carried out via temporary files.

In certain cases, however, the variable to be mapped was not a single quantitative attribute but rather a classified value. Lane (1981) has described how she inserted the cluster analysis program CLUSTAN between MIDAS and GIMMS and used CLUSTAN classification arrays as an 'area grouping' procedure, the results of which are qualitative but were still mapped by GIMMS and were used by her as comparisons with EEC standard regionalizations.

Generating the maps

With the exception of many national maps which were manually produced because they required symbol systems that could not be generated by available computer mapping packages only two computer mapping packages were utilized throughout this work. These were GIMMS 3 (and prototype versions of GIMMS 4) written by Waugh (1978; 1981) and a set of sub-routines written by Rase for point symbol mapping with hidden area suppression. One author (HM) implemented both GIMMS and the Rase package on an IBM 370/16 running under the Michigan Terminal System at the University of Durham, making a number of important modifications to speed up the latter software.

GIMMS is a large Fortran package which provides almost infinite flexibility to the cartographer through over 800 parameters — use of only a few of which is mandatory! It provides boundary data validation and polygon construction facilities, a manipulation of attributes capability and point symbol (dot mapping and a very wide range of other point symbols) and choropleth mapping capabilities. The latest version (Waugh, 1982) includes not only over twenty different alphabets but the ability to select features for plotting on presence within user-defined polygons, or distance from features (such as a river), and the capacity to be a general-purpose graphics system for making histograms, graphs and other graphics, all with high quality text and area shading. Even GIMMS 4, however, does not provide automated clipping of point symbols where they overlap.

In contrast, the software library of sub-routines created by Rase (1980) can only be used once a main program to handle input/output, etc., has been created by a skilled user. This software not only provides a range of basic symbols but permits the user to digitize 'macros', e.g. human shapes, outlines of trees, and to use these as symbols whose area is proportional to the value being mapped. The clipping procedure preserves the smaller of any pair of overlapping symbols at the expense of the larger; vectors such as area boundaries which are intersected by symbols are also clipped.

Ultimately, over 200 maps were produced by these means, all final maps being plotted on a multi-pen Calcomp plotter in monochrome with liquid ink on paper size of about 60cm across. They were then reduced photographically to an 18cm width format: this extreme reduction was larger than was originally intended but was necessitated by the increasing number of maps demanded by the author of the accompanying text (RH)! Considerable experiment was necessary to find shading densities which could still be printed satisfactorily after reduction: a maximum of five or six classes was used, using dot, line and crossed-line shading. Moreover, it was found that previewing maps on a graphics CRT such as a Tektronix 4014 was only a crude guide to the acceptability of the final map because of the coarseness of the lines on such CRTs when compared with those from large format pen plotters.

Because of the gross disparity in size of the level II regions, ranging in extent from the whole of Ireland to Berlin, low-density shading occasionally provided inadequate representation of the smaller areas. In such circumstances, critical cases were amended as necessary by hand. Even mapping national units did not obviate this problem, since Luxembourg is very small relative to the other areas. Similarly, the concentration of point symbols in and around the triangular area bounded by London, Paris and Amsterdam was sometimes impossible to interpret, even though hidden areas had been suppressed: to minimize such problems, the originally computed centroids of troublesome areas were edited further away from each other.

REFERENCES

Aldcroft, D. H. (1978) *The European Economy, 1914–70*, London, Croom Helm.

Alting von Gesau, F. A. M. (ed.) (1975) *Energy in the European Communities*, Leiden, Sijthoff.

Anderson, J., Duncan, S. and Hudson, R. (eds) (1983) *Redundant Spaces in Cities and Regions?*, London, Academic Press.

Arcangeli, F. (1982) 'Regional and sub-regional planning in Italy: An evaluation of current practice and some proposals for the future', pp. 57–84 in Hudson, R. and Lewis, J. (eds) *Regional Planning in Europe*, London, Pion.

Arcangeli, F., Borzaga, C. and Goglio, G. (1981) 'Patterns of peripheral development in Italian regions', *Dunelm Translations No. 2*, available from the authors, Department of Geography, Durham University.

Ardagh, J. (1977) *The New France: A Society in Transition*, London, Penguin.

Ardagh, J. (1982) *France in the 1980s*, Harmondsworth, Penguin.

Armstrong, H. W. (1978) 'Community regional policy: a survey and critique', *Regional Studies*, 12, 511–18.

Bagnasco, A. (1977) *Le Tre Italie*, Bologna, Il Mulino.

Bailey, R. (1976) 'Heading for an EEC common energy policy', *Energy Policy*, 4, 308–21.

Baker, A. R. (1961) 'Le remembrement rural en France', *Geography*, 46, 60–2.

Balassa, B. (1981) *The Newly Industrialising Countries in the World Economy*, London, Pergamon.

de Bauw, R. (1979) 'Energy', in Commission of the European Communities, *The Community Today*, pp. 80–92, Luxembourg, CEC.

Begg, I., Cripps, F. and Ward, T. (1981) 'The European Community: problems and prospects', *Cambridge Economic Policy Review*, 7, 2, Aldershot, Gower.

Bergmann, D. (1977) 'Agricultural policies in the EEC and their external implications', *World Development*, 5, 5–7, 407–15.

Bethemont, J. and Pelletier, J. (1983) *Italy: a Geographical Introduction*, Harlow, Longman.

Bird, E. (1980) *Information Technology in the Office: the Impact on Women's Jobs*, Manchester, Equal Opportunities Commission.

Blacksell, M. (1977) *Post-war Europe: a political geography*, Folkstone, Dawson.

Bleitrach, D. and Chenu, A. (1982) 'Regional planning: regulation or deepening of social contradictions? An example: Fos-sur-Mer and the Marseilles Metropolitan Region', pp. 148–78 in Hudson, R. and Lewis, J. (eds) *Regional Planning in Europe*, London, Pion.

Böhning, W. R. (1979) 'International migration in Europe: reflections on the past five years', *International Labour Review*, 118, 401–14.

Boissevain, J. (1980) 'Tourism and the European periphery: the Mediterranean case', in Seers, D., Schaffer, B. and Kiljunen, M. L. (eds) *Underdeveloped Europe*, pp. 124–35, Brighton, Harvester.

Borzaga, C. and Goglio, S. (1981) 'Economic development and regional imbalance: the case of Italy, 1945–76', *Dunelm Translations No. 6*, available from the authors, Department of Geography, Durham University.

Bowler, I. R. (1975) 'The CAP and the space-economy of agriculture in the EEC', in Lee, R. and Ogden, P. (eds) *Economy and Society in the EEC*, pp. 235–55, Farnborough, Saxon House.

Brandt, W. (Chairman) (1980) *North-South: A Programme for Survival – Report of the Independent Commission on International Development Issues*, London, Pan.

Brouwers, J.-C. (1979) 'The Community budget', in Commission of the European Communities, *The Community Today*, pp. 32–41, Luxembourg, CEC.

Burt, M. E. (1972) 'Roads and the environment', *Transport and Road Research Laboratory Report No. 441*, Crowthorne, England, TRRL.

Carney, J. and Hudson, R. (1979) 'The European regional development fund', *Town and Country Planning*, 48, 4, 125–6.

Carney, J., Hudson, R. and Lewis, J. (eds) (1980) *Regions in Crisis: New Perspectives in European Regional Theory*, London, Croom Helm.

Castells, M. (1978) *City, Class and Power*, London, Macmillan.

Castles, S. and Kosack, G. (1973) *Immigrant Workers and Class Structure in Western Europe*, London, OUP.

Clavel, P. (1982) *Opposition Planning in Wales and Appalachia*, Philadelphia, Temple University Press.

Commission of the European Communities (1975) *Stocktaking of the Common Agricultural Policy*, COM (75) 100, Brussels.

Commission of the European Communities (1978) *The Economic Implications of Demographic Change in the European Community, 1975–95*, Brussels, Directorate General for Economic and Financial Affairs.

Commission of the European Communities (1979a) *A Transport Network for Europe: Outline of a Policy*, Bulletin of the European Communities Supplement 8/79, Brussels.

Commission of the European Communities (1979b) 'Changes in the industrial structure of the European economies since the oil crisis, 1973–8', special issue of *European Economy*, Brussels, Directorate General for Economic and Financial Affairs.

Commission of the European Communities (1980) *Reflection on the Common Agricultural Policy*, Brussels, COM (80) 800.

Commission of the European Communities (1981a) *The Regions of Europe*, COM (80) 816 Final, Brussels, Directorate General for Regional Policy.

Commission of the European Communities (1981b) *European Economy*, July 1981, Brussels, Directorate General for Economic and Financial Affairs.

Commission of the European Communities Spokesman's Group (1978) *The European Community and the Arab World*, Brussels.

Commission of the European Communities Spokesman's Group (1980) *The European Community and the EFTA Countries*, June, Brussels.

Cornelissen, A. (1976) *Women of the Shadows*, London, Macmillan.

Counter Information Services, n.d., *The New Technology*, Anti-Report No. 23, London, CIS.

Davin, L. E. (1969) 'Structural crisis of a regional economy – a case study: the Walloon area', in Robinson, E. A. G. (ed.) *Backward Areas in Advanced Countries*, pp. 113–43, London, St Martin.

Denison, E. F. (1967) *Why Growth Rates Differ: Post-war Experience in Nine Western Countries*, Washington, Brookings Institute.

Despicht, N. S. (1969) *The Common Transport Policy of the European Communities*, London, Political and Economic Planning.

Drewer, S. (1974) 'The economic impact of immigrant workers in western Europe', *European Studies*, 18, 1–4.

Drury, P. (1983) 'Some spatial aspects of health service developments', *Progress in Human Geography*, 7, 1, 60–77.

Economist (1979) *Political Europe*, London, Economist Newspaper Ltd.

Eurostat (1976) *Regional Statistics, 1975*, Luxembourg, Statistical Office of the European Communities.

Eurostat (1978) *Regional Statistics, 1977*, Luxembourg, Statistical Office of the European Communities.

Eurostat (1980a) *Social Indicators for the European Community, 1960–78*, Brussels, Statistical Office of the European Communities.

Eurostat (1980b) *Basic Statistics of the Community*, Luxembourg, Statistical Office of the European Communities.

Eurostat (1980c) *Regional Statistics, 1978*, Brussels, EEC Commission.

Eurostat (1981) *Review, 1970–1979*, Luxembourg, Statistical Office of the European Communities.

Fielding, A. J. (1975) 'International migration in western Europe', in Kosinski, L. and Prothero, M. (eds), *People on the Move*, London, Methuen.

Financial Times, 7 July 1979.

Financial Times, 10 January 1980.

Financial Times, 14 January 1982.

Firn, J. (1975) 'External control and regional development: the case of Scotland', *Environment and Planning A*, 7, 393–414.

Frank, A. G. (1980) *Crisis in the World Economy*, London, Heinemann.

Friis, P. (1980) 'Regional problems in Denmark: myth or reality?', *Dunelm Translations No. 4*, available from the authors, Department of Geography, Durham University.

Frobel, F., Heinrichs, J. and Kreye, O. (1980) *The New International Division of Labour*, London, CUP.

Galtung, J. (1973) *The European Community: Superpower in the Making?* London, Allen & Unwin.

Godet, M. and Ruyssen, O. (1981) *The Old World and the New Technologies – Challenges to Europe in a Hostile World*, Luxembourg, Commission of the European Communities.

Gonen, A. (1981) 'Tourism and coastal settlement processes in the Mediterranean region', *Ekistics*, 290, 378–81.

Hafele, W. and Wolfgang, S. (1978) 'Energy options and strategies for western Europe', *Science*, 200, 164–7.

Hamilton, F. E. I. (1976) 'Multinational enterprise and the EEC', *Tijdschrift voor Economische en Sociale Geografie*, 67, 5, 258–78.

Hewitt, A., and Stevens, C. (1981) 'The Second Lomé Convention', in Stevens, C. (ed.) *EEC and the Third World: a Survey*, pp. 30–59, London, Hodder & Stoughton.

Hillman, M., Henderson, I. and Whalley, A. (1973) 'Personal mobility and transport policy', *Political and Economic Planning Broadsheet 542*, London.

Hines, C. and Searle, G. (1979) *Automatic Unemployment*, London, Earth Resources Ltd.

Hood, N. and Young, S. (1976) 'The geographical expansion of US firms in western Europe: some survey evidence', *Journal of Common Market Studies*, 14, 223–39.

Hudson, R. (1982a) 'Capital accumulation and regional problems: a study of north-east England', forthcoming in Hamilton, F. E. I. and Linge, G. (eds) *Spatial Analysis, Industry and the Industrial Environment*, vol. 3, pp. 75–101, London, Wiley.

Hudson, R. (1982b) 'Unemployment in the north', *Town and Country Planning*, 51, 1, 8–10.

Hudson, R. (1983a) 'Regional labour reserves and forms of capitalist industrialisation in the European Community in the post-war period', *Area*, 15, 3 (forthcoming).

Hudson, R. (1983b) 'Capital accumulation and chemicals production in western Europe in the post-war period', *Environment and Planning*, A, 15, 105–22.

Hudson, R. and Lewis, J. (eds) (1982a) *Regional Planning in Europe*, London, Pion.

Hudson, R. and Lewis, J. (1982b) 'The regional problem in the enlarged European Community', paper read to the Annual Conference of the Institute of British Geographers, Southampton, 8 January 1982.

Hudson, R. and Lewis, J. (eds) (1984a, forthcoming) *Accumulation, Class and the State in Southern Europe*, London, Methuen.

Hudson, R. and Lewis, J. (1984b) 'Capital movements and the industrialisation of southern Europe', in Williams, A. (ed.) *Southern Europe Transformed?*, London, Harper and Row.

Hudson, R. and Sadler, D. (1983a) 'Consett: anatomy of a disaster', *Northern Economic Review*, 6, 2–18.

Hudson, R. and Sadler, D. (1983b) 'Region, class and the politics of steel closures in the European Community', *Society and Space*, 1, 405–28.

Hume, I. M. (1973) 'Migrant workers in Europe', *Finance and Development*, 10, 2–6.

Ilberry, B. W. (1981) *Western Europe*, London, OUP.

Independent Commission on Transport (1974) *Changing Directions*, London, Coronet Books.

Jones, A. (1984) 'Contemporary change in agriculture in southern Europe', in Williams, A. (ed.) *Southern Europe Transformed?*, London, Harper and Row.

Kane, T. T. (1978) 'Social problems and ethnic change: Europe's guest workers', *Intercom*, 6, 7–9.

Kayser, B. (1977) 'European migrations: the new pattern', *International Migration Review*, 11, 232–46.

Kerr, A. J. C. (1977) *The Common Market and How It Works*, London, Pergamon.

Kielstra, N. (1984) 'Rural Languedoc: from periphery to "zone reliquaire"', forthcoming in Hudson, R. and Lewis, J. (eds) *Dependent Development in Southern Europe*, London, Methuen.

Kindleberger, C. P. (1967) *Europe's Post-war Growth: the Role of Labour Supply*, Cambridge, Mass., Harvard University Press.

King, R. (1973) *Land Reform: the Italian Experience*, London, Butterworth.

King, R. (1976) 'The evolution of international migration movements in the EEC', *Tijdschrift voor Economische en Sociale Geografie*, 67, 66–82.

King, R. (1984) 'Emigration, return migration and internal migration', in Williams, A. (ed.) *Southern Europe Transformed?*, London, Harper and Row.

King, R., Mortimore, J. and Strachan, R. (1984) 'The effects of return migration on economic and social development in Southern Italy', forthcoming in Hudson, R. and Lewis, J. (eds) *Dependent Development in Southern Europe*, London, Methuen.

Kofman, E. (1981) 'Functional regionalism and alternative regional development strategies in Corsica', *Regional Studies*, 15, 3, 173–81.

Kofman, E. (1984) 'Internal colonialism, dependency and regional development in Corsica', in Hudson, R. and Lewis, J. (eds) *Dependent Development in Southern Europe*, London, Methuen (forthcoming).

Kosinski, L. (1970) *The Population of Europe*, London, Longmans.

Lacroix, J.-L. and Perini, M. (1979) 'Europe and the developing countries', in Commission of the European Communities, *The Community Today*, pp. 168–79, Brussels, CEC.

Lane, A. M. J. (1981) 'Towards a geographical information system for EEC regional data', unpublished M.Sc. dissertation, University of Durham.

Laurençin, J.-P., Monateri, J. G., Palloix, C., Tiberghien, R. and Vernet, P. (1977) 'The regional effects of crisis on the forms of organisation of production and location of industry in the Mediterranean basin', in Massey, D. B. and Batey, P. (eds) *London Papers in Regional Science*, 7, 7–18, London, Pion.

Law, C. M. and Warnes, A. M. (1976) 'The changing geography of the elderly in

England and Wales', *Institute of British Geographers Transactions*, New Series, 1, 4, 453–71.

Le Cour, A. (1980) 'Policy and recent development', in Eurostat, *European Political Data*, 35.

Lipietz, A. (1980) 'The structuration of space, the problem of land and spatial policy', in Carney, J., Hudson, R. and Lewis, J. (eds) *Regions in Crisis: New Directions in European Regional Theory*, pp. 60–75, London, Croom Helm.

Lipietz, A. (1981) 'Inter-regional polarisation of society', *Papers of the Regional Science Association*, 40, 3–18.

Lucas, N. J. D. (1977) *Energy and the European Community*, London, Europa Publications.

Mackerron, G. and Rush, H. J. (1976) 'Agriculture in the EEC: taking stock', *Food Policy*, 1, 4, 286–300.

Madison, A. (1964) *Economic Growth in the West: Comparative Experience in Europe and North America*, London, Allen & Unwin.

Mandel, E. (1975a) *Late Capitalism*, London, New Left Books.

Mandel, E. (1975b) 'International capitalism and "supranationality"', in Radice, H. (ed.) *International Firms and Modern Imperialism*, pp. 143–57, Harmondsworth, Penguin.

Mandel, E. (1978) *The Second Slump*, London, New Left Books.

Mayer, K. B. (1975) 'Intra-European migration during the past twenty years', *International Migration Review*, 9, 441–7.

Mayhew, A. (1970) 'Structural reform and the future of West German agriculture', *Geographical Review*, 60, 54–68.

Mayhew, A. (1971) 'Agrarian reform in West Germany', *Transactions, Institute of British Geographers*, 52, 61–76.

Maynard, A. (1975) *Health Care in the European Community*, London, Croom Helm.

Merrett, C. R. (1981) 'Petrochemicals in Japan and western Europe: the need for restructuring in the 1980s', *Barclays Review*, November, 83–7.

Mesnage, M. (1980) 'Dissemination of statistics using computer facilities', Eurostat, *European Political Data*, 35.

Minshull, G. N. (1978) *The New Europe*, London, Hodder & Stoughton.

Mishalani, P., Robert, A., Stevens, C. and Weston, A. (1981) 'The pyramid of privilege', in Stevens, C. (ed.) *EEC and the Third World: A Survey*, pp. 60–83, London, Hodder & Stoughton.

Morgan, K. (1979) 'State regional interventions and industrial restructuring in post-war Britain: the case of Wales', *Urban and Regional Studies Working Paper No. 16*, University of Sussex, Falmer.

Mouzelis, N. (1978) *Modern Greece: Facets of Underdevelopment*, London, Macmillan.

Nairn, T. (1977) *The Break-up of Britain: Crisis and Neo-nationalism*, London, New Left Books.

O'Dell, P. R. (1976) 'The EEC energy market: structure and integration', in Lee, R. and Ogden, P. (eds) *Economy and Society in the EEC*, pp. 63–81, Farnborough, Saxon House.

Organization for Economic Co-operation and Development (1973) *Effects of Traffic and Roads on the Urban Environment*, Paris, OECD.

Organization for Economic Co-operation and Development (1976) *The 1974–5 Recession and the Employment of Women*, Paris, OECD.

Organization for Economic Co-operation and Development (1978) *Labour Force Statistics, 1965–76*, Paris, OECD.

Organization for Economic Co-operation and Development (1979) *Labour Force Statistics, 1966–77*, Paris, OECD.

Paine, S. (1977) 'The changing role of migrant labour in the advance capitalist economies of western Europe', in Griffiths, M. (ed.) *Government, Business and Labour in European Capitalism*, ch. 12, London, Europotentials Press.

Paine, S. (1980) 'Replacement of the west European migrant labour system by investment in the European periphery', in Seers, D., Schaffer, B. and Kiljunen, M. L. (eds) *Underdeveloped Europe*, pp. 65–95, Brighton, Harvester.

Parker, G. (1975) *The Logic of Unity*, London, Longman.

Parker, G. (1979) *The Countries of the European Community*, London, Macmillan.

Pearce, D. (1981) *Tourist Development*, Harlow, Longman.

Perrons, D. (1980) 'The role of Ireland in the new international division of labour; a proposed framework for regional analysis', *Regional Studies*, 15, 2, 81–100.

Pickvance, C. G. (ed.) (1976) *Urban Sociology: Critical Essays*, London, Methuen.

Power, J. (1978) *Western Europe's Migrant Workers*, London, Minority Rights Group.

Pugliese, E. (1984) 'Farmworkers in Italy: landless peasants, agricultural working class or clients of the Welfare State', in Hudson, R. and Lewis, J. (eds) *Dependent Development in Southern Europe*, London, Methuen (forthcoming).

Rase, W. D. (1980) 'Subroutines for plotting graduated symbol maps', *EDV Report 2/1980*, Bonn, BFLR.

Romus, P. (1979) 'Regional policy', in Commission of the European Communities, *The Community Today*, pp. 102–15, Brussels, CEC.

Salt, J. and Clout, H. D. (eds) (1976) *Migration in Post-War Europe: Geographical Essays*, Oxford, Clarendon Press.

Schlupp, F. (1980) 'Modell Deutschland and the international division of labour', in Krippendorf, E. and Rittenberger, V. (eds) *The Foreign Policy of West Germany*, pp. 33–100, Beverley Hills and London, Sage.

Schmid, G. C. (1971) 'Foreign workers and labour market flexibility', *Journal of Common Market Studies*, 9, 246–53.

Schröter, L. and Zierold, H. (1980) 'Economic development in the Ruhr: genesis of a crisis', in Hudson, R., Friis, P., Plum, V. and Toft Jensen, H. (eds) *Industrialisation Processes and Regional Labour Reserves in the EEC: Recent Trends in the International Division of Labour*, vol. 2, Final Report 637–79–8 EDU UK, pp. 116–40, Brussels, Directorate General of Science, Research and Education, Commission of the European Communities.

SOPEMI (Système d'Observation Permanente des Migrations) (1980) *Eighth Annual Report*, Paris, Organisation for Economic Cooperation and Development.

Stubenitsky, F. (1973) *American Direct Investment in Netherlands Industry*, Rotterdam, Rotterdam University Press.

Swann, D. (1975) *The Economics of the Common Market*, Harmondsworth, Penguin.

Taylor, R. (1980) *Implications for the Southern Mediterranean Countries of the Second Enlargement of the European Community*, Brussels, Commission of the European Communities Spokesman's Group and Directorate General for Information.

Thomson, M. (1976) 'Towards a European transport strategy', in Lee, R. and Ogden, P. (eds) *Economy and Society in the EEC*, pp. 273–87, Farnborough, Saxon House.

Tsoukalis, L. (1981) *The European Community and Its Mediterranean Enlargement*, London, Allen & Unwin.

Twitchett, K. J. (ed.) (1975) *Europe and the World: the External Relations of the Common Market*, London, Europa Publications.

United Nations Environmental Programme (1981) 'The Mediterranean action plan', *Ekistics*, 290, 400–7.

Warren, B. (1977) 'The EEC, the Lomè Convention and imperialism', in Nairn, T. (ed.) *Atlantic Europe? The Radical View*, pp. 96–110, Amsterdam, Transnational Institute.

Watkins, L. H. (1972) 'Urban transport and environmental pollution', *Transport and Road Research Laboratory Report*, 455, Crowthorne, England, TRRL.

Waugh, T. C. (1978) 'GIMMS reference manual', *Inter University/Research Council Series Report*, 30, University of Edinburgh, Program Library Unit.

Waugh, T. C. (1981) 'The development of the GIMMS computer mapping system', in Taylor, D. R. F. (ed.) *Computers in Cartography*, Chichester, Wiley.

Waugh, T. C. (1982) *GIMMS Reference Manual, Version 4.0*, Edinburgh, GIMMS Ltd.

Werner, H. (1974) 'Migration and free movement of workers in western Europe', *International Migration*, 12, 311–27.

Wild, T. (1981) *West Germany: A Geography of Its People*, London, Longman.

Williams, R. L. (1976) 'The misuse of area in mapping census – type numbers', *Historical Methods Newsletter*, 9, 4, 213–16.

World Bank (1979) *World Development Report, 1979*, New York, World Bank.

World Bank (1980) *World Development Report, 1980*, New York, World Bank.

Young, G. (1973) *Tourism: Blessing or Blight?*, Harmondsworth, Penguin.

Yuill, D., Allen, K. and Hull, C. (eds) (1980) *Regional Policy in the European Community*, London, Croom Helm.

AUTHOR INDEX

LOCATION INDEX

N.B. References to member countries of the Community, together with the two current applicants Portugal and Spain, are *not* given here; references to regions, cities and towns within these countries are given separately, however.

SUBJECT INDEX

This atlas offers a uniquely clear introduction to the conditions facing the European Economic Community. In its accessible maps and text the student will find up-to-date guidance to both the national and the regional problems of the EEC.

The scene is set in the first chapter, which examines the history, organizational structure, and powers and policies of the Community itself. The next four chapters deal in turn with key contemporary issues: the changing population; patterns and trends of employment and unemployment; economic performance and resources; and social conditions, consumption patterns and lifestyles. In the final chapter the authors look forward to the year 2000: can the Community meet the challenges presented by the economic and social trends of the late twentieth century?

The authors: Ray Hudson is a Senior Lecturer in the Department of Geography, University of Durham, and David Rhind is Professor and Helen Mounsey is a Research Officer in the Department of Geography, Birkbeck College, University of London.

Other titles in this series include:

An Atlas of North American Affairs
Second edition
D. K. Adams, S. F. Mills and H. B. Rodgers

An Atlas of World Affairs
Seventh edition
Andrew Boyd

An Atlas of African Affairs
Ieuan Ll. Griffiths

The Common Agricultural Policy
Past, present and future
Brian E. Hill

Competition and Industrial Policy in the European Community
Dennis Swann

The Common Fisheries Policy of the European Community
Mark Wise

University Paperbacks
are published by

Methuen & Co. Ltd
11 New Fetter Lane
London EC4P 4EE

Methuen, Inc.
733 Third Avenue
New York NY 10017

ISBN 0-416-30920-8

9 780416 309201